# HYPNOTHERAPY FOR TROUBLED CHILDREN

By
ROBERT E. DUKE, Ph.D.

Foreword by
STANLEY KRIPPNER, Ph.D.

IRVINGTON PUBLISHERS, INC.
NEW HORIZON PRESS PUBLISHERS
NEW YORK

Copyright© 1984 by Irvington Publishers, Inc.
All rights reserved. No part of this book may be reproduced in any manner whatever, including information storage or retrieval, in whole or in part (except for brief quotations in critical articles or reviews), without written permission from the publisher. For information, write to Irvington Publishers, Inc., 551 Fifth Avenue, New York, New York, 10176.

Library of Congress Cataloging in Publication Data

Duke, Robert E.
   Hypnotherapy for Troubled Children.

   Includes bibliographical references and index.
   1. Child psychotherapy—Case studies.
2. Hypnotism—Therapeutic use—Case studies.
I. Title.
PJ505.H86084    1984    618.92'89162    82-14849
ISBN 0-8290-1030-0


ISBN 0-8290-1030-0 (Irvington)

ISBN 0-88282-007-9 (Horizon/New Horizon)

Printed in the United States of America

# CONTENTS

| | | |
|---|---|---:|
| **Foreword** | | *v* |
| **Prologue** | | *xiii* |
| **Chapter** | | |
| 1 | *Bobby: Enuresis and Dyslexia* | 1 |
| 2 | *John: Fear and Failing* | 7 |
| 3 | *Richard: School Phobia* | 21 |
| 4 | *Larry: Stuttering* | 41 |
| 5 | *Billy: Sibling Rivalry* | 89 |
| 6 | *Timothy: Schizophrenia* | 101 |
| 7 | *Michael: Resistance to Hypnosis* | 127 |
| 8 | *Edward: Poor Self-Concept* | 141 |
| 9 | *Sandra: Suicide* | 163 |
| 10 | *Joe: Stealing* | 193 |
| **Epilogue** | | 199 |
| **Index** | | 205 |

# FOREWORD

*Dr. Krippner of the Saybrook Institute in San Francisco, California, pioneered the use of hypnosis to assist young people suffering from educational blockages. Dr. Krippner kindly allowed me the full use of the following as a foreword to this book.*

There is no such thing as instant creativity. A hypnotist cannot point his index finger at an individual, tell him to—Create! and produce another Leonardo da Vinci.

On the other hand, some creative workers enter into a state of consciousness in which their concentration is so intense that they may seem, to themselves as well as to others, in a trance. When this trancelike state occurs, it is not purposively generated, it happens spontaneously as a result of the creative process. Poet Brewster Ghiselin stated, "In short, the creative discipline when successful may generate a trancelike state, but one does not throw oneself into a trance in order to create." He further remarked:

"This self-surrender so familiar to creative minds is nearly always hard to achieve. It calls for a purity of motive that is rarely sustained except through dedication and discipline. Subordination of everything to the whole impulse of life is easier for the innocent and ignorant because ... they are not so powerfully possessed by convention."

It is for this reason that my own work with hypnosis has approached the creative process from the roundabout method. I have never told a subject "be more creative, write better" or "paint more skillfully." Instead, I have attempted to decrease tension, increase motivation, and facilitate concentration.

The basic approach has been demonstrated by an experimental study. The subjects were 49 elementary and secondary school children enrolled in a summer clinic for disabled readers. In response to a questionnaire, the parents of nine children (all of them boys) had requested that hypnosis be included in the treatment program for their sons.

For all 49 children, two hour sessions were held five times a week for five weeks. One hour of the session was spent in individual remedial work and one hour was spent in group work.

Form Z of the California Reading Test was administered on the first day of the clinic while Form X was administered on the final day. The children's scores on Form Z were subtracted from their scores on Form X to measure the amount of reading improvement.

The "experimental group" consisted of the nine boys receiving hypnosis as part of their treatment. The "control group" consisted of the 40 children who did not receive hypnosis. The groups were similar in terms of age and intelligence.

At the end of the five weeks, the groups as a whole had made five months of progress, as measured by the California Reading Test. All but one of the boys in the experimental group had made more than five months progress. Of the children in the control group only 24 of the 40 progressed more than five months. This difference between the two groups was statistically significant.

Although it seems likely that the difference was in part due to hypnosis, there are several alternate explanations. The extra attention paid to the members of the experimental group might have been an influencing factor, although great care was taken to see that the time spent in hypnosis was balanced off by additional remedial reading work for the control group.

It must also be remembered that the parents of the boys in the experimental group requested hypnotic treatment for them. It might be argued that this type of parent would have been so highly motiated that the child would have received additional help at home. On the other hand, it is just as possible that this type of parent would have exerted unreasonable pressure which would have made the child uncooperative at the reading clinic.

Although this study is one of the few reported in the field of hypnosis and learning to utilize a control group, it is apparent that additional research remains to be conducted. Even if the conditions were the same for both groups, there is no assurance that the same techniques, carried on without formal hypnotic induction, would not have produced similar results.

The nine boys in the experimental group were seen once a week, or five times during the course of the clinic. The sessions lasted about a half hour. The tutor, working individually with the pupil, was present during every hypnotic session. In each instance, the tutor and the hypnotist discussed ways in which they could use adaptions of hypnosis working with the pupil.

If the child had been told that he would receive hypnotic treatment, the word "hypnosis" was used while inducing the trance. If he had not been told that he would receive hypnotic treatment, the word "hypnosis" was avoided. Instead, words as "suggestion," "relaxation," and "concentration" were used to describe what was going on.

If the word "hypnosis" was not to be used, the child was only told that he would be given suggestions on how to concentrate and how to relax. He was also told that these suggestions would help him to improve his reading skills. The beginning part of the hypnotic induction generally included instructions which directed the child to sit in a comfortable chair, close his eyes, and listen closely.

If the pupil expected to be hypnotized, an informal conversation determined his expectations. Every effort was made to fulfill his expectations. One boy had seen a movie in which a man was hypnotized by staring at a ring. Therefore, a similar ring was used to assist the boy in entering hypnosis.

During these sessions, hypnosis was employed to decrease tension while reading, increase the motivation to read, and maintain attention and concentration for longer periods of time. Each one of these procedures has implications for creativity as well as for reading improvement.

## TENSION PROBLEMS

Anxiety about the reading process characterizes many poor learners. Sometimes their undue concern is the result of past failures. Sometimes it serves as a cause as well as an effect and brings about further blocks to efficient reading. Hypnosis was often used with pupils in an attempt to reduce tension and produce a more relaxing muscle tone while reading.

In many instances, acute anxiety lies behind poor visual skills and blurred perception. In one remarkable case, a pupil attempted to recite the words on a basic word list and made 17 errors out of 20 words. Under hypnosis he was told that his second reading would be more successful because the eye muscles would relax and function properly. He would be able to see with his eyes "wide open" and would be able to perceive, "all the letters in each word." The second reading of the word list produced only five errors. The first reading of a different word list produced only seven errors out of twenty words.

Similar instructions can be given to creative individuals to help them work in a relaxed manner. I have worked with university students, attempting to facilitate their educational goals. In one instance, a music student was helped from suffering a pre-examination anxiety. In part, these are the instructions given him once he had entered hypnosis:

> As you relax, you begin to stop worrying. You stop worrying about your examination. You begin to think about how much you like music. You begin to think how interesting the material is; you have to study. You know that you can be more interested in this material if the muscles of your body are relaxed. If your muscles are relaxed, you will be able to pay closer attention to what you are studying. You want to relax your muscles just enough so that you will be at ease when you study.

A number of sessions helped the music student reduce nervous tensions as he studied. As his tension and anxiety decreased his interest increased and he did well on his examinations.

As might be expected, those students without clearly defined goals or with little concern for their future have the most difficulty in benefiting from the type of hypnotic suggestion that attempts to replace stress with interest. Hypnosis, after all, rarely implants new ideas into one's thought processes. It merely reinforces ideas that have been there all along. If there is nothing to reinforce, hypnosis is generally ineffective.

For the music student, specific suggestions on examination procedures were made once his tension decreased. He was told that no outside noises would bother him while taking the test. He was also told that his self-confidence would be very high as a result of his thorough preparation for the examination. He was told that because he was well-prepared, and his confidence was high, there would be no reason for him to develop fear reactions towards the test.

A small amount of anxiety often helps to sharpen one's reactions during an examination. More than that, however, it hampers one's effectiveness. Therefore, the music student was told that he would approach the test situation with an alert, but not anxious attitude. He was told to be attentive, but not tense, while answering questions.

## MOTIVATION PROBLEMS

Motivation and interest in learning were stressed with the members of the experimental group of elementary school children during their hypnosis sessions. It was suggested to the pupils that while they were in hypnosis, they would become more interested in reading as time went on and that each successful attempt would increase their desire to do well during the following attempt.

Perfection was never put forward as a goal and no statements were made regarding specific grade evaluations or letter grades in school. However, it was realized that the difference between a capable pupil and a poor one is often a matter of motivation. A pupil with a high persistence and continuous interest generally does well in his work. He prepares his assignments. He follows a schedule for study. He applies himself energetically.

Sometimes, what a well-motivated pupil lacks in mental ability he compensates for by his purposefulness. On the other hand, many bright pupils do poorly because they have little interest in the learning process and strong motivation to succeed academically.

For several sessions these feelings were discussed, both in the waking state and while in the hypnotized state. Once pupils became fully aware of these feelings and resolved them, their motivation improved, their grades improved, and most of all their writing talents continued to flourish and develop.

## CONCENTRATION PROBLEMS

Poor concentration, a lack of attention, inability to study without becoming distracted, and poor recall for what has been read characterized many pupils attending the summer reading clinic. If serious emotional disturbances were behind these problems, psychotherapy and family counseling were advised. It is usually futile to work on any phase of a pupil's reading disability if it is symptomatic of a deep-seated emotional problem.

If serious personality disturbance is not evident, hypnosis can help develop better study habits, sharpen attention, make possible longer periods of concentration and increase recall. Several sessions are usually needed to eliminate the poor habits and introduce improved ones. At the end of that time, in most cases, the pupil can go ahead on his own and put the new procedures into practice.

Attention and concentration difficulties are frequently reported by creative individuals. If they have not developed internal discipline over the years, their thoughts are often restless and activities embrace so many facets of life that they find it difficult to settle down for a period of intense work.

A hypnotist can't assist an individual into hypnosis and expect him to create. However he can work with a hypnotized subject on the improvement of attention and concentration in the hopes that the creative individual will put this knowledge to use when it is needed. Many people can be taught self-hypnosis for this purpose.

A seminary student whose assignments included the writing of several theological treatises was taught self-hypnosis and given suggestions on what to tell himself once in a hypnotic state. For example, when he was about to work on one of his assignments, he would go into hypnosis and tell himself to ignore room temperature, ignore thirst sensations, ignore hunger pangs, ignore conversations that he might hear in the hallway. He also told himself that his periods of concentration would increase in length, that his interest in his work would grow, and that he would become so involved in his work that he would do an excellent job.

In the case of the seminarian, the suggestions worked. In other cases, they have not. Hypnosis is not a panacea; it is only one of many approaches which can be attempted to assist the creative process.

## REACTIONS TO EDUCATIONAL HYPNOSIS

Critics of hypnosis have offered several adverse comments to the procedure—some as follows:

> When one mind 'suggests' and repeatedly 'suggests' a thought or idea to another receptive, weak or passive 'listener' there is such power centered in the 'suggestion' that

it dominates, outshines, the living light of independent thinking in the subject. Here is the evil, to take away for a time, or for all time, if continued, the independent self-control of a human mind.

The dangers of hypnosis have been cited and tales have been told of subjects who have been ruined for life, etc. It is more likely that much educational hypnosis evokes no permanent change. However, to claim that it is extremely hazardous displays an ignorance of the facts. Hypnosis in any of its forms is perfectly safe when utilized by a competent practitioner. Psychiatrist M. Erik Wright stated:

> In applying these principals to the creative individul with faulty motivation, it is usually best to take a nondirective approach. It would be futile to tell a hypnotized chemist, 'You will go into your laboratory and make a great discovery.' This is not the way creativity functions.
> 
> If the creative person has entered a phase of low productivity or if he complains that he has lost inspiration, he can often be assisted into a hypnotic trance and the discussion is continued. A hypnotic interview of this nature will often reveal factors that would never come to light if the matter was discussed in the waking state.
> 
> For example, a college student who was interested in creative writing complained that she began to find college difficult and said that she could do well academically only if she liked the professor, enjoyed the course content, and found herself, 'in the right mood for studying.' Her writing was suffering, she complained, and she felt she had lost whatever 'creative spark' with which she began.
> 
> This discussion was continued after she had entered a hypnotic trance. She began to discuss her home life and revealed that her parents had discouraged her creative pasttimes, branding them 'impractical' and 'useless.' At first, this criticism had only stimulated the student and each success was a further proof that she was correct and that her parents were wrong. Eventually, however, unconscious guilt feelings arose as she imagined that she was using her talents to strike back at her father and mother.

> The problems associated with the use of hypnosis ... arises far more from misconceptions about it, and from limited professional training in it, than from the intrinsic characteristics of the hypnotic state. ...

The physician Herbert Mann added:

> The fear that hypnosis may promote intense dependency cannot be justified by factual evidence. The patient who seeks a dependency relationship does not need hypnosis to develop and satisfy his emotional need.
>
> The opposition to hypnosis still persisting in the American culture is primarily due to a suspicion of all forms of consciousness outside of logical, rational thought. The result of this prejudice has been to retard the advance of hypnosis in medical, dental, psychological and educational fields.

Stanley Krippner, Ph.D.

# PROLOGUE

## WHY I GOT INTO EDUCATIONAL THERAPY

The head of the psychology department of a New England college recently remarked to a class of graduate students that included me, "In England, the work in psychological medicine is 40 years ahead of the American effort." The professor might be wrong in suggesting that this gap embraced 40 years but he might be correct otherwise because as a principal of an elementary school I've been frustrated again and again at the lack of meaningful psychological help available for boys and girls in trouble scholastically and socially. It seems possible that the English are way ahead of us.

Most New England school systems employ guidance counselors, school adjustment counselors, remedial specialists, doctors and nurses and have access to hospitals, colleges and clinics having psychological, diagnostic and remedial services. There is a tremendous wealth of material and personnel available. Why with this formidable array of power for the relief of children's problems do we frequently fail to help the child who needs help most of all.

My search for help for these young people turned to England where it seems true that they are ahead of America in this struggle. The English doctor whose work drew me out of pessimism suggested in one of his books that a comparison study be made—children with similar problems be paired, one group with hypnotherapy and one group without hypnotherapy. In full agreement with his thoughts I became involved in this work.

I visited Dr. Gordon Ambrose, a London psychiatrist who is in the foremost ranks of psychosomatic medicine, an author in this field and a member of the International Congress of Psychosomatic Medicine and Hygiene. His publications in the field of child guidance drew me to his London office.

Like others in the teaching profession, I have been responsible for sending large numbers of children who were having difficulty in school to child guidance clinics and to remedial specialists. In most instances, they were children of average or better abilities, but children who, for some reason, were failing in their work or were becoming antisocial in their behavior. Unfortunately, most of the children so referred were returned to us, not changed, but armed only with additional information about their problems. This added information frequently followed a pattern suggesting that the child needed additional guidance, remedial work and more individual attention.

It appeared that the children who came to attention because of their problems and were sent to specialists, returned to their work with the cause of their problems detailed to a greater and more helpful degree. They still had their problems, and were still crippled, with no realistic solution and with precious little individual therapy, to help them reorient their lives.

I don't want to depreciate the efforts of the many dedicated workers in child guidance and remedial instruction. The efforts of these teachers is appreciated. They are working hard at the job assigned to them. But only occasionally are their efforts rewarded with complete success. This is not due to lack of effort on the part of either the adult or the child but comes from the complex nature of the problem they face together. The younger the child is with a problem the better job they can do. The young child has had less time to develop a general expectation of failure and to develop ingrained academic problems.

Many of the children with reasonably good intelligence levels are problem readers because they have simply failed to discriminate between the letter sounds, or have developed wrong eye movements. Although the causes of an educational disability are numerous, a search for a single factor is apt to prove insufficient. Seldom does a single factor cause an educational block in any of the academic disciplines. A good remedial teacher attempts to discover the composite conditions causing the problem. First of all, she searches for physical deficiencies as a contributing cause. She seeks an examination of the visual and hearing organs of the child. She also knows that speech

## PROLOGUE

and various motor adjustments as well as glandular deficiencies cause learning disabilities. Brain damage can also be responsible for educational deficiency.

The solution to educational problems is also complicated by the many differences found in children and in their environments. No two cases present the same situation and solution. The more complex the problem the more detailed and penetrating is the search for a solution. In such problem cases the services of a physician are needed.

The various emotional factors arising from the physical impairment are disabling, and these factors remain to plague the child long after the physical situation is corrected. The child already in trouble academically becomes tense, aggressive and sensitive. Apathy can develop with some children to eventually lead them into withdrawal characteristics, anxiety and disorganization. The circle of tension that often surrounds the skill defect makes the solution of the defect almost an impossibility. There is still another vicious circle. As in the familiar question what came first, the egg or the chicken, in this case we ask, what came first, the learning deficiency or the emotional problem connected with it that unfortunately grows and grows with each new failure.

Children laboring under an educational disability are also laboring under stress which can be transformed into other disabling characteristics, shyness, poor concentration, stuttering, nail biting, and tendencies to give up easily. Still other children may acquire all of these and become over aggressive. Such children disrupt their classes and seek attention by poor compensating devices.

Some unfortunate children arrive at school with emotional problems on their very first day. While most of the children are confident, poised and happy to be in the classroom, there are others who are shy, timid and are so self-centered that they are unable to get along with their classmates and cannot adjust to their classroom activities.

Because they have these problems and are so easily upset they are often referred to as being emotionally immature. They may become handicapped academically. Teachers are not always as alert to the emotional involvement and general instability of the pupils as they should be. Such pupils are all too frequently labeled immature and as such are ignored until they mature which, of course, they don't always do. The immaturity label that is sometimes attached to a child may result from just a casual observation of an improper classroom behavior and is impossible for the average teacher to uncover.

Research by experts in the field of scholastic disability are in considerable agreement that there is high incidence of emotional problems among the disabled students. Among the personality handicaps observed by these clinicians are: over-interest in personal problems, shyness and a lack of confidence in personal abilities. There is apt to be considerable tension and a great deal of antagonism toward school. The unfortunate pupil is apt to become truant in order to seek something better or to escape from the unpleasantness of the scene of his failure. Such a pupil is likely to be difficult if he seeks attention in an obnoxious way. As his school or home situation worsens, his behavior regresses accordingly. To escape from extreme frustration, these pupils may become school dropouts.

Children who fail usually develop the idea that they are stupid. Frequently their grouping in school helps to develop this feeling. The class in which they are placed may have three or more groups of children grouped by "ability" with the most insecure child of all usually in the slowest of the groups. Sometimes these children are grouped together in one class where they may have to endure name calling from schoolmates not in their class. In one local junior high school, these children are called the 'one ohs' by the other children of the school for the simple reason that the number of their home room is 101. Whenever a child from this class is encountered in or out of the school situation, he is immediately referred to as a 'one oh.' There may be some able children in the 'one ohs' who like the others there are daily devaluated through the caustic words of the brighter-appearing young people as well as by the attitude of some teachers. Fortunately most young people enter school happy and eagerly attend the daily sessions and if they meet with success and the approval of their teacher their growth is to be assured. But some children meet with immediate frustration perhaps as a result of an incompetent teacher pushing them into materials for which they are not ready.

A child's home situation is not always the cause of his woes in school as many teachers would like to believe. An unthinking maladjusted teacher can be devastating to the personality adjustment of her pupils.

# PROLOGUE

There are children who have become emotionally insecure prior to coming to school, a result of some unfortunate incident during the pre-school years. Unless their attitudes are modified or improved upon, such children could be expected to make very little progress in school. Some difficulties are deep-seated and may require the services of a psychiatrist. Many others may not be deepseated at all and can be readily modified. Sometimes a child can hear an unfavorable statement concerning his teacher from another member of his own family and as a result of such careless talk learn to fear the teacher and do poorly in the class. He may think that there is no escape.

Many young children sit in needless fear of their teachers all day and do nothing about it. Daily stomachaches and sleepless nights may be their physical reactions to the predicament. They can't be expected to do their best work or make the progress in school that their natural talents would normally allow.

While at home, children sometimes may not only hear derogatory remarks about the school teachers but sometimes listen to their own efforts being devaluated. Quarreling parents, a broken home, overprotection or dominance by one of the parents will produce disabling tensions for their child. It has been said many times that an anxious parent will produce an anxious child.

Some unfortuante children become the center of a battleground between two fighting parents. They are torn with a divided allegiance and struggle to maintain loyalty to each of the quarreling parents. A child struggling against parental domination exists on one end of a scale while a child who lives with parents who are unconcerned about his difficulties lives on the other end. Both children are apt to develop the same kind of personality maladjustment. The tensions built up by the maladjusted child cannot help but aggravate his learning problems to such a degree that standard progress is impossible. How can the average remedial teacher be expected to cope with such odds? When children are emotionally upset they can hardly be expected to respond to the regular efforts of remedial teachers. Before such children can be expected to respond to remedial instruction, they have to be helped emotionally and achieve some kind of adjustment to their situation. Without a satisfactory attitude toward school and the learning situation, it is foolish to expect the child to achieve any real success in school.

When a child does poorly in school, some of the professional staff members of the school are apt to point out deficiencies that exist in the home life of the offending pupil. If the parents of the child and the professional staff of the school should get together, then the combined anxieties of the home and school descend upon the unfortunate child who has failed to live up to everyone's expectations. The child usually bears the blame and suffers the consequent guilt for having developed a problem that he is expected to solve. His superiors of the school and home usually reach some kind of agreement. They may require that he perform a daily task usually centered upon his homework with his parents ensuring that he does the work with the school making sure that they know of what it consists. By joining forces, the home and school will require the child to perform some kind of mechanical academic task. Such arrangements do little in solving the child's problems.

Rarely does a school criticize itself for failing to solve a learning problem for one of its failing students. In fact when a school is confronted with a questioning pupil or even worse a questioning parent, the school gathers its forces together to meet the challenge. Professional ranks can be quickly closed against anyone challenging its expertise. A junior or senior high school student who gets into trouble with one of his teachers may find that his other teachers will also condemn him. Parents are aware of the cohesiveness of the profession and for this reason try to avoid getting into conflict with any one of their child's teachers. The safest target for criticism is the child. He is least able to fight back. There are reasons for some educational difficulties of many pupils. A child just learning to read can encounter a frustrating experience that is sufficient to give him a personality maladjustment. Children become ready for reading instruction at different ages. Some are ready to begin reading as soon as they get to school but others, who may also be bright, need more time to prepare themselves for formal instruction. Frustration is bound to develop in the youngster who is pushed into a learning situation for which he is not ready.

A school curriculum that rigidly adheres to grade standards and not achievement by individual pupils will surely cause widespread reading failure for many of its pupils. Promotion policies that enable a poor reader to drop farther and farther behind his contemporaries will surely cause him to become emotionally disabled. He cannot help but feel inadequate, inferior and insecure as he loses his ability to cope with daily assignments. He may eventually learn to hate, not just the subject, but his teacher, the school and anyone connected with it. In due time, the chances are good that he will not only become a school dropout, but that his rebellion against the school that humiliated him will spread to other segments of the society aligned with school. Unfortunately, delinquency is sometimes born in school.

Incompetent teachers or good teachers having to use dull and ineffective methods can create an unfortunate attitude towards the school. A disproportionate amount of drill can kill the interest of the brightest pupil. A teaching method that concentrates upon isolated elements of a subject such as overemphasis upon the phonetic elements of words is a dull procedure that can be guaranteed to kill a child's interest in reading.

Motivating a child to want to learn calls for methods that are interesting and important to the child. A good learning situation develops from something that is going on in class. If the child can see a reason for studying then his interest and motivation are assured. His total learning experience should be integrated and not taught as isolated fragments of a whole.

Over emphasis upon fragments of a subject may be more detrimental of the pupil's mastery of the subject than under-emphasis of the same fragments. But some teachers drill their students on fragmentory knowledge to such an extent that some of their pupils tend to become academic casualties. Some children become so intent upon sounding out words that they are unable to grasp word meanings. Their sight vocabulary may be so neglected that they cannot make use of context clues for word recognition. A good curriculum centers upon a balanced growth of the large number of skills that are part of any subject.

If the child's teacher is sympathetic to the emotional needs as well as the integrated curriculum needs of his pupils and if he is well trained and is able to maintain the orderly development of subject skills, then the child is indeed fortunate. A pupil will be in difficulty if he finds himself in the classroom of a teacher who can only follow a fixed routine and is unable to adjust the instruction to fit the varied needs of the pupils in his room.

Unfortunately, there are some teachers who cannot maintain a satisfactory relationship with all students. The teacher's personality is such that he can't help but adopt an unfortunate attitude toward some pupils. A bright pupil who asks too many questions of an insecure teacher may find himself the object of that teacher's hostility.

Some teachers seem to actually drive their pupils away from learning and so become responsible for creating academically crippled children.

If a child's academic problem is allowed to continue long enough to become affixed with an emotional block around the problem, the remedial teacher who may later work diligently toward a solution of the academic problem will fail. The negative emotional blocking effect upon the child's mind can effectively close his mind to the help that he desperately needs.

Another type of problem frequently encountered is the student who arrives at school with an emotional problem that triggers an academic difficulty. Here again a remedial specialist may work doggedly to close the educational gap, but if he is unaware or is unable to resolve the emotional block that caused the problem in the first place, he most assuredly fails to help the child.

When an emotional block becomes involved with an "educational gap," it probably would be impossible for the teacher to determine which came first, the skill defect or the emotional problem, but at that point it really wouldn't matter. In any case, the emotional problem will block the academic progress. It is with these children that this book is generally concerned. These children are the ones most in need of remedial help, but are equally unable to appreciably profit from it.

## ROLE PLAYING

During the many parent-principal conferences held in my office, I have often watched unhappy children who are failing in their work turn alternately to their parents and then to me. I've had the unpleasant task of presenting to the child's parents the damning evidence: the child's report card. I've listened to the children earnestly promise to try harder in school, and I know they sincerely mean every word of their promise. The school teacher and the parents are relieved and released from some anxiety upon hearing the child's solemn promise. But many years of experience with such well-meaning parents, teachers and children, have made me be privately pessimistic of the final outcome. These conferences, however, are always terminated with a cheery note of optimism all around.

Unhappy sequels to many of these conferences would be another onference with the parents continuing to seek solutions to their child's educational problem. Reprisals against the child, who has let them down, are frequently mentioned: no television, no bicycle, no summer camp and "grounded" every day after school, etc. It seems that in spite of everything, most of the children who are doing poor work in school continue to do so in the face of threats, promises, rewards, non-promotions, spankings, humiliations and extra help. There are exceptions—there are always exceptions—and the significant question is why? Explanations suggesting the increasing maturity of the child or that he is a mysterious "late bloomer" seem shallow reasons for a child finding himself.

Dr. Ambrose's pioneering efforts in child guidance puts some of the parts of this puzzle together. His publication offers a new understanding of why some of the children who were in need of help have succeeded and why others with similar problems have not. More than that, he has explained a way to help most of these children, a way that is both quick and easy. But perhaps most importantly, he has called attention to the fact that many children's problems that appear to develop at school, and as a result have become the focus of academic attention, are apt to be "the red herring" symptoms of something else.

It may be that the fortunate child who found his way through normal remedial procedures to average or better performance functions as an emotionally well adjusted person. A child who through prolonged absence and failure to pay attention at a critical time perhaps through faulty teaching lacked a fundamental skill upon which to build new skills. Such a child must have been so emotionally stable as to remain unaffected by his school deficiency. When his knowledge gap was bridged he could "bloom forth." There are probably many emotionally healthy children who have determined solutions for their own academic needs and have also done something about them with or without the aid of remedial experts. But the more sensitive child or perhaps the one with parents who unintentionally contribute negatively to their susceptible child's woes, the same initial lack of a fundamental skill becomes a different story. This child's knowledge gap leads to school failure to give the child still another obstacle—"the failure" as an entity complete with self censure to accompany the new entity. This child who has missed one or more of the fundamental skills may also have picked up a sense of personal failure that the other children in his class do not have. If he didn't have an emotional problem or learning block, he is now about to acquire one. Should he fail again and be called to task for it, then, lacking other assurances, he is at the threshold of becoming involved in the three great nemeses of growing up emotionally healthy, *frustration, conflict* and *repression*.

The child's normal desire to succeed or even to excel has conflicted with the substance of having done poorly in school and being pointed out because of it. He is frustrated when he sees the fruits of his endeavors reviewed and criticized. Tensions feed upon the child's deteriorating self-image. While the situation that I am describing is serious, it, like many of the emotional problems of children, can be thought of as still superficial.

The book is primarily addressed to individuals who work with children having problems that can be defined as "superficial." Fortunately, this designation covers the vast majority of children's problems. Children with these problems seldom require the extensive use of psychotherapy.

There are some self-destroying children who subconsciously desire to fail so that they may, in this way, punish someone close to them. These unfortunate children may require the extensive treatment of expert psychiatry. But such children are unusual. It should be noted that while most emotional problems of children can be described as superficial, in time, they could become ingrained and require extensive adult treatment if they are to be resolved.

When an initial problem of a defective skill becomes surrounded by the vicious circle of tension, as described by Dr. Ambrose, it does not seem possible for any normal form of remedial help to succeed. The child's injured opinion of himself, isolated by the vicious circle of frustration, conflict and depression is standing in the way. He may earnestly try harder and make promises to his parents, and they, in turn, may do what they want to do with him, but all to no avail for the child cannot will away the harmful thoughts and impressions that have become rooted in his subconsciousness.

There are many obstacles other than scholastic disability for troubled children to face. Scholastic failure is often an attention-getter relating to the child's home situation. An all too common factor for children found in the vicious circle of tension is a feeling of being unwanted. Almost all parents want their children, but not all of them succeed in impressing their children with that fact. There are some children who are completely unsure of their parents' love and this can lead to insecurity and a desire to attract attention as a means of reassurance. With these can come the whole slippery path of nervous disorder, tics, habits, enuresis, nail-biting, asthma, and delinquency. The rising circle of tension that creates an anxiety reaction in one child compels a delinquent reaction in another. While two children may react in two different ways, the stimulus in both instances might be similar. Psychic energy may manifest itself physically or mentally. Neurotic adults are also obstacles for some children when they are in close contact with each other. An anxious mother, and even an anxious teacher can produce an anxious child. How can we erase the vicious circle of tension that limits the academic growth of these children? There is therapy ranging from the familiar psychoanalytical process to the play therapy of Lydia Jackson and Kathleen Todd. But in these techniques is a time-consuming factor and the services of a team, that adds a cost factor. Lately psychiatry has been under considerable criticism. Andrew Salter has some rather interesting comments about psychoanalysis in his book, *Conditioned Reflex Therapy*. He suggests that the process might well lose itself in some remote part of a distant graveyard not unlike the elephants who are said to drag themselves off to an elephant graveyard. He indicates that this form of therapy lacks the firm bedrock of scientific procedure—that it is confusing and extremely inefficient as universally practiced. His work seeks to develop a scientific basis for psychotherapy.

In some instances the expensive use of both time and money as demanded by psychotherapy may be mandated by the serious maladjustment of the child. But fortunately the majority of the children have "superficial problems." Their symptoms are not deepy ingrained. For these children there is a therapy that is not demanding in its treatment and cuts across the time factor. It also cuts across the cost factor as this therapy can be offered by trained individuals whose services are frequently free for the asking—clergymen, guidance counselors, etc. This therapy is offered through hypnotism.

Hypnotherapy, as it is called when employed for reeducative purposes, offers new hope for the early cases of maladjustment. Alone, hypnotism is almost a parlor room oddity. Alone it cures nothing, and it should be noted that there are some who believe that improperly used it can remove symptoms that may, without the reeducative therapy, develop into another form, perhaps even less desirable than the one removed. Although this particular point is debatable, Melvin Powers, author of the Foreword in L. T. Woodward, M.D.'s *Sex and Hypnosis,* is one who debates the issue. He writes,* "It has not been the experience of those who daily use the tool of hypnotism that the removal of a symptom is followed by another symptom . . . possibly one more serious than the one removed."

The viewpoint that is held by Powers, and others, is that without reeducative therapy the symptom removed may soon return or not be fully vanquished in the first place. It follows that unless some form of reeducative therapy has been used, real success in removing an objectionable symptom cannot be expected. In some instances, a substitute might be offered in the place of reeducation. This may consist of something that is socially acceptable and very simple in its nature. To give a subject a pure and simple suggestion, such as 'from this moment you will not bite your nails again' is doomed to fail—but a socially accepted substitute may be offered to take the place of nail biting. Better still would be hypnotherapy—and this would be finding the cause and reeducating the habit away.

## WHAT IS HYPNOSIS?

Perhaps at this point hypnotism should be defined, though its construction is elusive. Theorists have offered various explanations but they tend to conflict with each other. The definition of hypnosis offered by Dr. S. J. Van Pelt seems reasonable to me.

Van Pelt describes hypnosis as a state of exaggerated suggestibility. He explains that the mind has "units of mind power" capable of carrying out suggestions. A stream of suggestions in the ordinary waking state can only hit a few of the "units." They are ordinarily well dispersed by the labyrinth of ideas always present in the mind. As a result a suggestion is correspondingly weak. In hypnosis, these "units" are considered to be concentrated so that a stream of suggestions hits every unit. While the subject is paying attention to the hypnotist, he is completely oblivious to other things, even physical pain. Scatterbrained people make poor hypnotic subjects, being sometimes unable to concentrate long enough to bring about the great concentration required in hypnosis. Van Pelt's "Units of Mind Power" concept also explains the nature of a traumatic episode and its striking effect upon the mind. Here the total impact of a shocking situation causes all of the "units of mind power" into 100 percent concentra-

---

*Powers, M.; Foreword, *Sex and Hypnosis*, Woodward, L. T., M.D., Hollywood: Wilshire Book Company

PROLOGUE                                                                    xxv

tion. Thereafter the mind units return to their normal scattered pattern, but they leave the subject with a concentrated effect to permanently plague him. It would seem that an incident capable of producing a trauma momentarily (*Dr. S. J. Van Pelt, *Medical Hypnosis Handbook,*) produced a hypnotic situation in that all of the "units of mind power" became concentrated and produced an exaggerated suggestible state. A relieving reversal of the traumatic-producing state would seem to be possible by using corrective hypnotic suggestions.

There are many ways of producing hypnosis, and books describing the various processes are legion. It seems superfluous to describe again hypnotic procedures that are similar fundamentally. They are well publicized and there are methods that suit every individual subject. It's up to the hypnotist to adjust his methods to suit the subject and that is something that comes with experience. However, the methods used with the children discussed in this book are consistent.

The first or light stage of hypnosis produced in each following case was described and perhaps devised by Dr. C. Gindes in his book *New Concepts of Hypnosis*.**Dr. Gindes suspended an object suspended an object from the subject's finger. He caused the subject to look down past the suspended object to a cross drawn on paper. His subject was told that the object would become increasingly heavy until at last it would be too heavy to hold off the cross, etc. I changed this procedure and used a selection of Moire patterns on cellophane over an opaque glass with fluorescent lights under them. A draftsman's copying device provided me with this dramatic modification. The child looked down the string and object to illuminated pattern. The second or medium stage of hypnosis was usually induced by a method described by Dr. Gordon Ambrose as the recount method. This method is fully described in his book *Hypnotherapy with Children.*\*\*\*

Although we will refer to deep hypnosis in reference to the case studies, my reference does not refer to the deep hypnosis as described by Ambrose who suggests that the deep stage of hypnosis be left to the expert psychiatrist or psychoanalyst. He explains that the

---

*Van Pelt, Dr. S. J., *Medical Hypnosis Handbook,* Wilshire Book Company, 1965 ed.

**Gindes, C. *New Concepts of Hypnosis,* Hollywood: Wilshire Book Company

***Ambrose, G. *Hypnotherapy with Children,* London: L'Staples Press

first and second stages are adequate for treatment of the superficial symptoms usually found in children and are sufficient to help children become relaxed, less tense and able to concentrate better upon their work and to get along better in school. Hypnotherapy has a rapid effect on the child's ability to concentrate which, as Dr. Ambrose writes, is not surprising as no child could be expected to sit in school, unhappy, worried, tense and anxious, with his mind clouded by doubts, suspicions, guilty, fear or other unhappy emotions associated with insecurity and anxiety, and be expected to excel in school and behave at home.

A child who is busy attempting to work out why he seems to be unloved or unwanted at home has little chance of holding his own against the competition of a healthy, happy, well-adjusted pupil. Of special interest to educators is his report of a boy treated each day for six days. This boy was brought to Dr. Ambrose because of an anxiety problem. It seemed that all reassurances by the boy's parents, teachers and family doctor had been to no avail. His anxiety seemed to center around his school work. His report card stated that he should repeat the year. After hypnotherapy, the report from the school a year later showed that he had made a healthy advance in knowledge, even to the point of reaching the top of his class in two subjects in which he previously did poorly and that he did not seem to understand.

Dr. Ambrose suggests that research is needed and indicates that two groups of children, a controlled group and an experimental one, be arranged. All of the children would, of course, have similar problems and backgrounds. The hypnotherapy and appropriate suggestions would be given to one group but not to the other. The idea behind this arrangement would be to prove or disprove the theory that children having difficulty in school could improve their standing by receiving direct and simple suggestions such as, "You will find schoolwork easy, and you will want to work harder. You will be able to concentrate easily and remember the things taught you, and you will go to school, feel at ease there and will look forward to going to school each day." Such suggestions could be given by counselors, teachers, and doctors, as well as by the few psychiatrists who are available to children who lack the money necessary to pay for their services.

The ten students of this following study submitted themselves to hypnotherapy and were given a little more therapy than is suggested by Dr. Ambrose. The research suggested by Ambrose still remains to be done.

A few years ago researchers at the Children's Hospital in Boston developed a project personality test for young people called the TED (Tasks of Emotional Development). Children taking this test make up stories about several tasks represented by a photograph. A child's response to these "tasks" is intended to give an insight into the child's emotional development. It was decided to give this test to the students asleep as well as awake thinking that the hypnotized student might possibly divulge information more freely that he would while awake.

It was also decided to construct a word association test and to administer it to the child in both the waking and the sleeping state for the same reasons. This is another way to locate pathological material troubling the child. Other testing consisted of the Binet or Otis-Lennon Mental Ability and the Gates-MacGintie Reading Test (Drs. G. Richard and H. Cohen).

## THE METHOD

One of the best descriptions of the hypnoanalytic method of analysis is described by Robert M. Lindner in the forepart of his best selling book, *Rebel without a Cause*. In this book Dr. Lindner writes in detail of his work with a psychopathic personality. He saw this subject fifty times and described each session in considerable detail.

The children who are in this book have superficial problems and are not at all like the subject in Robert Lindner's book, *Rebel without a Cause*, but there is a relationship in methodology; his work is definitive and instructional. In every instance the children that I am writing about have had trouble with their school work and some have come into conflict with the law. Their problems can be termed superficial when compared to the problems of the subject of Lindner's book, but they are serious problems to the individuals concerned and are not considered lightly.

The various methods I have used to bring about the hypnotic trance are discussed in detail with each case history. They take up a considerable portion of the work. In most instances treatment has been combined with the induction of hypnosis right from the beginning because the subject/client needs practice if he is to achieve his goals.

Perhaps my limited use of hypnoanalysis could be called something else although it seems to me that the use of hypnoanalysis really involves a philosophy rather than a detailed and carefully formulated explanation. A feature of hypnoanalysis as practiced by Dr. Lindner is his use of hypnotism as a means of preparing for the therapy . . . and I somewhat followed his way.

He points out that, in some instances, analysis is only a little more than a diagnosis. Hypnosis as an instrument for analysis can be used to probe into the darkest area.

I agree with Dr. Lindner that hypnosis, used only as a suggestive therapy, is little more than a symptom dispeller and, as such, is almost certain to lead to failure. It is possible to suggest, under hypnosis, that relief will allay a symptom, or a habit, but the energy that created the offending symptom may not have dissipated and be just as strong as ever.

Freud has been accused of having used hypnosis to build the foundations of the psychoanalytic school of treatment that is associated with his name. Having done this, it is said, he foresook this tool but only because he could not hypnotize everyone. It seems that he sought a method that would work with all people. Lindner agrees with Freud that some people cannot be deeply hypnotized. Although, Lindner also writes that everyone can reach a hypnotic trance with some degree of success.

Perhaps there are thresholds of suggestibility in the same way that there are thresholds of stress resistance. It is now agreed that all people can be broken down by stress if it continues over a prolonged period of time. It is not really a matter of breaking down under stress but rather how much stress can an individual take before becoming disorganized.

Some individuals are easier to hypnotize than others but all are suggestible to some degree. For some reason there are such high levels of resistance to suggestions that hypnosis is difficult for some individuals. Perhaps persistant effort and adroit handling of the art might eventually reduce the strongest bar to suggestion long enough to allow some degree of hypnosis to develop—exception being only those few individuals that are "scatterbrained" or psychotic.

The fact that hypnoanalysis can shorten the time that is needed to search for pathological material and at the same time be accurate in revealing the material should earn the art, a special respect. Hypnosis can be used to search for pathological material and then to almost immediately alleviate its affects.

# PROLOGUE   xxix

Lindner begins a little differently than I do. He seems to use a training period lasting for several weeks. During this time his client is taught to achieve the trance state with a minimum of time and effort. This skill is taught through practice until at last the subject is able to pass into the hypnotic state quickly and easily. The therapist may employ several methods of inducing hypnosis if reaction to any one process is encountered. Lindner writes that it is possible to encounter multiple personalities during the treatment, each one requiring special treatment. Such an encounter can force a redirection of the hypnoanalytic method. My own subjects are not as difficult to work with and if I meet such a person in therapy I would immediately refer him to a qualified psychiatrist.

The reversed motion picture process of age regression is also well defined by Lindner. With this technique he tries to remove the subject's 'conscious' control over his statements. There are times when the subject initially resists making any statements at all. Dr. Lindner writes that the hypnotic training period should include mastery, by the subject, of post-hypnotic suggestion. In particular, the subject should be able to quickly forget or to accurately recall what has taken place during a session.

*Before entering into the analysis,* Lindner believes that the subject should be trained to enter into deep hypnosis almost as soon as he is told to go into it. From this trance he must be able to recall earlier parts of his life without any hesitation. The subject who is carefully trained in post-hypnotic suggestion is equally well trained in amnesia.

When a subject comes into an analysis session he is encouraged to bring with him anything that he wishes to discuss. The hour opens with the subject's free association of material. Hypnosis is brought into the session when it becomes obvious to the therapist that the subject is resisting the disclosure of some material. Under the influence of hypnotism, the subject is encouraged to reveal this material on to which he has been holding. Before awakening, the subject is cloaked with amnesia regarding this admission.

The key association to this questionable material is retained by the therapist for ready representation although it can be expected that the subject will repeat the material after the hypnotic session, only if the material was memorially valid and not just a screen memory. One of the greatest values of this procedure is its use as a tool to estimate the validity of revealed material and to enable the therapist to overcome future resistances.

In spite of the inducted amnesia, the sensitive material can be expected to come forth post-hypnotically almost as though no obstructin to its readmission had been introduced.

Robert M. Lindner* has entitled the two types of memories that come forth under hypnosis as regressive and revivified. The regressive memories are in terms of the subject's regard for the past. This type of memory could be responsible for developing that which is called the subject's 'frame of reference.' Regressive memories are frequently accompanied by an admission of judgement of worth. In the revivified memory, the subject relives his past experiences unhindered by regressive memories. An observation of the subject's physical activities during the session can enable the therapist to distinguish between revivified or regressive memories.

The hypnotherapist can use the tools of the psychiatrist. He can employ free association as developed by Sigmumd Freud, but he can also readily abreact a situation. He can interpret a response and in addition to this he can also employ post-hypnotic suggestion to enforce understanding and acceptance of new attitudes and patterns of behavior. It can be a reeducative process to enable the therapist to redirect the subject's energies into new and prescribed paths.

The subjects of this study are, for the most part, children who have yet to develop ingrained patterns of personality disorder or deep rooted causes for the difficulties that they face so the process is cut short and is so simple that it can be practiced by almost any educator charged with child guidance and with only a minimum amount of specialized training. There are many children who can benefit with just a minimal amount of help. There are not enough psychiatrists around to see and work with everybody and so their time is occupied by the really serious cases.

Acquiring skill in the fascinating art of hypnosis is just one part of this work. It is not only the most interesting part of the therapist's job, but it is also the easiest. The more challenging part of the work

---

*Lindner, R. *Psychoanalysis—Therapy through Hypnosis*, Wilshire Book Company, Hollywood, California. p. 213.

*Regressive memory*—The client readily recalls past events, but interprets them as he is *now*.
*Revivified memory*—The therapist helps the client to relive the past events—by going back in time and seemingly reparticipate in the event.

## PROLOGUE                                                     xxxi

is the exhaustive search for proper suggestions to be made during the hypnotic trance. Again I must emphasize that it is never enough to just tell a hypnotized person with a problem that he will get better or that he will overcome his problem if he will only try. A hypnotized subject can hardly be expected to overcome a problem with such a simple suggestion any more than a person not hypnotized.

Hypnosis is a powerful tool for focusing the complete attention of the subject on a problem, but it does not work miracles. The therapist can't expect to suggest to a hypnotized subject that his problems will disappear; it just doesn't work that way.

The work of the therapist is to dig out the causes of his subject's problem. In psychiatry, much of the burden of this job seems to be upon the subject. Here the subject, already weighed down with problems close to overwhelming, is guided into his past to uncover the frightening episodes that triggered him into coming to see the therapist. This search into his own background may cost the subject several expensive years in time and money, but there may be times when the time and cost factor is mandated by the seriousness of the subject's problem and maybe for some people there may be no other way to reach the roots of his dilemma.

In hypnotherapy, the responsibility for discovering the dynamics behind the subject's problem is upon the therapist rather than the subject. It is the therapist's duty to find the words, ideas, activities that have caused the subject to react to a situation or to behave in a manner that created the problem.

Somewhere in the subject's background there are keys to the problem. Somehow he has become conditioned to react to a situation in the wrong way. His conditioning might have taken place over many years or in just one traumatic moment. There is always a cause and effect relationship. The therapist has to find the cause and modify it *for the subject*.

He can often do this while the subject is under hypnosis. The therapist can choose to protect the subject's consciousness from past experiences that are painful. Under hypnosis the therapist can cull the subconscious memory for pathological material and leave it there or recall it to the conscious memory of the subject as the situation demands. Most importantly the therapist has a choice. This use of hypnosis is fundamental to the search for reeducative suggestions he will later make to the hypnotized subject.

Finding the right hypnotic suggestions is the most important part of the therapy. This is one thing that separates the ordinary hypnotist from a hypnoanalyst. Hypnosis itself is a realtively simple matter of finding the proper suggestion or knowing what to say or not. The suggestions that will help overcome the subject's problems is a product of the analyst's understanding of the subject and his problem. The analyst's depth of knowledge and experience in educational psychology are key factors in his ability to formulate a successful reeducative suggestion.

There are some teachers who seem to be able to intuitively understand people and their problems but most have to depend upon textbooks for a knowledge of human behavior.

There are many tools that can be used to aid in understanding children's problems. In the following cases you will read of some tools I have used in seeking clues to their problems. The most elemental tool of all is just taking the student's case history—in a proper fashion.

When I receive an application for reeducative therapy, I sometimes send the student an adjustment inventory. Hopefully this inventory will be filled out by the student's teacher or guidance counselor. The student is expected to bring the completed inventory when he comes for his first appointment.

One such inventory is the *Pupil Adjustment Inventory,* published by the Houghton Mifflin Company of Boston, Massachusetts. This company publishes two versions of their inventory, a short one and a long one. This particular inventory enables the teacher to rate the pupil in the following broad areas: academic, social, emotional, and physical, school influence, and home background.

When the inventory is completed it is possible to draw connecting lines from the 55 marks representing the teacher evaluations for each of the 55 scales on the inventory. Should the profile veer off to the left of center in any one of the areas, the therapist knows immediately that there is a problem in that area. The profile points up the area where there is need for investigation.

It is not always possible to have the pupil adjustment completed by the student's teacher. Some don't wish to do this work and sometimes the pupil doesn't want the school to know that he is seeking help outside of the school's own guidance offices. In these instances, the pupil may rate himself using the *California Test of Personality,* published by the California Test Bureau of Los Angeles, California.

The California test measures the personality of the pupil in six broad areas: personal adjustment, social adjustment, family relationship, school relationship, occupational relationship, and community relationship.

This test also lends itself to the construction of a helpful profile and offers a percentile rank for the individual in the several areas. It does much more than just indicate that a problem exists in one of the broad areas. It delineates the problem. It does not suggest the cause of a maladjustment or treatment, but it does a good job of locating the problem quickly . . . and sometimes the elusive reeducative suggestions can be found through these two personality instruments.

One of the most interesting instruments is the picture-instigated stories that the students have to make up with the *Tasks of Emotional Development* personality test. This instrument was developed at the Children's Hospital of Boston a few years ago. It probably could be considered a structured projection test of the second level in test standing if we consider the California test to be in the third level and the Rorschach in the first level.

Diagnostic tests to determine specific educational disabilities are readily available. Reading tests are especially abundant for the hypnotherapist who wants to deal with children. The Bond-Clymer-Hoyt *Silent Reading Diagnostic Tests* published by Lyons and Carnaham Publishing Company of Chicago, Illinois is a good example. This is an analytical type of test that gives detailed information about the strengths and weaknesses of a pupil's reading. Specific measures of a child's diagnosis is given in the following reading skills:

The location within a word where the child makes his errors.
Recognizing words in isolation.
Recognizing reversible words in the context.
Locating word elements.
Syllabication.
Locating route words.
Knowing word elements.
Recognizing the beginning sounds.
Letter sounds.
Knowing how to synthesize words.

There are many other reading tests that are not necessarily diagnostic but are helpful in working with children. One is the *Inventory Survey Test,* published by the Scott-Foresman Company of Chicago, Illinois. Other tests used with a great deal of success is the very comprehensive *Iowa Every Pupil Tests* published by Houghton Mifflin

Company of Boston, Massachusetts. Still another is the *Stanford Achievement Test Battery* of the Harcourt Brace and World Company of New York.

The *Revised Stanford Binet* intelligence test is an excellent and easy means to obtain the intelligence quotient of a student. Unlike some other tests, its use requires special training. It is an individual test and is a true performance test. It is a time consuming test, especially so with a bright student who will test on and on, passing sub-test after sub-test. There are a multitude of "paper and pencil" intelligence tests—the therapist has to pick and choose.

There are a number of intelligence tests published by Harcourt Brace and World Company of New York. Some are developed especially for children who are in the first three grades. For these children such a test might be considered a true performance test if it is not dependent upon the pupil's ability to read. Reading factor usually enters paper and pencil tests for children who are in grades four through twelve. And a pupil with a reading disability will score an I.Q. less than his true potential. Reading disabilities always depress scores since tests require reading competency.

A different type of test that is highly recommended is the *Flannagan Aptitude Classification Test* published by the Science Research Associates of Chicago, Illinois. This test is useful in guiding students seeking help in establishing educational and vocational plans. There are 19 separate tests in this comprehensive battery that identify a student's aptitude for 37 occupational areas. Dr. Flannagan suggests a timetable consisting of three sessions of three hours each. I have given this test to some individuals in just one day and they seem to have come out well.

There are many other test instruments just as good or better than the ones mentioned. Present tests are always being revised and new ones are always being constructed. The selection of the test instrument is an individual choice. The most important thing to remember is that test values must be interpreted by the analyst in relationship to the various factors that go to make up his subject's personality. No score is absolute. All scores are subject to interpretation. The most objective instrument available is at times subjective. The value of the various tests lies in understanding their limitations, and the therapist must remember that an individual with a great amount of drive towards a goal can confound the most objective test.

# CHAPTER ONE
# BOBBY: ENURESIS AND DYSLEXIA

The enuretic child's problem may be caused by a physical condition and if it is, no amount of hypnosis is going to assuage the enuresis; but if the original cause for the condition has become reinforced or replaced by a mental condition (fear/worry) then hypnosis can help.

The many worthwhile drugs used in the treatment of enuresis may fail if the physician doesn't include, along with his drugs, some needed reassurance and affirmations. If the physician and the hypnotherapist will work together as a medical team then the chances of the patient overcoming his enuretic condition seems to be assured.

Bobby had been to see his physician before coming to see me. The physician and I didn't know about our mutual interest in the child, but we coincidentally complemented each other's work. The physician attended to the child's physical condition and I stumbled upon the child's mental condition and cured the child because that is what the child expected me to do.

Bobby's teacher said that he suffered from dyslexia because the child wrote some numbers and some letters backwards. I suppose the teacher used one or more of the following test instruments to help come to that conclusion: VM, BGT, the Detroit, the Wepman, the Slossen and the Frostig. The trouble is that all of the commonly used tests have been carefully scrutinized and found to be both unreliable and invalid. They don't measure what they are supposed to in the same way repeatedly.*

---

*Howards, Melvin, Ph.D. Director, Reading and Learning Clinic, Northeastern University, Boston, Massachusetts. Boston Sunday Globe Dec. 6, 1981.

It is interesting to note that the dyslexic child (Bobby) read and wrote *some* of the letters and numbers backwards, but not all of them. I wondered why.

Bobby was as handsome as a young boy could possibly be. His brown eyes sparkled and his dimples winked pleasantly at me while he answered my questions. He seemed confident and well adjusted, but he wasn't. He had some serious problems. Bobby was a school failure and he suffered from enuresis.*

Following my usual custom, I asked Bobby to tell me about every important success that he had enjoyed, in or out of school. He couldn't think of any. When I asked him to tell me about his failures he was eager to talk. These are his exact words, "It happened when I was not promoted. I think about it a lot. I feel bad about it. My friends made it, but I didn't. I am stupid."

Bobby liked his friends, his family and his teachers. He even liked the teacher who made him repeat a grade. Bobby blamed himself and not his teacher for his failure. He appeared to like just about everybody, but he did consider some of his sisters to be, "pains in the neck."

I administered the *California Test of Personality*. Bobby required some help in reading a few of the questions, but that help didn't affect the outcome of the test except to clarify some of his responses. Bobby's overall test rating was fairly good, but there were a few personality low spots that we could work with later on.

Bobby's California Test profile contained these scores:

I. **Personal Adjustment**
   - A. Self reliance — 69%
   - B. Sense of personal worth — 50%
   - C. Sense of personal freedom — 90%
   - D. Withdrawing tendencies — 80%
   - E. Nervous systems — 80%

II. **Social Adjustment**
   - A. Social standards — 60%
   - B. Social skills — 30%
   - C. Antisocial tendencies — 50%
   - D. Family relationships — 30%
   - E. School relationships — 30%
   - F. Community relationships — 90%

---

*Bed wetting

The test profile revealed that Bobby had a few problems in the social skills. His mother had already told me that he couldn't get along with other children: that he was quick to lose his temper and strike them, that he wouldn't play with other children just because they wanted to play. Bobby would play with other children only if he felt like playing and then he would play with them if everything went his way. I couldn't help but wonder if this was Bobby's way of regaining some of the status he lost when he failed to get promoted.

Bobby didn't want to go to school any more. He wanted to stay home where he felt safe. School had become a disaster area for him. He believed, "I'm stupid."

Bobby was a bed wetter. He had been doing this every night for as long as he could remember. His mother had taken him to see a doctor, hoping to find a cure. In fact, Bobby had been to see several doctors. One of the doctors had prescribed a blanket fitted with an electrical device that caused a bell to ring after the boy had urinated upon it. The device worked very well. It woke the boy up, but it also woke everyone in the house. The bell rang after the urination had taken place and that was the trouble with it. Regrettably, it could not be set to ring before the urination act for that would have solved the problem.

Bobby's doctors couldn't find anything wrong with the bladder nor any related linkage. He had been given some medication that was supposed to cure his enuresis, but it hadn't worked at all. Bobby was enuretic and there seemed to be nothing that anyone could do about it. His parents had finally given up trying to cure Bobby and their surrender may have helped. Bobby had learned to take care of himself and his bed clothes, after his accidents, and that may have been helpful.

Bobby's mother explained that he had no trouble in learning how to walk or to talk. He accomplished both of these things when he was only one year old. He was toilet trained when he was about two and one half years old. When he was three he was able to go outside and play with the other children in the neighborhood. He played in a very aggressive manner and soon became the neighborhood terror. It was reported that he once put sand in the gasoline tank of a neighbor's automobile. Bobby readily accepted the blame for the incident even though it developed that an older boy had put him up to it. Bobby became interested in fires that caused his mother to give up her job and spend more time at home with him. Interestingly enough, Bobby's fire setting activities ceased after she quit her job. I wondered if his bed wetting problem had any connection with his fire starting inclinations.

Bobby had the pleasing ability to make friends easily, but when his new friends went home equipped with a new enlarged vocabulary acquired while playing with Bobby, their parents quickly put an end to the developing friendships. As a result Bobby's use of profanity was slowing down. Bobby's teachers characterized him as being withdrawn, quiet, immature and possessing a short attention span. They also said that he pushed other children around.

Bobby preferred to play with older boys rather than with boys of his own age. The older boys enjoyed having him around. This may have been because Bobby would steal money from his parents and buy them candy. Bobby had failed to ingratiate himself with his neighbors and his family, but to me he was a loveable, highly entertaining and very intriguing boy. But then I didn't have to live with him.

I decided to give Bobby the *Frostig Development Test of Visual Perception.*\* This is a test that explores the effect of a visual handicap upon school learning. There are five separate tests in this instrument. The first test involves exercises that check the student's eye and hand coordination. The second test determines a child's ability to perceive figures against a background of increasingly complex designs. The third test checks the child's ability to recognize various geometric shapes. The fourth test determines the child's ability to recognize reversals and rotation of shapes in space. The last test checks the child's ability to handle spacial relationships.

Bobby did very poorly with this test. It developed that he was in the lowest quartile. His percentile was only 4. Bobby needed immediate training in all of the areas covered by this test. It was no wonder the child was experiencing school problems. His teacher's comments seemed to confirm the test results. Bobby had learned next to nothing while he was in the first grade. He was, at the time I worked with him, in the second grade, but it was his third year in school. He was doing very poorly in the second grade.

Bobby was a very trusting individual. He loved coming to see me. He was receptive to positive suggestions and so he responded well to meditation therapy.\*\*

---

\**Development Test of Visual Perception,* Marriane Frostig, et al. Consulting Psychologist Press, Palo Alto, California—Follet Publishing Company

\*\*Hypnotherapy

I gave Bobby the *Otis Mental Ability Test* Level One, Form J, to find out if he was as intelligent as he appeared to be. In spite of his educational handicap Bobby did very well and achieved an I.Q. of at least 98. His mental age, as determined by this test was 8 years and 11 months. The score was only two months behind his chronological age. The boy was perceptually handicapped and it appeared that he had learned nothing during his first year at school, and was getting very little out of his second year.

Bobby said that he could hardly wait for our visits together. To my surprise, during one of our visits he told me that he had almost stopped bed wetting. I was surprised because enuresis had not been mentioned. While his mother had mentioned this to me I never spoke about it to the child, thinking that it might be embarrassing to him. Later on, I discovered that his mother had informed him that his bed wetting problem was one of the reasons she had sent him to me. I don't attempt to provide therapy for enuresis feeling that this is a medical problem that is more appropriately handled by the physicians. Bobby had listened to his mother and believed that he was receiving therapy for enuresis and as a result had wet the bed only once in the past several weeks. He was disgusted with his younger brother who wet the bed. He was refusing to sleep in the same bed with him.

I saw Bobby eight times and during each visit used meditation/therapy that included these thoughts, "You are a very intelligent boy therefore you will have no trouble in learning to read. You will soon like reading." In the middle of his meditation I roused the boy and had him read a few paragraphs from an appropriate test. Bobby made mistakes and they were immediately corrected and the paragraph re-read correctly and then we would continue with the meditation. "Tomorrow, in school, you will read just as well as you have done here tonight."

Bobby couldn't make the number five correctly. "I have trouble with numbers, especially the fives . . . I make them backwards."

I asked the boy to do some arithmetic for me and sure enough the boy constructed all of the fives backwards. He seemed to be unable to construct a five correctly unless he was carefully guided each time that he made one. His mother explained that he had always made his fives backwards. I wondered if his teachers had labeled the boy dyslexic. While the boy was deep in meditation/therapy I instructed him, "You will begin to make fives the right way, you are going to remember to make them the right way from now on," with this short comment I guided his hand through several fives. Later on during the same session he did some arithmetic problems for me and this time there were no errors with his fives.

Bobby came again the following week and he could hardly wait to say, "I don't make my fives backwards anymore. My teacher noticed this and asked, 'What happened?' I explained, I go to see Mr. Duke."

Bobby was eager to demonstrate his prowess in number writing so he made a lot of fives for me. I made up a few problems that contained fives in their answers. Bobby wrote his fives correctly every time. He wasn't fooling; Bobby had overcome this dyslexic type problem with just one lesson in meditation/therapy. His attitude towards school was improving. Bobby read from his school text. He stumbled a few times but quickly recovered and without any help from me continued to read. Later, during the meditation/therapy sequence of our session, I again counseled, "You will remember the words...."

I only saw the boy one more time after the arithmetic episode. Bobby came at my request and stayed for just a short time because someone was impatiently waiting for him. Bobby did a few arithmetic problems for me. They had fives in their answers. Bobby slipped up once. He quickly spotted his own error. Bobby apologized for this single error. I assured him that no apology was necessary, "After years of making fives the wrong way, what's one error every now and then. The important thing is that you spotted and corrected it immediately."

There wasn't enough time to check his reading progress, but he claimed that he was doing great. I was inclined to believe him because he had been so frank about everything else. It was obvious that the boy was now oriented toward success. He didn't mention the bed wetting problem and neither did I.

## CHAPTER TWO
# JOHN: FEAR AND FAILING

John, like any other child, needed to succeed in something more than just a foot race on the playground. Some failure is inevitable and it can become a foundation for success, but a history of failure in school can only lead a child to expect more failure in school. John's fear of failure was about to cause an emotional disturbance.

John had failed so often that he had come to the conclusion, "I can't read so good ... I don't know the words."

John's expectations and self image changed because he quickly responded to hypnotherapy. In just a few months he lost his perturbed, anxious and unhappy feelings. John changed his self image and came to the new conclusion, "I'm doing fine ... I don't need any more help."

### FIRST SESSION

John is a handsome nine-year-old boy who had to repeat a year in school. I would like to find out why this happened to John and see what kind of effect this had made upon him. Later I will try to formulate hypnotic suggestions to help him through any difficulties that he might have as a result of his failure.

It was Friday and this night is the traditional schoolboy's night out. While I was sure that John wouldn't be going anywhere, it was equally certain that he wouldn't be interested in continuing with a long test session. He was given only the first part of the Otis-Lennon Mental Ability Test Elementary Level 1 Form J. This is a fairly pleasant activity. Following the test session, I lightly hypnotized the boy. John sat, as requested, beside the drafting machine. This is a metal box with a ground glass top illuminated from beneath with fluorescent bulbs. On top of the glass I had placed a design to create an optical illusion. He extended his forefinger so that I could fasten a thread holding a small weight at the other end. John leaned over the glass to aim the weight at the center of the intricate pattern. I explained that he would soon enjoy a feeling that would resemble sleeping, but would not be the same, a pleasant, lovely moment of half awakeness that occurs sometimes just as his mother is calling him from sleep. "How lovely is that feeling of half awake and half asleep . . . etc."

Soon his eyes closed and with one of my hands resting gently on the back of his head and the other on his forehead I guided his head to rest upon the drafting table and then I shut off its light. I implanted just one suggestion in his mind, "You will look forward to coming again . . . you will feel good about the work that we are going to do together."

## SECOND SESSION

John came in smiling for his second session. He had been looking ahead to this session with eagerness—could our last post-hypnotic suggestions have contributed to his anticipation? His first task was to finish the Otis-Lennon Mental Ability Test that he had begun the week before. This test was a good one for him because it doesn't involve reading. Most paper and pencil tests of mental ability consist of so much reading that a student with a reading disability taking the test would be seriously handicapped. His derived I.Q. score would be far below his true power.

On this 1967 edition of the test, John got 52 correct responses out of 80 to give him an I.Q. of 99 or just average. His mental age according to the test was 9 years and 3 months and his chronological age was 9 years and 3 months which is an exact correlation of mental abilities to mental age. In the percentages, he was ahead of 48 percent of those who have taken the test in his same grade, but it must be remembered that this boy is repeating the grade. The test did indicate that John has a good solid ability to work and that he should be doing much better than he is.

It was too early in the session for John to enter the hypnotic sequence so he was instructed to begin work on the *Iowa Every Pupil Test of Silent Reading Comprehension,* Form L, the elementary battery for grades 2 through 5—one of the older editions. It developed that the boy could not comprehend the reading at all and that his vocabulary development was almost too low to score. He was given the reading test immediately after finishing the mental ability test.

I am inclined to believe that the results of his reading test were not depreciated by the earlier test and that John not only couldn't read, but this was directly responsible for his non-promotion in the fourth grade. The boy's good mind indicated that he would be a good prospect for remedial reading, but this wasn't offered at his school.

Out of 58 possible correct responses on the comprehension part of the test the boy only scored 8 right. The publishers do not give a grade equivalent for a score this low. On the vocabulary part of the test he only got 6 correct responses out of a total of 40 possible ones. Again the publishers do not give a grade equivalent for such a low score. His total score of 14 the grade equivalent was grade one and eight months.

The boy was again placed under hypnosis. While "asleep" he was given a simple word association test mostly to help him get accustomed to making responses while under hypnosis. He was also given the same word association while awake. The results of this word association test while awake and under hypnosis is as follows:

| **Stimulus** Word | Awake Association | Sleep Association |
|---|---|---|
| Dark | Light | Light |
| Sickness | Hurts | Hurts |
| Mountain | High | High |
| Girl | Boy | Boy |
| Boy | Girl | Girl |
| Beautiful | Handsome | Handsome |
| Smooth | Hard | Hard |
| Big | Small | Small |
| Small | Big | Big |
| Slow | Fast | Fast |
| Man | Woman | Woman |
| Brave | Scared | Scared |
| School | Learn | Learn |
| Woman | Man | Man |
| Ruler | Measure | Measure |

In both instances the boy responded to the stimuli in the same manner and there was no significant or unusual deviation from what is referred to as normal.

I decided to use another method to hypnotize the boy. This time I carefully took his pulse and set a metronome to beating in time with his heart. To mask other noises from the neighborhood I started up a soft sound maker. He soon showed signs of going into a trance. My hypnotic patter reminded him how easily he had entered a trance the time before, "Your arm got so heavy that it sank to the table and your head soon followed ... to make sure that it didn't happen too quickly I put my hand on your forehead and as it came down I let it rest upon my hand."

As this was only the boy's second visit I concluded with suggestions that would lead to greater success under hypnosis and then gently brought him back to awareness.

### THIRD SESSION

John's case history had revealed his affection for his parents, "They are good to me ... they buy me things."

Children associate love with food or other gifts given to them. It is unfortunate that they feel, sometimes erroneously, that the bearer of a gift is also giving some love along with the gift.

John likes the other members of his family and also claims to have two close friends. He likes to go to school and there he appreciates art, physical education and recess, in that order. John doesn't like any academic subjects.

The greatest happiness that he can remember is a family outing at a pleasure park in New Hampshire where they all enjoyed rides and had a picnic. I reflected on how his greatest happiness was such a simple thing and suspected that his parents got as much happiness from the outing as John did.

John does not feel misunderstood by his friends, parents, teachers or brothers and sisters. He isn't searching for his "real self." He recognizes that he has a problem. He shyly admits, "I can't read so good ... I don't know the words."

When I asked John to talk about his success stories he could only admit to running well. It developed that the children of his school engage in foot races during recess and John wins. To me this was an indictment of his school and of the teachers who work with the boy. Everybody, but especially a vulnerable child, needs to be successful at something other than just running. It seemed to me that a part of each teacher's day should be devoted to finding something that would enable each child to be successful within the classroom, because success generates more success. This boy failed to be promoted in the first grade because he was 'immature' and couldn't read. Today this boy was in the third grade, but he still couldn't read. Was it because he was still immature? After more than three years of school he couldn't remember a successful school experience other than a foot race on the playground. His present reading level was only that of a good first grader, and the boy was of average intelligence.

His greatest "hate" was to fail, "like in football and you don't do so good ... the other kids say things at you ... you feel sad."

"Has anything like this happened to you?" I asked.

He answered, "Yes."

John couldn't remember having any trouble with strangers, family, etc. He remembered a man who rode around in a car and sometimes stopped and looked at him. "What did you think about this?" I asked.

"It made me feel funny," he answered.

John's greatest fear was of the dark. "Sometimes when I have to go home from my friend's house ... it is dark ... and I have to pass the woods (a small park on one side of the street) ... Sometimes there are men in there and they drink beer," he explained.

It was hard to determine if his greatest fear was of the dark or or the men whom he feels are in the woods at night. When John was asked if he had any special problems that he wanted to tell me about at school or at home with his family he replied, "Yes ... at school ... I want to be smart."

"Have you ever seen anyone hypnotized?" I asked.

"No," he replied.

"Do you feel that you were hypnotized last week?" I questioned.

"Yes, I did go to sleep," he replied.

"How did it feel?"

"It felt good," he replied with a smile.

"What is hypnosis like?" I asked.

"It's like falling to sleep without trying," he replied.

John relaxed in the leather chair that was much too large for him. When most of the lights were turned out I held a small penlight in front of his eyes and continued to talk in a soothing manner. While talking I lowered the light from a position of several inches above his eyes to several inches below. His eyes followed the sinking light and were soon tightly closed—and he went to "sleep." He then received suggestions stating that he will soon learn to like words ...

that any boy as intelligent as he would have no trouble with words. Because he had only reached the shallow stages of hypnosis up to that point, I also implanted the suggestion that he would go deeper into hypnosis the next time.

## FOURTH SESSION

After an unavoidable absence of several weeks, John seemed glad to be back with me. This time, because he had done so poorly on his reading achievement test yet so well on his intelligence test, I decided to give him the Intermediate Durrell Sullivan Reading Capacity Test. This is an interesting examination that consists of many pictures. Each one answers a question from stories that the examiner reads. There are two parts to the test. First there is a WORD MEANING section where the child's hearing vocabulary is tested by having him find the pictures that illustrate the words pronounced by the examiner. The second part is PARAGRAPH MEANING. Paragraphs are read to the child and he seeks a picture to illustrate his ability to understand the paragraph read.

John did well, his results are as follows:
WORD MEANING—Score 30, his Grade Equivalent—3.8, Age Equivalent—9.1.
PARAGRAPH MEANING—Score 26, his Grade Equivalent—3.8, Age Equivalent—9.1.
TOTAL MEANING—Score 56, his Grade Equivalent—3.9, Age Equivalent—9.3.

John's reading capacity, as measured by this test, was very different from his actual reading achievement. How could this have happened? Did he develop reading block at an early age that arrested his progress? Was he a victim of poor teaching?

His previous hypnotic trance had been so shallow that I decided to return to the drafting device that first fascinated him. I decided to spend much of this session developing and strengthening our rapport in hypnosis. John's hand was quickly pulled down to the glass followed immediately by his head.

His eyes closed according to my suggestions and he was quickly in a light hypnosis.

I told John that he would be more comfortable in the leather chair and would remain 'asleep,' but with opened eyes, while being assisted into the chair. The flashing metronome was placed in his hands. He was instructed to keep his eyes upon the light. The audible part of the machine was turned down very low. It wasn't long before his eyes again closed. He was asked to remain in hypnosis, but to open his eyes once more so that I could again hypnotize him. I piled hypnosis upon hypnosis until at last he could hardly open his eyes (even upon command).

It was then explained that there were several levels of hypnosis, level one, two, three, and so on. "Tell me what level are you now in?" I asked.

"Two," he softly replied, but I don't believe he really knew.

"You know that if you are really in the second stage I can insert a needle into your hand without your feeling it," I stated.

"I know," he stated.

"Then is it all right with you if I do just that," I continued.

"Yes," he replied.

With this I pricked his finger with a sterile needle and he didn't change his expression or move a muscle. I know there was no effort being made to trick me—not by this boy—I'm always a little cautious as previous subjects have done exactly that—pretending to be hypnotized when they were not.

I told him that school would become easier for him each day because he was intelligent. I explained again how we had discovered this to be true with our testing program, and because he had such a good mind it would be easier for him to remember things taught to him in school. I explained that it wasn't his fault that he had had some difficulty in school, but it was all over now . . . this was a new day and he was going to make the most of it.

John was introduced to a definite post-hypnotic suggestion. I sounded a small gong and remarked, "John, I'm going to use this gong to later return you to the state of hypnosis that you are now in . . . I'll sound this gong in this way and say sleep . . . sleep . . . sleep. When I do this you will again enter the sleep state that you are now in, but this sleep will only come over you if I ring this particular bell." It was important to state that he wouldn't fall into hypnosis should someone else ring a bell. He needed to understand clearly that only my ringing this particular bell would produce the effect. I didn't want the boy to enter hypnosis by accident or by another person.

John was awakened and we talked for a while about his experiences under hypnosis. He remarked that he felt good and couldn't remember anything that was done or said to him.

"Do you remember this?" I asked as I rang the gong and chanted with each beat, sleep . . . sleep . . . sleep. John's eyes soon closed and he was again under the influence of hypnosis. "What stage of hypnosis are you now in?" I asked.

"Stage two," he answered.

"If you are truly in stage two then you will feel no pain should I stick this needle in your finger. Do you mind if I try?" I somewhat viciously asked.

"I don't mind," he returned.

His response satisfied me that he was in a deep stage of hypnosis and that he had attained that stage in just a few minutes. Could he hold this post-hypnotic suggestion until the next time we met which would be at least a week away, possibly two weeks?

John again received the same suggestions concerning his school work that he had heard a few minutes earlier and was then brought back to the waking stage. He felt fine when awakened possibly as a result of the suggestion that I always make to an awakening subject— "You will feel better than ever when you have awakened from this refreshing sleep."

## FIFTH SESSION

It was three weeks before the boy returned and he came with his interested mother. While the boy and I talked together he continually darted his eyes at her and I became concerned about the effect upon the session. I had the pictures of the TED (Tasks of Emotional Development) ready for him. This is a projective personality test developed at the Children's Hospital in Boston. John's mother was interested in seeing the pictures, but remained only long enough to hear his responses to the first picture. I think that he was relieved at this. She may have noticed that she was distracting the boy's attention. After she had left I asked John, "Did your mother's presence make you feel a little bit uncomfortable?"

The boy smiled and replied, "A little bit."

This was a good example of why it is usually best to have the parents of children wait in another room. It is better still to have the parents leave the child and pick him up an hour later.

The TED indicated that John is experiencing trouble growing up. He failed to score well on a number of the *tasks*.

The first picture was of the task of learning to socialize. Here John readily perceived a boy in position to join with other boys, but regrettably he perceived that the teams had already been picked, and his boy, in the picture, didn't get to join in the fun. In fact his boy felt sad because he was left out. He just watched the other boys play. John's response to the same picture under hypnosis was about the same. It seems that John has the problem of socialization.

The second picture was one of developing trust. Here John scored well in all four areas represented by this picture. He quickly perceived a lady giving a boy some cookies though I wondered why the lady giving the cookies to the pictured boy was not the boy's mother, but instead the mother of a friend. Was this significant? Even so the boy took the cookies from the 'mother substitute' and was happy to get them. Again, under hypnosis, John's responses were about the same.

The third picture was one of aggression, because he scored only a two on several of the categories represented by this picture. He was in a fight situation, but didn't permit the fight to develop. John seemed so hesitant that I wondered if he was trying to figure out what I wanted to hear from him about his story of the picture. Did he feel that I believed that boys should not fight and so he made up a story accordingly? Under hypnosis John changed his story only slightly. When awake he was asked, "How did the neutral boy feel when the other boy was threatening him?" John replied, "Angry."

Later, and under hypnosis, John said the boy was "Scared."

The fourth task is one of learning. While it is obvious that John has a problem in school, I had to score him a "one" which was good because in all of the dimensions tested by this picture John not only readily perceived a student doing his homework, but stated that the boy was happy to do it. He has adjusted to school, but just can't get going.

John's response to the next picture was very significant. This represented the task of conscience development. John immediately saw a boy in a position to steal some money, which he did. His boy in the picture not only took the money to buy things for himself, but was happy about the whole thing. John failed this developmental task for he not only had the boy steal the money, but his make-believe boy showed no remorse about it.

Task six is separation from the mother figure. John completely failed this task. In this picture there is a boy on a threshold, going in or out at the same time, responding to a woman. John perceived the boy coming in from the outside, and the mother worried because he had been out so long. Both the mother and the boy felt better now that he was home. Again, his responses under hypnosis were about the same as while awake. I am reasonably sure that John has a serious problem in separating from his mother and pretty sure that there is nothing that I can do about it because the problem, most likely is with the mother and not the child—can she separate from him?

The boy leaned back in the chair in anticipation of hypnosis, looking very serious, "I don't think that I am going very deep in hypnosis."

"You will tonight," I replied. The boy began to breath deeply as requested and to the accompaniment of the gong I chanted, sleep . . . sleep . . . sleep. Soon his eyelids closed and I could see the movement of the eyeballs under the lids. "Have you reached that stage where you can't open your eyes?" I asked.

"Yes, I have," he responded.

"Good, you are doing very well tonight," I complimented. "Let's try a test." I clasped my hands over both of his and remarked, "If you have been successful in reaching deeper into hypnosis then your hands will stick together after I remove mine from yours." This was repeated several times and then I asked, "Why don't you try now and see?" John struggled mightily to get his hands apart but could not do it. "You are doing very well with hypnosis tonight, aren't you?" I asked. John nodded his head.

"You want to go deep into hypnosis tonight so I'm going to pile hypnosis upon hypnosis. I'm going to have you remain asleep, but do open your eyes and watch the light from my penlight sway from eye to eye." John opened his eyes and I could see the pale blue irises dilate as the light struck them. "Think of hypnosis as a tunnel or cave with you at the beginning of it. You are looking down into the tunnel and you are going deeper and deeper inside . . . you want to see what is there . . . keep moving in, deeper and deeper." John's eyes closed again in response to the light and suggestions. It can be assumed that he was more deeply hypnotized as a result.

"We will try another test of hypnosis," I remarked. "I am going to rub your right hand like this and as I do, it will get numb . . . numb . . . numb, until at last you will lose all feeling in it." Finally, I remarked to the boy, "Let me pinch both hands. First I will pinch the back of your left hand. Does it hurt?" I asked. John made no effort to withdraw the hand, but admitted that it did hurt. "How about this hand?" I asked as I pinched the back of his right hand. "I know that you are pinching it, but it doesn't hurt," he replied. And so I know that I had developed a deep rapport with the boy—and that he was ready for the following.

"Tonight, I will implant some suggestions in your mind and they will become a part of you to remain forever." With this comment the suggestive therapy began. "You know that you are intelligent and that there is no reason for your not doing well in school. You have the ability to do well. It is all up to you. You are going to like school better and better each day because you are going to do better and better there. You are going to remember the things that are taught to you there."

I opened a third grade reading book and opened it to the middle. "Remain in hypnosis, but open your eyes and read what you see on this page," I requested. John did as he was instructed. He read, but his efforts were pitiful. When he had finished the page I remarked, "You will again read the page and as you do I will correct your mistakes. You are to remember each correction so that when you read it for the third time you will be able to do so without making any mistakes."

It was fascinating to see him do exactly as he was told. He correctly read the page without mistakes the third time. He read fast and easily. I asked questions and saw that he comprehended what he had just read. After all, the words were a part of his speaking vocabulary. "John, you read without any trouble and so it will be when you go to school tomorrow. Remember to pay attention to your teacher and you will do well. You will not daydream but will pay close attention to your teacher. You will remember and do better and better each day."

While John was receiving these suggestions, I wondered about the results of the TED test. Had his separation problem negatively influenced his work at school? Could his reading disability be a home-related problem? I will never know.

### SIXTH SESSION

It was the day after Thanksgiving and later on that day several of my friends and their children were coming to view a rather exciting color TV program. Color TVs were relatively new at the time. We planned to have refreshments for the children. John was invited to stay and join in the fun after the lesson. The boy wanted to stay and did so. The interesting point in all of this is that his mother phoned twice during the evening to see if her son wanted to come home. He didn't need transportation as there were plenty of cars available and people to drive them when he was ready to leave. His mother demonstrated the anxiety that had been poignantly revealed the week before in the TED test.

John had done so poorly on that part of the TED that it was impossible to score his story. He had created a story of a boy who had failed to separate from his mother ... the TED test had acquired, in my eyes, a new element of credibility. I wondered if John had school phobia in grade one? I chose not to age regress in order to find out.

The relationship between the therapist and his client is very close, with the client usually wanting to keep other people out of the relationship. John went into a trance readily, but he had to work harder to obtain it than he had the week before. Again, the hypnosis was deepened by piling more inductions on top of the first one.

"I will again give you the same suggestions, for emphasis, that I did last week," I said. "But before we do that will you remain in hypnosis but open your eyes and read a page of this book?"

Once more John opened his eyes and read from the third grade reader and made a few mistakes. The boy was corrected and told to read again, but without making any mistakes at all. He did exactly that.

I closed his eyes with a slight pressure from my fingers and gave him the same message that he had heard before, "You read very well today. There is no reason why you can't do it every day. First of all you know that you are an intelligent boy. I have told you that before. You took an intelligence test and that proved the truth of what I have been telling you. Now you will not only read better in school, but you will find it easier to remember the things that are taught to you there. You will like words and you will like school and you won't have time to daydream because you will be so interested in doing your schoolwork."

Remembering his poor performance on the TED picture for conscience development I added, "You tell me that you go to church on Sunday. I'm glad to hear that because that means you know right from wrong. You feel your conscience speak to you when you have been wrong, don't you?"

John murmured, "Yes, I do," and with this admission he was awakened.

## SEVENTH SESSION

John came for his seventh and last session full of bounce. He seemed to have developed an almost complete faith in me. His eyes twinkled with boyish humor. He went readily into hypnosis. We tested him in the usual manner and found that his trance was adequate.

I wanted to try a test for an induced amnesia—one that hadn't worked with him before. I gave the boy three words: blue, black, and white. He was asked to hallucinate a blackboard and then to see himself writing those words upon his blackboard. He was then asked to erase the first two words. Each time that he mentally erased a word from his imaginary blackboard I rubbed my hands over his forehead and asked that the word also be erased from his memory. We repeated this activity several times before he was asked to see if he could remember the words. He thought for a moment and did remember the words . . . he might not have done so . . . post-hypnotically.

"Why don't we try for a deeper hypnosis," I suggested. "Perhaps then we will succeed." John opened his eyes and I played the pen light back and forth across his eyes. Again I suggested that he think of hypnosis as a long tunnel and that he would like to explore by going deeper inside it. Once more the boy's eyes closed and it seemed he had entered into a deeper stage of hypnosis. We repeated the blackboard experiement and this time we were successful. John was unable to remember the first two words. He was given several minutes to try. His brow furrowed as he struggled to recall the words. Finally he was told that they were blue and black.

"Oh yes, now I remember," he called with apparent relief.

John was awakened in the usual gentle manner with positive suggestions about feeling well.

## FINAL MEETING

It was a year before I again saw John. He hadn't felt the need for additional therapy, in fact he protested when asked to come to my office. "I'm doing fine . . . I don't need any more help." The boy came as he was requested, not to receive help, but to participate in a test.

According to the boy's mother and teacher, John was doing well in school. Very importantly, he believed that he was doing well and he enjoyed the feeling of success. He had lost the pathetic "hangdog" expression that he had exhibited a year ago. Very few of his problems had been resolved. But he was doing better in school and that was the object of our work together.

Once more, the boy took the *Iowa Every Pupil Test of Silent Reading Comprehension*. It was the same test that he had done so poorly in the year before. I suppose that it could be said that since he had previously taken the test, the results of the second time were augmented by the first time. This might be true had not a full year lapsed. There was no "halo effect."

The results were as follows:

| OCTOBER 1967 | OCTOBER 1968 |
|---|---|
| **Reading Comprehension** | **Reading Comprehension** |
| So low that his response could not be scored. | 3.3 grade |
| **Vocabulary** | **Vocabulary** |
| So low that his response could not be scored. | 4.2 grade |
| **Total Response** | **Total Response** |
| 1.8 grade | 3.7 grade |

The difference between the two test results was striking. The fact that the boy made this advance in reading without even the benefit of remedial reading instruction is of extreme interest. Nothing new was added to the boy's life. There was no tutor. His advancement was the result of educational hypnotherapy that consisted of just seven involvements with a prime purpose to change his self-image.

# CHAPTER THREE
# RICHARD: SCHOOL PHOBIA

A phobia is a functional abnormality due to some maladjustment in functioning. It is caused by an unfortunate, unusual and vivid earlier experience. The special association phenomena of a phobia is an uncontrollable fear. There are many different abnormal and uncontrollable fears. In order to treat a phobia it is necessary to discover its cause and then to re-integrate the emotions with the personality.

Richard is a good example of a child suffering from this psychoneuroses. Richard is afraid to leave his mother—something might happen to her.

## FIRST SESSION

Richard *is* only seven years old. His eyes are a pale blue and he has long blonde hair with just a trace of a wave in it. His size and weight are about normal for his age. He is an attractive boy with a problem. He doesn't want to go to school. If we were to attach a label to his problem it would read "school phobic."

Ricky is repeating the first grade. One admitted reason for this failure is a large number of absences from school. In the morning, just as it becomes time to go to school, Ricky was likely to develop pains in his body, particularly in his stomach.

The boy saw his doctor for these pains, but there appeared to be nothing medically wrong. They remained to plague him. There was no doubt that his aches were real, but only his mother's concern for his health and the final ringing of the school bell would soothe his aching body, but by that time it would be too late to go to school.

When the doctor was unable to locate anything medically wrong, his parents decided that the boy was making up his sickness and that his malingering must come to an end. They took a firm hand and sent him off to school together with all his aches and pains. At school his pains would grow greater and so he cried. The tears were a distraction to the other children so Ricky would be sent home from school. What the boy had been unable to accomplish at home he was able to at school. Ricky needed to be home with his mother or his father. He was afraid to leave them and go to school and run the risk of coming home and finding them gone. It seemed, he didn't want to run the risk of being separated from those he loved.

School phobia[1] may result from a number of conditions. In Ricky's case, a separation anxiety from his mother was certainly indicated. She appeared not to be overly dominant or overprotective; if anything she seemed to be just the opposite. Perhaps this was the problem. Could the boy have imagined that he was unloved? Could he be apprehensive as a result of having heard negative things said about the school from his older brother? Maybe we will never know the dynamics of his particular phobia and maybe it will not be necessary to seek them. Perhaps a few simple suggestions to ease his anxious mind will be sufficient.

We talked about his father for a while. "Sometimes he is good to me and sometimes he is not," he stated.

"Well, he yells at me for things that sometimes I don't do," he replied.

"Could you tell me about this?" I asked.

Ricky began to show excessive motor activity. "He called me but all the other boys were on top of me ... I couldn't hear him so when I got home he hit me." The boy's breathing was coming hard and fast. Perhaps we should pursue the father/son relationship just as diligently as we had planned for the mother/son relationship.

"What is your mother's first name?" I asked.

"———, he replied.

"How do you feel when you are with her?" I inquired.

"Mostly good," he returned. "She lets me hold the baby ... I *love* the baby," he continued with what seemed to be an over emphasis upon the word 'love.' It was interesting to note how quickly he jumped from the inquiry about his mother to their two

---

[1] Coleman, James C. *Abnormal Psychology and Modern Life,* Scott Foresman, 1964

week old baby. He hadn't been asked about his feelings concerning their new arrival, but he had hastened to assure me of his love for the infant. What was the boy really saying?

"How do you like your teacher?" I continued.

"She is nice," he returned. "We color paper and match up dots and things like that."

"What do they call that kind of thing?" I asked with real interest.

"I don't know," he replied.

"Have you been out of school a lot this year just like you were last year with stomachaches and other things like that?" I politely inquired.

"Yes, sometimes I have a stomachache and stay home . . . my mother gives me aspirin and sometimes aspergum."

"Does that help the stomachache get better?" I asked.

"Yes, but sometimes I have to go to bed," he replied.

"Does it hurt sometimes so much that you have to cry?" I asked.

Ricky avoided answering this question for a while. Perhaps he didn't want to admit that a boy his age would cry over something like that. Finally he admitted, "Sometimes I cry, a little."

"They tell me that you are repeating the first grade. How do you feel about doing this?" I asked.

"I felt bad about not going into second grade . . . my mother didn't tell me about it for a long time . . . I don't know . . ." With this admission he fell into a subdued silence.

"Are you doing better in school now that you are repeating?" I asked.

"Yes, I'm doing good in reading, but I don't like arithmetic and stuff like that."

"Do you feel better about going to school or do you still have the same old health problems?" I asked.

"I have an earache already," he answered. "Sometimes I have belly aches and colds." This admission reminded the boy of his health problem so he coughed several times . . . right in my face.

"Ricky, I want to thank you for being so helpful. You have told me a lot about yourself, of how you feel about things, important things that will help me help you with your arithmetic. Do you want to pay a game with me, one that I think you will enjoy?" I asked.

He brightened up. "Sure."

"Fine, sit behind this table that will light up from beneath.

Look at the figures until at last they seem to move."

Ricky watched the Moire patterns for a short time and remarked, "I can see yellow colors there." The patterns are all black and white.

"Good," I replied. "Let me fasten this small object to your finger ... now look down the string to the object and aim it at this point." With these instructions I drew my finger down the string, touching the object and then the center of the figures.

"Some interesting things are now going to happen to you, first of all the object fastened to the thread will seem to get very heavy and then it will pull your hand to the table. Soon after that your head will be pulled down to the table, perhaps to rest upon your hand already there." These suggestive instructions were firmly repeated several times until at last he fell gently into a sleep.

I picked up the boy and transferred him to the comfortable reclining chair stating, "This will be more comfortable ... now open your eyes and look at my little penlight." This small light was waved slowly back and forth in front of his eyes with the suggestion that his eyes would get heavy and close again.

"I see two lights," he remarked with excitement ... there was only one.

It wasn't long after that before his eyes closed. "You will find that they have stuck together and that they will remain that way for a while ... why don't you see for yourself." Ricky made an effort to open his eyes but was unable to do so. To augment this success I continued. "Hold your hands together ... fingers between fingers ... now squeeze them together and you will find that, like your eyes, they will also stick together."

This suggestion was repeated several times. Finally, he was asked to test the suggestion. "See if you can pull your hands apart." Ricky's muscles bulged as he tugged. He could not get his hands apart.

It seemed that he was now ready for suggestions. "Tonight you will sleep very well knowing that your mother and father love you very much ... You are a very good boy and are well liked by your friends. You will sleep well tonight and when you awake in the morning you will feel good. You will be ready for school."

The boy was awakened in the usual way. He blinked a few times and commented that he felt good, "Like I had been to sleep."

## SECOND SESSION

The first thing that I asked the boy was, "Did you get to

school today?" and to my disappointment he replied, "No."
"Didn't you feel well enough to go?" I asked.
"I felt all right, but I didn't get up in time."
This response added to my disappointment. "Didn't your mother get up in time to get you off to school?"
"No, she slept late this morning. When we got up it was too late for me to go to school."

I wondered just how many times during the past unsuccessful school year his mother had failed to get him up and off to school . . . perhaps this was an isolated case, although I doubted it. Without the boy's mother's support how could I succeed?

Ricky's older brother had a special message for me from their mother. She was unable to make the trip across town due to other commitments and so entrusted her older son with the responsibility of getting his young son to my office. She wanted to inform me that the tearful goodbyes that were encountered as Ricky left home for school usually occurred after the boy's father had played with him during the morning. His father had a habit of picking him up and playing with him in a loving manner and it seemed that the boy wanted to stay at home and hopefully get more of the same thing. It was more fun to stay home and play with his father than it was to go to school. I gathered that this was the mother's diagnosis of her son's problem—if she was right, what did she expect me to do about it?

Richard was given the *Otis Lennon Mental Ability Test,* Elementary Level, Form J, for grades one and two to work on. He was able to complete the first two parts before entering the hypnotherapy phase of our time together. According to the boy he had been successfully hypnotized during the last visit. He claimed that he could not open his eyes or pull his hands apart.

On the basis of our past successful experience with hypnosis, it seemed unnecessary to begin again with the cumbersome drafting device so we began our induction using the penlight with the little fellow reclining comfortably in the chair. The lights were reduced as usual and the soft sound machine was turned on to mask any noises that might disturb him.

After a few minutes of working with the boy I realized, "I'm not hypnotizing this boy." I pressed on and on, but it was obvious that I was not succeeding very well this time. The boy's eyes would close to very narrow slits to be immediately opened wide. We would quietly begin again and as soon as the boy's eyes would close he would just as quickly reopen them and stare about the room.

He was resisting hypnotization. Why was he doing this when he had seemed so pleased with it the week before? Had someone talked with him about hypnosis since then in a negative fashion?

We went again to the drafting board. Ricky sat behind the board and dutifully obeyed every request. His hand soon dropped to the board as did his head. Was this more physiology than hypnotism? His eyes closed, but with the appearance of obedience rather than hypnotic influence.

This time he was helped rather than carried to the big chair. He moved readily and with assurance not as though he were in a trance. In fact, he opened his eyes to see where he was going and closed them again as soon as he was in the chair. He quickly opened them when asked to do so. He again looked steadily at the penlight and again I worked diligently to produce the trance although it was obvious that there was to be no hypnosis that night. I could and should have terminated the induction earlier with a remark that another night would be better and just offer assurances.

There were several negative thoughts generated that evening before we began the hypnosis. First of all, I was personally disappointed that he had failed to go to school that morning. He had not been chastized for this failure, but nevertheless, there were negative thoughts generated. Secondly, I might have hypnotized him had I begun the induction immediately upon his entrance to the office. He may have come to the office primed and ready for hypnosis, but when he was given time to reflect upon the prospect he may have rejected the idea, especially if it could make him go off to school when he preferred to stay home. Dr. Gindes[2] has remarked that a hypnotist is like a salesman with a prospect. He feels that a hypnotist and a salesman must complete their transaction when the prospect is ready. He says that many sales have been lost when the prospect has been given time to think about the transaction.

Richard was dismissed for the evening with the positive comment that we would succeed next week. No suggestions of a therapeutic nature were given to the boy.

### THIRD SESSION

Ricky wanted to talk about his friends and school. He was en-

---

[2] Gindes, *New Concepts in Hypnosis*

couraged to talk. His talk was the usual small boy variety of conversation and did not seem to contain material that could be thought of as significant. His chatter could also have had some "cover up" significance.

Remembering last week and our lack of success, I decided to give a choice of what we should do first. "Do you want to finish the test that you started before or would you prefer to go into hypnosis first?" I had debated with myself the advisability of avoiding the term 'hypnosis' in favor of the terms 'sleep' or 'suggestion' and had decided to label what I was doing by the accepted name. I doubted that I could fool this seven-year-old boy with hypnosis under a disguised title. It was almost certain that one or even both of his parents had explained the nature of what we were doing together. He was also a reasonably alert boy and a devotee of television where he could also have learned of hypnosis.

Ricky decided to finish the test. From a total of 80 possible correct responses he got a total of 30 correct ones. This gave him an I.Q. of 94, better than might have been expected. His mental age was 6 years and 11 months. This is just a few months lower than his actual chronological age.

This intelligence test is a good one, especially for his age level because there is nothing for the student to read. He is only required to listen to directions. A hearing disability would reflect a lower score, but I didn't believe the boy had a hearing problem. The score was probably accurate.

Why did he go into a trance state the first time but not the second time? The boy volunteered, "I don't like the lights shining in my eyes . . . they hurt." I had planned to use the drafting device but immediately changed my mind.

"Do you find the penlight bothersome?" I asked.

"Yes, that hurts too," he claimed, "but that doesn't hurt as much as the other thing." (drafting instrument)

I wondered about his objections to the drafting device. This device is illuminated from underneath by two powered fluorescent bulbs that shine through a ground glass window and several layers of plastic upon which the Moire patterns are etched. This is the device that has brought everyone, including Ricky, to some state of hypnosis. This has been the beginning of hypnotic conditioning for all of the children. It was the first device he had encountered and it had been successful. Was this why he wished to avoid it?

I turned off all of the lights except the soft red one of no more than 5 watts. The soft sound machine was turned on to mask any outside distractions that might take his attention away from what we were doing. Something new, to him, was placed in his hands—the flashing metronome. The machine had been set to flash at 120 flashes per minute. This machine can also make a beating sound. He was told to keep looking at the softly flashing light and to listen to the sound of the machine saying sleep . . . sleep . . . sleep.

It was so dark in the room that I could hardly see the boy's eyes. I talked for a while to let the impact of the setting come upon the boy. He snuggled down to watch the flashing light. Again I explained the nature of hypnosis. "If you are successful tonight, you will go into a very pleasant sleep. It won't be the kind of sleep that you go into every night where you can't speak or hear the voice of another person. In this sleep you will be able to hear everything that I say. Not only that, you will be able to speak to me and tell me how you feel."

The responsibility of entering the hypnotic trance should be placed upon the subject. It is he who succeeds or fails to enter into the trance. With this induction I continued, "Tonight you will find that your eyes will get heavy until at last they will close together. It will be as though they were glued together . . . etc."

This dialogue continued until his eyes closed, but then he would scratch them and cause them to reopen. From time to time, his eyelids would flutter as frequently seen in a subject about to enter a trance. This sequence of events continued until I finally brought his hands together and asked that he keep them firmly clasped together. Occasionally he would start to unclasp his hands probably to scratch his eyes and so I would close my hands over his to prevent it from happening.

My left hand rested lightly upon his clasped hands and my right hand rested upon his forehead. While saying, "Your eyes will close . . . ," my fingers slid down over his eyelids to force the closure. I held them this way saying, "Your eyes will stick together tighter and tighter."

Finally I removed my hands and asked, "Have your eyes stuck together as we had hoped that they would?"

"Yes," he claimed, "it's like they were glued together."

At this point it probably would have been smart to offer the evening's suggestions and to have been satisfied with our progress. Instead I chose to deepen the hypnosis so I asked that he open his eyes to look again at the flashing light. This time I did not force his eyes to close with physical pressure. I had expected to use only the power of suggestion, but I was wrong. I tried, but I could not bring about another hypnotic trance with just the power of verbal suggestion.

The time allocated for the boy was expiring, but there would be another day. I thought that we had made good progress because it seemed certain that he had achieved hypnosis sufficient for eye closure. It was a beginning . . . I hoped.

This boy is about the youngest child with which I have worked. Could it be that a six-year-old is too young to hold a trance, or perhaps not mature enough yet to concentrate sufficient for hypnosis? I have found that older children can come out of a trance by a simple act . . . being asked to examine a picture will sometimes break the trance . . . any sudden noise or unexpected touch will surely do it. It is always necessary to be very careful of what is said to a subject in the trance or the subject will awaken. They can almost always reject any suggestion and immediately awaken. Usually when they are asked to perform any physical task, it is well to precede the request by suggesting that the task will lead them into deeper hypnosis.

## FOURTH SESSION

Ricky was beginning to "warm up to me" according to his mother. He was anxious to make these visits. Could it be because he got candy every time he came? Children do associate gifts, especially those of food, with love. The giving of any gift is symbolic of giving love and that is why I keep a large supply of handsome lollipops on hand for children like Ricky . . . hopefully it is not just the candy.

"Tell me about school," I requested.

"I got my report card and I got all 'A's," he proudly stated.

"That is great, you must like school to have done that well." He admitted that he liked it "just a little."

"Were you able to get to school every day since our last lesson?" I asked. He disappointed me again. "No, I had a headache one day and another time my mother didn't get up . . . she was tired."

Wondering about the boy's relationship with his mother, I decided to offer him the separation picture from the TED test.

Ricky thought a long time before responding to this stimulus. It almost seemed as if the boy was trying to fathom the reasons behind the task assigned to him . . . making up a story about the people in the picture.

Eventually he perceived a boy about to separate from the mother figure. His make-believe boy was going out to put his bike away. Ricky had to receive a good score for perception although his subsequent comment raised some thoughts. "That boy looks like me, he feels unhappy."

"Why do you say that he feels unhappy?" I asked.

"Because he has to go down into the cellar with his father . . . it is cold down there."

There may not be a real separation problem with his mother, but what about his father? Why the identification with a boy about to go into the cellar with his father? We will go into that later . . . time was running out.

"We will try a very light hypnosis tonight," I remarked, thinking that I might be fortunate to get even that much. "You may like the experience because it is so restful. You will experience a pleasing drowsiness that will help you feel much better in the morning."

Ricky reclined in the chair and I waved the penlight back and forth in front of his eyes. But instead of continuing to emphasize his eyes where there seemed to be so much resistance, I decided to direct his attention to other parts of his body, "Your arms are getting heavier and heavier . . . arms . . . legs . . . body," etc. Finally we returned to his eyes, "Your eyes are also getting heavier and will soon close just as they have done before . . . it will be just as though they were glued together." Once more my right hand moved down his forehead, over his frontal lobes, over his eyebrows, but not closing his eyelids shut.

Yes the boy's eyes closed and remained that way. It became apparent that he was trying to open them. His eyeballs appeared to be moving frantically under his eyelids. Several times he screwed his eyelids together very tightly and then stretched his eyebrows up as far as they would go trying to open his eyes. During all of this I continued to talk—to misdirect his attention. "You have done very well . . ." Not once was he told that he could not open his eyes. I wanted to avoid a contest. Finally he seemed resigned to the fact that his eyes were closed and that he could not open them . . . and he stopped trying.

"Relax and listen carefully. You know that your parents love you a lot. They want you to go to school and to do well there. You have said that you do like school and you are going to find that you will like it better each day. In fact, you will hardly be able to wait for the school doors to open. You know that going to school is a part of growing up. This is your job and one that you can and will do well. You will like doing your job." I concluded with another post-hypnotic suggestion, "You will go more easily into this sleep the next time."

Hopefully this post-hypnotic suggestion would end our troubles in bringing this boy into hypnosis. He was awakened with the usual ten count interspersed with suggestions for feeling better than ever.

## FIFTH SESSION

The boy came bubbling with things to tell me, and he came to my office by himself, showing his independence. He had to travel several miles to do this. Knowing that one way to his heart was through his stomach I immediately offered him two lollipops, one for himself and another for his 'friend.' He responded to this act of generosity by rattling off the names of a large number of his friends. It was suggested that he save the extra candy for his *best friend*.

Ricky was anxious to tell about the Christmas party held at his school. "We had a Santa Claus, but we all knew that it really was Mr. ———" (the principal). He not only wanted to talk about the party, but also about his progress in school. "I'm now in the 'Tulips' in reading, but I wish that I was in the "Butterflies" . . . my friend R——— is in the Butterflies . . . they get more stars than we do."

The "stars" are a tangible measure of accomplishment. They are things the boy can understand. He talked excitedly about his Christmas activities. Adults experience a "lost feeling" at Christmas compared to the enthusiastic joy children have. For some of us Christmas seems to stir memories of our relatively secure childhood days as nothing else can do.

"How are things at home?" I asked.

"L——— (his two-year-old sister) screams at me," he replied and added, "She swore at me the other day."

"Where would a girl that age learn swear words?" I asked.

"From my mother and father . . . they swear at each other all the time . . . I don't like it so I walk away when they do." That told me something.

After listening to his parents' problems, I wondered if he was afraid to leave for school because he was wondering if they would be there when he returns. Could it be that if there was more love at home there wouldn't be these fights. The boy's school phobia appeared to be rooted in family disarrangement.

"You did very well with hypnosis last time," I complimented. "Do you suppose that you will do just as well today?"

"Yes," Ricky nodded, "I think so."

"I think so too," I added reassuringly. "Actually, I expect that you will do even better this week and that you will continue to improve as we go along."

The boy reclined in his chair and looked at me very expectantly. He was instructed to remove his wet shoes, lie back and breath deeply. With each of his deep breaths, I waved the penlight back and forth before his eyes. I spoke of the stillness creeping over the various parts of his body. At the same time my free hand was allowed to rest rather heavily upon his forehead. His eyes closed tighter and tighter as he complied with the suggestions. He was again reminded of previous successes, "Just as before, your eyes will stick together . . . just as though they were glued."

In three or four minutes, the boy's eyes were tightly closed and as before he made numerous, but futile attempts to open them. His eyebrows would arch and his brow would furrow in his attempt to open them. When it became apparent that he was making no more effort to open his eyes I asked, "Have you been successful tonight? Have you found that your eyes have stuck together?" Ricky only nodded.

"I'm so glad that you have been successful and I'm sure that you are pleased with your progress . . . you know that it means you will be helped to do well in school." With this assurance he received the following suggestions:

"You are going to like school more and more each day . . . as a matter of fact you are going to wake up in the morning wanting to get there to be with your friends and to study. You like to read and because of your liking for this interesting subject you will get better and better at it all the time. You are going to discover that reading is fun. You will want to go to school, not only for your own sake, but to please your parents who love you and want you to do well in school. It's too bad that parents don't always show their children just how much they love them, but they really do. Remember that, and remember that you will want to get up and get off to school each morning . . . you will feel well, well, well, well . . .

you will want to go to school and you will feel well, well, well."

Ricky had awakened during an earlier session without warning. He had accomplished this after he had successfully pulled his hands apart even though he had been given suggestions to the contrary. I decided to risk this happening again. "Place your hands together, clinch them together tightly."

He did as I requested and I placed my hands over his. "I think that you have reached a deeper stage of hypnosis so much that your hands will stick together, just as your eyes have done. There is only one way to find out. Don't worry about what happens. You know that you can reach the first stage of hypnosis very well and that is good enough." I hoped to protect the progress we had achieved so far and prepare for the possible failure of the hand test. Hopefully he would pass the hand test and prepare the way for even more dramatic exercises in the future.

"Just as your eyes have stuck together so will your hands . . . ." Each time that I repeated this suggestion I pulsated my grip upon his hands to emphasize the suggestion. Slowly I removed my hands from his and said, "Now see if we have been successful in reaching a deeper stage of hypnosis. See if you can pull your hands apart."

The muscles of his arms bulged and his face grew red as he tugged and tugged. I let him struggle for a while before again closing my hands over his saying, "That is wonderful, see your hands did stick together just as we both hoped they would. Now relax and you will be able to take them apart very easily."

"I'm very pleased with your success tonight and hope that you are just as pleased as I am." With this additional assurance he was brought out of his trance with the usual count of ten interspersed with suggestions of feeling well. "You will awaken feeling fine . . . feeling great all over . . . isn't that wonderful?" At ten his eyes opened and like other children who have had a successful trance experience, he seemed pleased with himself.

## SIXTH SESSION

Due to the Christmas holidays, several weeks passed before we were able to get together again. When he did come he could hardly contain himself. He was so glad to be with me. He had brought with him a small object filled with real swamp water that he wanted me to see. It received a thorough examination and hearty admiration.

Again I brought out two lollipops. "One for you and one for your friend."

"I didn't give the other one to my friend," he remarked.

"Why not?" I asked. "I thought you were going to give one to your best friend."

"My sister L——— saw me eating mine so I gave her the other one," he explained.

"In that case," I generously offered, "Take three, one for you, one for L——— and one for your best friend," and so we established a sound basis for the work that we would do this session.

We examined the pictures of the TED test while he was in the waking state, but I omitted its use during the sleep state because I had been getting the same results during both conditions. There have been a few variations, but not enough to affect the scoring of the test to any appreciable degree.

Ricky did well with the test, better than expected. There seems to be only one troublesome task. He performed creditably with the first task, Socialization. He readily perceived the outside boy who was new to the neighborhood joining a group of boys. Ricky saw all the boys playing together and going into one of the boy's homes.

He did just as well with the second picture, Trust. Here he saw a boy being called in by his mother so that she might give him something to eat. What was it that the mother was giving her son to eat? Grapes. This is the first instance of my ever hearing of this particular gift being given, usually it's cookies.

Ricky did equally as well as with the third picture, Aggression. He readily perceived two boys about to fight. These boys were mad at each other and finally ended up fighting. When the fight was over they both departed for home to make up another day.

Ricky did reasonably well with the fourth picture, Learning. This picture may not be appropriate for a seven-year-old boy who is still in the first grade. Such children usually have little homework and seldom use a desk for serious study. Even so, Ricky did well making up a story about a student who got up to study in the morning when all the other members of the household were still in bed. Possibly some of his older siblings did this. Ricky was showing his individuality. He was not exactly like other children. As a matter of fact, no child is exactly like any other child. All children want to be recognized in their own right as individuals. A child does not want to be just a face in a group. In a school there are hundreds of children saying, each in his own way, "See me."

Ricky's response to the fifth picture, Conscience, was the response that indicated a problem of growing up emotionally healthy. He failed to perceive a boy in a position to steal money. Instead, he saw a boy receiving a wallet containing money as a birthday present. This failure to perceive the situation meant Ricky's responses to the other dimensions of the picture was not scoreable.

Ricky had been given the sixth picture, Separation, several weeks ago. He did reasonably well with the stimuli.

The boy's overall performance on the TED indicated that his one difficult problem in growing up emotionally healthy was in the area of conscience development.

Ricky's mother informed me that he no longer cried when he had to go to school although she thought that he still didn't like the place. He had missed only a few days of school since his last visit, but he had missed them for reasons that are valid, colds. He appeared to be prone to colds. His nose was dripping and he was coughing, frequently right in my face.

His mother was asked if she believed in giving cod-liver oil to children who are prone to colds. Her solution was to give him aspirin—which could hardly prevent him from catching colds.

The boy reclined in the chair while I turned down the lights. The soft sound machine was turned on to mask other street sounds that might distract him. I placed his hands upon his abdomen and requested that he keep them there until we had finished with the hypnosis. He still had a habit of scratching and moving about and rubbing his eyes. I held down the penlight in front of his eyes and moved it up and down. "Take twenty deep breaths," I requested. An unusual amount of oxygen in anyone's lungs causes him to feel faint—a small trick played on the child might help.

"You know from past experience that your eyes will soon get heavy ... so much so you will soon not be able to open them." I droned on in my special 'hypnotic tone' of voice. In a few minutes the boy's eyes were tightly closed. For a while his eyes could be detected moving beneath his tightly closed eyelids. He was unable to open them. There was some movement of his hands. He had tested to see if he could open his eyes and found that he could not. He then wanted to see if he could move his hands and found that he could. He was about to rub his eyes and then remembered that he had been told not to remove his hands from his tummy.

I droned on. "You know that you are an intelligent boy and that you come from a family where there is much love, but your family is like a lot of others because there are arguments. We have learned to accept these arguments because we know that they have no real meaning. Your parents love you and want you to go to school and do a good job there. You will like going to school because you know that it will please your parents who love you and because it is fun to be there with your friends. You also know that school is important ... you will like going there more and more each day. You will like being with your friends and reading the interesting books. You will like doing arithmetic which is easy for you, you will like going to school...."

These re-educative suggestions were repeated several times before he was awakened with the usual ten count. He left the office feeling fine, no longer coughing and with his nose no longer dripping.

### SEVENTH SESSION

According to the boy's mother, he was doing something that he he had never done before, going to school without causing a scene and equally as interesting, bringing home library books. At the end of the school day, Ricky would drop into the library, fortunately located in an annex of the building, where he would obtain a few first grade books. At home he would ask his mother to read them for him. She was gratified to see his interest in books developing. They read these books together although it seemed certain that he would be reading his library books alone soon.

Ricky was coughing again and complaining about it. Hopefully he wouldn't cough in my face as he usually did. He was handed two lollipops, "One for you and one for anybody that you care to give it to."

"Did your mother get you any medicine to build you up where you wouldn't get so many colds?" I asked, thinking about my suggestion to her a few weeks ago.

"No," the boy replied, "She just gives me aspirin ... sometimes she gives me a cough syrup."

"Didn't she try some vitamins or cod-liver oil with you?" I persisted with dying hope.

"No," he replied, but brightly added, "Sometimes she gives me aspergum."

"Well, you look very healthy. She probably figures that's all you need," I pleasantly lied. "If you needed vitamins or stuff like that she would get them for you. There's no doubt about that."

# SCHOOL PHOBIA

"How are you getting along in school?" I asked.
"O.K.," he replied.
"Do you still like your teacher?" I continued.
"Sure," he returned as though surprised that I could question his relationship with his teacher.
"Everything all right at home?" I inquired.
"Yeah," he brightly offered and then began a lengthy discourse about this. He had a great deal to say about his small world.
The boy confidently leaned back in his reclining chair and looked expectantly at the penlight brought out from the desk. "Will you sleep for me tonight?" I asked.
"Yes," he pleasantly and trustfully replied.
The boy took the twenty deep breaths that he was asked to take. He kept his eyes upon the penlight swaying back and forth in front of his eyes. In a moment his eyes were closed. For a while there appeared to be a struggle. His eyebrows arched up a few times, but eyes remained tightly closed. "Have your eyes closed so that you are unable to open them?" I asked.
"Yes," he responded.
There were no more tests of hypnosis and no more additional hypnosis piled upon hypnosis. The suggestions for this session were about the same as those given to him from the previous session.
"You will come to love school better and better as you get to know the school and your teacher. You will feel better and better about going. You can relax in school knowing that your parents love you. Your school is important to your future . . . even now you are getting ready to grow up . . . learning about things that are important. I'm glad to know that you are taking a good interest in books . . . that you are going to the library to get books for home so that you can also read there. This interest in reading will grow and grow and as it does your reading will get better and better."
The suggestions were repeated several times. All suggestions given to a hypnotized subject need to be emphasized as strongly as possible. If some kind of drama could be attached to the suggestions, they might be even better.
Ricky was awakened with the usual ten count with the count being interspersed with suggestions for his well-being. He awoke feeling rested and free of tensions. His cold no longer seemed to bother him. This was a short session lasting no longer than twenty minutes.

## EIGHTH SESSION

Ricky now loved to come and "visit" with me so it was decided to let him come again for a very short visit. There seemed to be little need for additional therapy because he was going to school without any problems. I honestly commented upon how well he looked. His physical appearance was better than I had ever seen it. He wasn't coughing, sneezing, etc. There was no evidence of any kind of health problem. His eyes were bright as he began his story.

"I got all S's on my report card." The boy beamed as he related this. Not knowing what exactly the S's meant I commented, "That's great ... I suppose S's are about the highest one can get in your school." (satisfactory, C's)

"No," he admitted. "You could get an S plus, but not many kids get that." He continued, "I'm reading a book called *On Cherry Street*. It is a third grade book. Our reading group is called the Tulips."

Ricky was wrong about his reading book being a third grade level text. It is a first grade book in the Ginn reading series, but it is the second book or hardest of the first grade books.

"How are you getting along with the kids in school?" I asked, expanding our conversation.

"Good," he said and added, "We have a new girl in our class. Her name is A———. I am smarter than she is," he boasted in the way children like to do.

"Tell me about your mother and father and the way that you are getting along with them."

"They treat me real good," he happily responded.

It will be remembered that this boy was brought to see me because he was "school phobic." He wanted to cling to his home and to his parents and even became ill when forced to separate from them in order to go to school. He had cried so much during his first year in school that he was sent home so many times that he was called upon to repeat the year. This second year in school started out in the same unfortunate manner. He was sickly and cried to stay home.

When hypnotherapy was first attempted with this boy, it seemed that there would be no hypnotism. He resisted hypnotism successfully through several sessions. We almost came to the conclusion that he would not go into trance at all, for reasons of his own. It wasn't until we had persisted and developed a special rapport that we were able to accomplish hypnosis. He took longer than most of the other children seem to need, but he was eventually conditioned into receiving hypnotic suggestions. These suggestions were successful in helping him through a difficult adjustment.

## FINAL VISIT

Ricky returned one year later to again take the Otis-Lennon Mental Ability Test. His I.Q. on the retest improved.

### TEST RESULTS

|  | 1967 (December) | 1968 (November) |
|---|---|---|
| Correct Responses | 30 | 43 |
| I.Q. | 94 | 98 |
| Mental Age | 6 yrs. 11 mo. | 8 yrs. 3 mo. |

There is an important difference between these two tests. His Intelligence Quotient gained 4.00 points and his mental age gained one year and four months. It should be noted that this improvement occurred in less than a year.

There is an important improvement in measured mental ability as indicated by these two tests. It would be presumptuous to state that hypnotherapy was entirely responsible. There are many variables that enter into a testing situation, but we can't toss out the possibility that hypnotherapy did expand his mental abilities.

One possible account for the boy's improvement is the better attitude that he developed toward his school. "I like to go to school . . . my teacher is nice."

"How many days have you lost going to school so far this year?" I asked.

He looked surprised at the question. "I haven't been out any days."

I knew that he was telling the truth. He was going to school without any trouble. He was also doing well there. He read with the top group in his class. Perhaps his two years in the first grade helped build a good foundation for the second grade, but we see other children who did poorly in the first grade and repeated the grade to eventually be promoted to the second where again they floundered. This boy was on his way to a successful school career. There may come other blocks to impede his progress, but for now, the boy is doing fine. He believed that hypnotherapy was responsible for this and so did his mother.

# CHAPTER FOUR
# LARRY: STUTTERING

Bender writes that stutterers are, "more neurotic, more introverted, less dominant, less confident and less sociable than nonstutterers."* Bender's description of the stutterer certainly fits Larry who exhibits every one of those characteristics. Larry also exhibited an inhibitory personality and it appeared that his inhibitions preceded his stuttering problem. When Larry came under any kind of emotional stress his body changed significantly. This change was particularly noticable in his breathing. It became tense and disturbed. His face showed the tension he felt inwardly.

What was Larry afraid of? Was he simply afraid that he would stutter and so he did? Did he exhibit the stuttering syndrome in other stressful situations and when speaking was only imminent? If he did then his stuttering was a problem in psychology and all of the effort put forth by his school speech teacher was doomed to fail.

## LARRY
## FIRST SESSION

Larry is a tall well-proportioned 16 year old boy desperately seeking help for his problems that are almost too great for him to bear. Even though he is good looking, he has no girl friends and hasn't had one. Larry stutters and wants to overcome it. Stuttering prevents him from indulging in normal youthful relationships.

Larry attended a vocational school and was having trouble with his courses. He liked the school but couldn't understand math and

---

*Bender, J. F. *The Personality Structure of Stuttering*. Pitman Publishing Company, New York nouns, verbs, etc. taught there. Perhaps throughout his past years in school, stuttering helped him developed his present school problems. He may have been afraid to respond to his teacher's questions. He may have hesitated to read aloud in fear that some of his classmates would make fun of him.

Larry had a pleasing personality and when asked, "Do you feel that your mother likes you?"

He replied indignantly, "Yes, she does."

"How do you know that?" I persisted.

"She has always been good to me. I just know that she loves me," he replied in a manner that suggested that my question was ridiculous.

"How about your father?" I asked annoying even more.

"He does," Larry exclaimed, but with very little emphasis.

"Do your parents fight very much?" I queried.

Larry didn't like the questions, "Just the usual . . . sometimes they argue, but they don't hit each other."

"How do you know that?" I asked.

"Well, I have never seen them, if they have," he replied in a manner that indicated he would soon leave if I continued that line of questioning.

"Tell me about the other members of your family," I politely asked.

"I am the oldest," he answered. "——— is next to me, and he is only seven. I have a sister who is three. There is another child on the way."

"Tell me about your friends, who are they and tell me if you think they understand you," I requested.

"I have about five good friends, and they are all boys," he hastened to amplify this. "Of course, there are girls that hang around with us, but I don't have any girl friends, if that is what you mean." He narrowed his friends down, "I really only have one good friend . . . we sometimes argue that is, if he thinks he is right he stands up for it, and I do the same. We don't have any real fist fights."

"Do your parents understand you?" I asked.

"My mother understands me, but my father doesn't give me a chance. He hasn't hit me in a long time. He yells at me instead," he replied.

"Would you rather have him hit you or yell at you?" I asked.

"Well," he went on, "if he hits me it's over, but when he yells he keeps on . . . like five minutes later, he will start up again."

"Is this something that you particularly hate?" I asked him.

"Yes," he continued, "if he is wrong he will never admit it . . . he is right and you are wrong . . . you shut up or he cuffs you. I hate it when people are foolish like that."

"All of us have a little trouble from time to time, with our friends and with our family . . . but you have had a major trouble that you want to tell me about," I stated.

"I've told you about my friend . . . sometimes we argue, but we don't fight," Larry replied.

"Tell me about the important things," I demanded.

"I always had a feeling that my father wasn't my real father . . . and then one day I found out that it was true."

"How did you find out?" I asked.

"My mother told me," he answered. "She could see how we were together, so one day she told me that he wasn't my real father."

"How did you feel when you found out?" I asked.

"I wasn't surprised, because I didn't think that a father could treat me the way he did," he explained.

It took much of our time together to reach this crucial point. I wanted to get along to hypnosis which would be very important to the boy if he was to really overcome his tensions. Larry readily took a glass of water from me, and was about to drink, until I opened a small bottle of pills and shook one out. These pills are a pink placebo consisting of sugar. "The water is for the pill," I explained. Without any comment, he took the pill from me and quickly swallowed it. I also made no comment about the pill but continued questioning as though nothing had transpired. "What have you heard about hypnosis?" I asked.

"Well, I have heard that it can help you in things like reading . . . it has several uses," he replied with a little nervous laugh, "like if you are sick in the head or something like that."

"Where did you hear all this?" I questioned.

"I read it in a magazine," he continued. "I'm very interested in it."

"Have you ever been hypnotized before?" I asked.

"No."

"Have you ever seen it done?"

"No," he again replied.

"What do you think it will be like?" I questioned.

"I have no idea."

"Have you any idea how it is done?" I continued to question him.

"Yes," he answered. "You hold something in front of the eyes and swing it back and forth."

I had planted ideas about hypnosis in his young mind and now his imagination could go to work. "Tell me about your earliest childhood impression, the very first thing that you can remember," I requested, trying to redirect his attention.

"I guess that the first thing that I can remember is my mother pushing me around in a carriage . . . I think that we were living with my grandfather at that time," he replied.

"Was this a good feeling?" I questioned.

"Yes," he softly responded.

"Would you tell me about some of the troubles that you have had? Anything at all that has happened between you and strangers, as well as between you and members of your family." I looked at what remained of his glass of water and called him back to hypnosis. "Be sure to let me know if you feel warm or perhaps somewhat drowsy."

"Once, I was at a drive-in when a car drove up and a big kid, bigger than you," he added, "told me to come over. I did, and he put an arm around me and I didn't know what to expect. Some other kid in the car said to make it quick . . . then he hit me in the face real hard . . . later on that same night, I heard that he raped his girl friend. Her father was a cop, so they took him to court."

"Anything else?" I asked.

"I told you about my father . . . I feel a little dizzy," he added.

"I'm glad to hear that," I replied. "Perhaps you also feel a little warm."

He nodded. "I have just a few more questions to ask," I casually remarked. "Why don't you stretch out and get as comfortable as you can. Shortly we will talk more about hypnotism and then you will be hypnotized." We still avoided trance induction even though he seemed conditioned and receptive to hypnosis.

"We all have certain fears and hates, which is perfectly natural. I am going to list some things you might be afraid of. Pick out one or add to the list if you want to." With this, I read the list, father, mother, brothers, sisters, men, women, dark, school and food.

"You didn't say dying," he added, "that would be the thing I fear most."

"Anything else?" I questioned.

"Dark," he replied.

"And what would come after that?" I continued.

"Something you didn't list, either," he answered. "Sometimes I get a closed-in feeling." His contributions were significant.

"Are there any other problems about school, family or friends that you haven't told me about?" I asked.

"I don't have any problems around my friends," he replied, omitting any reference to his family, "but at school, I haven't been able to do math, and sometimes the English bothers me . . . I've had trouble with nouns, verbs, and things like that."

"What about reading?" I persisted.

"I knew the words, but couldn't say them," he replied.

"Could you understand what you read?" I continued.

"It was just saying the words. I think that I knew what I was reading about," the boy replied.

Larry's eyes were half closed. He was breathing deeply. "Let me tell you about hypnosis." I explained that it would be a pleasant experience; a kind of half sleep, so pleasant that he would look forward to the next time with eagerness. By now, the "pill" had produced a good effect. He could have been hypnotized by some other method, but I chose this indirect method at first and then slipped into a more direct one. He sat before the drafting device with a tiny weight strung on his finger. The hush sound machine was turned on and the lights dimmed. The usual suggestions were made and he responded quickly. His hand followed the small weight to the table. The concentric circles appeared to revolve automatically. He was told that deeper sleep would come upon him as he moved into the leather chair. He was allowed to open his eyes enough to see as he changed chairs. When the boy reclined in the chair, I placed the flashing device in his hands. I asked him to just open his eyes and look at the light that was operating at 120 flashes per minute. The audible section of this machine was turned to beat with the same rhythm. The boy sank deeper and deeper into hypnosis. The audible beat was turned off, but I continued making suggestions to deepen the hypnosis. His hands failed to support the machine so I removed it. He was ready for suggestions. To help him to pass quickly into a deep stage of hypnosis the next time, I gave him a post-hypnotic suggestion. "You will remember the hypnosis that you are now in, and will return immediately to it at the next session."

In order to cut some of the tensions that have bothered Larry, I also suggested, "You will be less tense from now on since you have done nothing wrong. You are a sensitive boy, do not feel bad about things for which you haven't been responsible. You will do better work at school knowing that you don't have to feel guilty."

When Larry was gently brought back to the waking state, there was an immediate noticeable reduction in stuttering.

## SECOND SESSION

We began talking about his family relationships. "As you know, love and hate kind of go together. We can't love and hate someone at the same time so we alternate our feelings. Do you sometimes hate your father?"

"Yes, I sometimes do hate him," he replied with a fierceness that contrasted to his response of the week before when he spoke of love. The inflections in his voice snarled and left no doubt about his meaning.

"Why?" I smoothly continued.

"He is always down on me for something. When something is missing he blames me. . . , (the younger brother) came in smelling of it, so I know he used it, but I still got the blame."

"Are you afraid of him?" I asked.

"Not now," he boasted (unconvincingly). "When I was young I was afraid of him. If he came up behind me I would cringe like this," Larry pulled up his legs as if to give some protection to his front and pulled his head down to be somewhat covered by his arms. His position was fetal in appearance and I wondered if it meant that he desired to return to the security of his mother's womb.

"Why did you do that?" I continued.

"My mother said that he hit me such a blow when I was little that it took several days for the marks to disappear. Now I am as big as he is . . ." he ended ominously.

"You told me last week that you liked guns and that the happiest moment of your life was the day when your father let you buy a shotgun with your own money. What is there about guns that interests you?" I asked.

"They are smooth and feel good. They help me feel calm," he answered.

"Do they also give you a feeling of strength?" I asked.

"Yes, they do," he replied.

Larry had opened several doors that needed to be looked

through. Had Larry been emotionally castrated by his stepfather? If he had, then when his father allowed him to buy the gun the boy felt that he had gained some of his manhood back. Could the gun represent a man's long penis?

"Can you tell me more about your mother and your relationships with her? Where did the two of you live when he wasn't with you?" I asked.

"We lived with my grandfather until I was eight years old," he answered.

"When did your stepfather come to live with you?" I asked.

"He came when ——— was born," the boy replied.

"Did you sleep with your mother before he came?" I asked. He may have evaded this question as he answered, "I don't know." "Did you stutter when you lived without him and just with your mother?" I asked.

"I'm not sure if I did or not," he admitted.

"Does it bother you to know that your mother was not married when she had you?" I asked, wondering if I was intruding too much.

"It did when I was young ... but it doesn't anymore," he quickly replied without conviction. We had entered into Larry's unpleasant background hoping that he would lose some of his tensions through discussion, but he stuttered more and more as we invaded his privacy and most of all when we talked about his father. Perhaps we could continue this discussion under hypnosis with less discomfort to him.

"I gave him the first picture of the TED test to examine. This is the picture of socialization and as could be expected, he failed to score well. Larry saw the outside boy, in the picture, in a position to join a group going home instead. Larry told the story of the picture, the boys in the group were making fun of the outsider so that his boy wasn't sure if he wanted to join them.

The second picture was of trust and Larry did surprisingly well with it. He saw a mother who had made some cookies and wanted to give some to her son who accepted them, but with a surprising twist ... his boy didn't like the cookies, but took them anyway, "in order to be nice." I wasn't sure how to score his response to that picture.

The third picture was one of aggression. He handled it well. Larry perceived that a fight was imminent with the neutral boy opposed to fighting; however, he fought when forced into it. The reason for not wanting to fight was good. The two boys in the picture had been friends with the neutral boy wanting to continue the friendship, not wanting to lose it in a fight.

The fourth picture was about the learning task. Larry scored well in all areas of the test, perception, outcome, affect and motivation. He saw the boy in the picture working at homework. His boy finished his work and then went on to do something more pleasing.

The fifth picture is about conscience development. Larry failed to score well. It would have been surprising had he done so. Larry readily perceived a boy in a position to steal some money from a wallet lying on a table. The boy took the money, but later returned it to the wallet. His boy didn't return the money as a result of having felt guilty about stealing, but rather out of fear of getting caught. Again, Larry was expressing fear of his own stepfather.

The sixth picture represented the task of separation from the mother figure. Again, the boy scored poorly. Larry had a separation problem. He was tied to his mother in a way that was not normal. For some reason, he felt guilty about leaving her. His story told of a boy wanting to go out with his friends. The boy's mother didn't want him to go out. She didn't like his friends because, "they drink." She finally gave up, telling her son to go, but warned if he got into trouble being with them, he couldn't come back to her. His boy went out with his friends, but was unhappy about it.

The TED test was later given to Larry while he was under hypnosis. There were no real differences in his responses from those given during the waking state. We could conclude from Larry's reaction, along with others, that the TED test works equally well with the subject awake or under hypnosis. The TED revealed that Larry had several problems in adjustment, adding to those of which he had spoken.

1. He was reluctant to socialize with people of his own age level, and perhaps other age levels as well. He may think that people are talking about his speech defect or even his illegitimate birth. He wanted to socialize, but was inclined to give up to avoid the possibility of being hurt.
2. He had failed to develop a controlling conscience. His tendency to do right was a result of his fear of punishment rather than a guiding conscience. The punishment that he feared was both physical and emotional.
3. He could leave his mother, but at the expense of his emotions; he felt guilty. It was possible that his mother used

him as an object of her physical love when she was without a mate. Tonight, he will be hypnotized and aroused and hypnotized. Hypnosis will be piled on top of hypnosis. He will be conditioned so that he will enter hypnosis at the sound of my Japanese gong. We will want to be able to talk to him while he is hypnotized, awake him for discussion, then immediately re-hypnotize him. By gaining more hypnotic control, the boy can be protected from admissions made under hypnosis that are repressed and should be left that way. This boy's problems are greater than those encountered in the usual school adjustment case . . . I was not confident of the outcome.

As Larry leaned back in the reclining chair, I remarked, "Sit back and relax, look steady at the flashing object that I'm going to place in your hands. You know what is going to happen . . . You will feel drowsy . . . sleepy . . . Your eyes will get heavy and close." I repeated this for a few moments and he responded by going into a trance. He was told to open his eyes again and we repeated the procedure. Once more, I told him to open his eyes, this time to look into my penlight moving back and forth slowly in front of his eyes. He sagged more and more. At last, there could be no doubt that he was deeper into a trance than usual.

I reinforced his acceptance of hypnosis by practicing posthypnotic suggestions. "I'm removing something from your pocket (his cigarettes) and placing it upon the desk. You are not to feel or remember anything about this. You will also listen to a lovely gong and know that when you hear me sound it and say 'sleep' that you will return to the hypnotic state that you are now in." These words were repeated several times before he was awakened from hypnosis and asked about his cigarettes. After the first practice, he stated that he could feel a light touch, but didn't know what I was doing. At last, with three or four more practice sessions, he was unable to feel anything when I removed the cigarettes, or later when I put them back. Larry readily went into hypnosis each time he heard the signal, but appeared to need the reinforcement of an additional hypnotic stimulus in order to reach a deeper stage.

I concluded the session with the following suggestions: "You are one of God's children and, as such, equal to any man on earth. You are intelligent or you wouldn't have been able to reach the deep state of hypnosis that you have. You have shown that you have the power to concentrate." These suggestions would help him to overcome his tensions and to raise his self-esteem. He was awakened feeling so much better that he wanted to know if I would help his brother. He explained that ——— cried a lot and not only failed to be promoted in school, but didn't want to go any more.

## THIRD SESSION

Larry brought a report card for the work he had done for the first quarter of the school year:

    English 3 ............... 65 (just passing)
    Math .................. 55 (below passing)
    Physics ............... 65 (just passing)
    Auto Mechanics .......... 60 (below passing)

His school record was a dismal one. The average grade for his efforts during the firest quarter was below passing. If he continued to do as poorly during the remainder of the year, he would fail. He had been absent seven times and dismissed once. The school that Larry attended arranged classes according to the ability of the pupils. There are four ability groups: Accelerated, Honors, Standard, Basic. The two courses that Larry passed were both in the lowest group.

I wanted to obtain his intelligence quotient, therefore, I gave him a test that was easy to administer; the Otis-Lennon Mental Ability Test, Intermediate Level, Form J. His score was probably retarded by his reading disability.

Larry did well on the intelligence test. He obtained a raw score of 50 correct responses out of 80 possible onces. According to his age, his derived I.Q. was 95. It was reasonable to expect that his true mental ability might be higher. He was easily hypnotized and that corresponded with good intelligence. The less intelligent subjects are harder to hypnotize.

This time, before hypnotizing him, I asked him to read from an old text book.

"At Maple Grove School, the children were getting ready for their Christmas party. They had invited all of their neighbors.

"They trimmed their tree with glass bells of different sizes and ropes of silver. They hung stars on it and put the biggest star on top.

"What a beautiful sight the tree was, all gold and silver and red and green."[1]

Larry stuttered painfully through the passage. The words beginning in 'b' were particularly difficult for the boy, although there were other words that caused him to stumble. It wasn't easy to listen to him. His teachers may have had him read orally during his elementary school years, but probably as seldom as possible.

He leaned back in the chair, and I gently sounded the gong. As a result of the week's previous post-hypnotic suggestion, I had expected that a few strokes of the gong together with an appropriate suggestion would send him into the trance state, but this wasn't the case. He did enter the trance state using that method, but it was necessary to strike the gong firmly with at least twenty strokes before his eyes fluttered and closed. Once or twice they opened, but closed as I continued to strike the gong. Finally, his eyeballs could be detected rolling beneath his eyelids and at last, there was no more movement.

To test his hypnosis, I picked up both his hands and placed them together in a firm manner with my hands over his, and said, "Right now you could hardly be expected to take your hands apart with my gripping them so firmly, but, in just a moment my hands will be removed and when they are, I want you to try very hard to take your hands apart. You will find that you will not be able to do this because they have stuck together." With this, I removed my hands and watched the muscles of his arms and hands bulge as he tried but failed to separate his hands. "You have done well," I praised him. "Now relax completely and take your hands apart if you want to." Larry separated his hands and placed them upon his legs.

The reclining chair was pushed into an upright position. "You are to read aloud again, but you will remain in the hypnotic state that you are now in with your eyes opened so that you can see the page of the book. This time when you read, you are not to stutter. Your tongue will be free of the tensions that have bound it ... you have no tensions ... open your eyes and read." He did exactly as he was told, except that he stumbled over the one word "silver." He was remonstrated firmly for stumbling over the word and told to reread the passage, "this time without any trouble." He was able to do this several times. Larry was complimented

[1] *Streets and Roads*, 1941 edition, Scott Foresman and Co.

upon reading so well. If he could read without stuttering under hypnosis, why couldn't he also read just as well awake? Would he ever be free of this burden and tensions connected with it?

The boy reclined again and I took the book away. His eyes were still opened so he could see the light from my penlight moving back and forth in front of his eyes. I whispered, "From the state of hypnosis that you are now in, you will travel deeper and deeper ... deeper. Your eyes will again close and as they do, you will travel a long way to a pleasant depth of hypnosis." Larry's eyes narrowed to slits and remained that way for a while, but eventually they closed tightly together.

"You will go back into your younger years tonight," I commanded. "You will imagine that you are in a motion picture theater and there, you will see some important scenes from your past life. Open your eyes. Can you see the screen?" I asked.

"Yes," he replied with eyes that opened and seemed to look beyond the blank wall.

"You are 16 years old. Tell me what you see upon the screen," I said.

There was a long silence before he replied, "Nothing."

"All right, then, let's go back to the age of 15. Can you still see the screen?" I asked.

"Yes," he replied. The boy was going to require a great amount of prompting.

"What are you doing?" I asked.

"I'm doing nothing," but after a while he continued, "I get a job ripping down walls ... in a school."

"What else do you see yourself doing?" I asked, wondering about the nature of his memory; was it memorial?

He answered, "Buying a shotgun ... on the lay-away."

"Can you see yourself doing something with the gun?" I asked.

"Shooting skeet," was his prompt reply.

"Can you see yourself doing something else?" I asked.

He changed the subject. "Going out for football ... I don't like it and quit."

"Do you know why you quit?" I returned.

"I just lost interest in it." With this answer, Larry fell silent.

"Travel back another year to 14. Can you see yourself doing anything?" I continued.

There was a long silence followed by the single word, "No."

"All right, then, I agreed thinking that his memories were memorial. "Take yourself back another year to age 13. Tell me what you can see."

"We moved to ———," Larry answered, using the past tense.

"Tell me what you are doing," I demanded, in the present tense.

He replied as though he was there. "I'm sitting in my room alone . . . I'm thinking of all the new friends that I will meet."

"What are you looking at?" I asked.

"I'm looking out of the window at all of the kids playing outside," he replied.

"Do you go and join them?" I asked him.

"No," he returned somewhat sadly, "I'm nervous about going out there. I don't know them."

"Let's go back another year. You are now 12 years old. Tell me what do you see?" I asked.

We waited for a while and then he answered, "Nothing."

After a long pause, I went on, "You are back to the age of 11 years. What do you see now?"

After a long pause, he answered, "I don't know where I am . . . maybe Vermont."

I responded, "What do you see yourself doing?"

"Just having fun skating," he slowly replied and relapsed into a long silence.

"Travel back another year," I asked, "to the age of 10. What do you see?"

Larry blinked his eyes several times, as if to clear the picture, "I can't see anything . . . I'm not sure where I am. Maybe I'm in a ———."

"All right," I decided to direct him, "you are in school. Can you see yourself in the classroom?"

"Yes, I can see it," he admitted.

"Who is your teacher?" I asked.

"It's Mr. B———, no, it's Mr. A———. He is sitting at his desk," he replied.

"What are you doing?" I asked.

"I'm listening to him," he replied. "He is asking questions about my homework."

Our progress was slow and painful, but I said, "You are doing fine. Go back to the age of 9. What do you see?"

"I can't see anything," he replied.

"Let me put my hand on your forehead to help you clear up the picture. You should be able to see yourself in your classroom."

With this prompting, he was able to continue. "The teacher is yelling at me . . . she said that it was my fault."

It seems to me that we had uncovered something significant. I eagerly probed, "And was it your fault?"

"No," he replied, "it was an accident."

The accident must have been very funny, he began to smile. "Tell me about it," I requested.

Larry's uninteresting laconic reply was, "A kid sat on my pencil." I suspected that Larry must have held it in the proper position for the kid to sit upon, but didn't convey my suspicious thoughts to him.

"What can you see yourself doing at home?" I asked.

"I'm babysitting . . . wouldn't shut up," he replied.

"What do you do about it?" I queried.

"I just let him cry, for about an hour, he finally went to sleep."

"Does the crying bother you?" I asked.

"A little," he admitted.

"Can you see your father?" I asked.

Larry began to breathe hard and became tense. "Yes," he admitted.

"What is he doing?" I asked.

"He is yelling at me," he replied.

"Is he hitting you?" I asked.

"No," he quickly returned. As the boy talked about his father, his speech changed from normal to bad stuttering.

"Let's go back just one more year to the age of 8. Tell me what are you doing?" I asked.

"I'm swinging on a rope," he stuttered.

"Are you alone?" I asked.

"No, there is a neighbor with me."

"Can you see your father?" I asked.

"Yes, he is yelling at me." With this comment about his father, we ended age regression for the night and came back up the years . . . year by year, to the present year.

Larry's eyes had been open to help him hallucinate. I now had him close his eyes and he received the following suggestions. "You are one of God's children. As His son, you are equal to anyone on earth. He is the Father of us all. Should you feel nervous and troubled about anything, you can go to Him for help. Remember, you are an intelligent boy, in school to learn an occupation. You can look ahead to a worthwhile career, money, and the independence that comes with these things. You are a young man growing into full power as a man . . . nothing can stop you. You have done nothing to feel guilty about . . . all of us have made some mistakes, that is part of being human. None of us are perfect. You are not responsible for the mistakes of other people. Look to the future, as you do, you will find your life becoming pleasant. Your school work will be easier as you relax more and more. Your stuttering will also begin to leave you. You found out, tonight that you can talk and read without stuttering. You know how to do it. Every day, in every way, you can become better and better."

## FOURTH SESSION

As Larry settled in the reclining chair, he was instructed to take several deep breaths. "This will help you relax and as you know, the more relaxed you are, the more quickly you will be able to pass into deep hypnosis." I didn't tell him that a sustained hyperventilation will cause anyone to become faint. The stage was set, most of the lights were dimmed, and the sound machine was turned on. "You remember that the last time that you were here you were told to go to sleep whenever I struck this gong." He could only vaguely remember something about the gong. Hypnotism was becoming more and more amnesic with him. He appeared to slip deeper into hypnosis each time and remember less about what was said and done under its influence. Confidence and trust in me were the real factors. He was convinced that he could be helped by the suggestions made to him while he was in the trance.

The gong was sounded several times and the boy looked as though he was trying to remember something. I rang it repeatedly, but with no apparent effect. His eyes remained open and no trance ensued. Sleep suggestions were then combined with the sound of the gong and he then went rapidly into the trance state. Was it the new sleep suggestions that put him to sleep instead of the previous posthypnotic suggestions and the gong? To deepen the trance, Larry was told to open his eyes so that he could see the light. He was rehypnotized with the usual suggestions to go into a deeper and deeper sleep. He did exactly what he was asked to do. Those words were repeated again, but with a new comment, "Think of hypnosis as a long, long cave ... you are somewhere near the beginning ... going in ... going in ... in ... in ... deep into the cave ... deep ... deep," etc.

I told him that his hands were to rotate about each other and when they did, he was given the following post-hypnotic suggestions. "When you are awake, I will ring the gong and your hands will begin to rotate just as they are now doing." These demonstrations were made to reinforce his belief in the power of hypnosis.

"The last time you went back in time until you had reached the age of eight years ... do you remember?" I asked. The question had to be repeated several times before he would respond. Had he entered into such a deep hypnotic trance that it was hard for him to respond to questioning?

The question was rephrased, "The last time when you were here, you saw yourself in a motion picture theater watching pictures upon the screen. They were pictures from your past. Pictures of scenes that were important to you as you grew up. Go back to that theatre and to that seat ... Tell me when you can again see that screen." Larry had to be asked several times before he could see the screen and then I wondered if he really could. I remarked, "Go back to the time when you were eight years old. Can you see yourself at eight years?" After some moments of silence, he said that he was unable to see a thing. I insisted, "Just try harder and the picture will clear up ... see yourself at Christmas time. What are you getting for a present?"

"I got a train," he finally admitted using the past tense. "It's an electric train."

"Where are you living?" I asked. He responded but I wasn't able to understand him.

"Can you see yourself in a classroom?" I asked.

"Yes," he softly admitted.

"Where are you in the classroom?" I asked.

"I'm sitting in the back of the room," he returned. This time he spoke of the past as though it was the present.

In every classroom, Larry has had a back seat. I wondered why? Was it because he stuttered so that he sought an anonymous rear seat?

"Who is sitting in front of you?" I asked.

"——— sits in front of me," he replied.

"What is the name of your teacher?" I asked.

"Miss ———," he answered.

Getting responses from the boy had always been hard. He did not volunteer information freely and had to be prompted for every response.

"Do you like her?" I questioned.

"Do you like to read for her?" I continued.

"No, I don't like to read," was his surprisingly quick reply.

"Why not?" I returned.

"Everyone looks at me," was his response.

I had to repeat the next question several times before getting an answer. "Why are they looking at you?"

"Cause I stutter," for some reason he added . . . "Watch me."

"Go back to seven years old, to Christmas . . . is there a tree with presents under it?"

"There are lots of things under the tree," he answered, without naming any of them.

"Who is with you?" I questioned.

After some probing he admitted that his father and mother were with him. Larry was willing to talk bout his school and the problems that he has there but was reluctant to say anything about his family.

The family repressions must have been stronger and also the cause of his trouble.

"What is the name of the school that you go to?" I asked.

"The ——— Elementary School."

"Who is sitting in front of you in your classroom?"

Larry flashed, "———."

"Do you like her?" I continued.

"She is old and she hollers all the time." His mind was upon the teacher and not upon my question.

"Do you read well for her?" I questioned.

"I won't read," Larry answered with all the petulance of a seven year old child.

"Why not?" I continued.

"I don't like to read . . . I stutter a little . . . I don't like to read."

"You are doing a good job," I praised, "Now continue going back to six years old. Can you see yourself at Christmas?" After some silence he said that he could not. "Can you see yourself at school?"

"Yes," he admitted.

"Who is your teacher?" I asked.

"Miss ———," he answered.
"Do you like her?"
Larry replied with his usual short answer, "No."
"Why not?" I pressed.
"She hurt me," he answered with child like anger in his voice.
"How?" It was my turn to be laconic.
"She grabbed me," he returned.
"How could this have hurt you?" I quizzed.
He was a little more explicit. "Her fingernails dug into my chest."
"How did this happen?" I returned, hoping that he would open up.
"I got out of line," was his answer.
"Why did you do this?" I continued.
"My father called me," he replied.
Maybe this is leading somewhere after all, I thought. What happened then, I wondered. His memory was real.
Larry was breathing fast and turning his head from side to side, reliving the episode. "He swore at teacher."
"Did you cry when this was going on?" I softly asked.
"I cried," the boy admitted.
"The pictures are coming to you just as they should. Go back to your fifth year. Can you see yourself at five years?" I inquired.
"I can't see myself," he hesitated.
"You go to school and you are in the first grade. What do you see?"
"I don't like it," he firmly stated.
"Why don't you like it?" I asked.
"I don't know," he replied.
"Yes you do," I prompted.
"Tell me about your teacher."
"I liked Miss ———, at first." He stopped short after that admission.
"What happened to change your mind?" I inquired.
"She hollered at me for nothing," he replied belligerently.
I waited for a while to see what else he might say. His lips moved slightly but the words were not audible.
"You were saying something, but I couldn't hear it . . . now say it again."
"She put me under her desk for punishment," he cried out.
"What did she do while you were under the desk?" I queried.

"She sat there," he answered.
"Were her legs under the desk?"
"Yes," he replied.
"Were her feet on you?" I pressed.
"No," he replied breathlessly.
"How do you feel under the desk?"
He replied, "I feel bad . . . I want to get out from under the desk . . . It's hot under there!"
"Does she put boys and girls under the desk?"
"No," he returned, "she just puts boys under there."

I decided to return to this episode at another time. "How do you feel toward your father, now that you are five years old?"

"I feel good . . . I miss him when he goes away," he answered.

When I referred to his father under hypnosis he seemed to feel less hostile towards him than he did while awake. If there was something traumatic in his filial relationship he was not willing to talk about it, at least for a while.

"Who are you living with?" I asked.
"We are living with my grandfather," he answered.
"How about your grandmother?" I asked.
"She died."
"Go back to four years old and tell me what you see," I ordered.
He replied, "I can't see myself."
"In that case," I returned, "go back to the age of three and tell me what you see."

It was obvious that the boy was tiring. His head was rolling back and forth faster and faster.

"What is happening to you?" I inquired.

Larry didn't answer but continued to roll his head silently from side to side.

"You have done well tonight . . . you have handled age regression without any trouble. It has been an exciting experience for you but it is now time to return up the ladder of age levels." With this brief prelude, I quickly reviewed the information that he had divulged at each level, age by age to the present, and his breathing returned to normal and his head stopped its movement.

"You know that you don't stutter while speaking under hypnosis. You can speak the same way while awake . . . you have a speech habit that soon should end. Repeat the Lord's Prayer after me but do so without stuttering."

The boy did exactly as requested.

"You can say this prayer while awake, too, without stuttering. Please practice it daily. Now listen carefully to suggestions that will remain with you. You are one of God's children; as such you are the equal of anyone. He is our true Father," etc. The same suggestions were given before, hoping to ease the tensions that caused his stuttering. There was one new addition. Larry had spoken of trouble with math and requested some help with it.

"You are going to pay careful attention to the words of your math teacher . . . You are to listen carefully to what she has to tell you about math. You will spend more time with your math homework. These things will make math more interesting, so much so that you will come to enjoy the subject . . . ."

Larry was awakened with the usual ten count but complained about feeling tired. He looked sleepy. He had received some posthypnotic suggestions. Were they holding him slightly in a trance? Did he want to hold on to some of his problems and therefore resist the awakening? I would return him immediately to a light hypnosis for reawakening. He was rapidly put into a trance and just as quickly awakened but armed with several positive suggestions about awakening. This time, he came all the way out and felt fine. We reminisced about his experiences under hypnosis. "It felt cool, weird this time," he remarked.

## FIFTH SESSION

Larry came to this meeting wanting to talk, and that was somewhat new. He sat back in the chair and began explaining why he wanted to drop his course in auto mechanics and take up the graphic arts. He spoke of his long time interest in art. According to him, there were people who thought that his art work was good. He claimed to have taken some of his drawings to the school where an art teacher examined and praised them. It could be that he had talent in this field, but it could also mean that he was not getting along with his auto mechanics instructor, that he was failing the course and would like to run away from it and needed to rationalize his flight. He talked on and on, trying to sell me, and possibly himself, on the idea. He was encouraged to talk. Art and music are valuable ways to work off tensions and anxieties, and many people use the fine arts for just that. Larry was encouraged to draw, and also to give a lot of consideration to other factors that would be involved in changing courses at that time of the year. I explained that, after all, automobile mechanics was an excellent profession, the money was very good, and there were plenty of job openings as well.

Larry had something else to say. Something that seemed especially ominous and it came out as an apparent last minute remembrance, an "Oh, by the way" type of comment: "My mother is concerned because I used to make coffins all the time. She thought that I made one the other day, but it really was a cigarette box." The boy wanted some kind of a response to explain his revelation.

"When you made the coffins you could have been thinking about death and if you were, then you were doing exactly the same thing that all of us have done at one time or another. It is normal for us all to want to escape troubles, and you certainly have had your share of trouble, but, the fact that you can sit here and tell me about coffins, etc. is an indication that you are all right. You have had problems that still trouble you and you are facing them showing the strength of your character. Do you want to tell me about the time when you first began to wonder who your father is?"

"Well," he began, "I used to lie in bed when I was small and wonder; sometimes I would cry and pray at the same time, I would pray that he was my father, but he didn't treat me like I really was his son. I used to watch the boy next door playing with his father. My father didn't play with me like that. I knew that something was wrong, but I didn't know for sure. One day after he hit me, my mother told me the truth."

"You know that your story is not unique, don't you? There are many boys and girls who face the same thing. As you grow into manhood, you may remember what this has done to you, and become a better father to the children you may have some day. Your own experiences should enable you to become a better father." Larry replied, with great earnestness, "Don't worry, I will."

Larry settled back in the chair, expectantly. The lights were turned down and the hush sound machine was turned on. The soft yellow glow from my small desk lamp gave a gentle soothing air to the normally well lighted office. Larry slid smoothly into hypnosis. To explore the depths of the trance, we ran through the simple tests that have been detailed in other parts of this book. He could not open his eyes, or pull his hands apart. When I rubbed the back of one of his hands and then suggested he would be unable to feel a pinch there, he could not. "Can you see a blackboard if you try?" I asked.

Larry became silent for a minute before claiming that he could.

"Take a piece of chalk and write three words on it ... pencil, paper and pen. Have you written these words on the board?" I asked. Larry said that he had written them. "Good," I continued, "now pick up a rag and erase the first word ... now erase the second word ... as you erased the words from the blackboard, you also erased them from your memory so that only word on the board and in your memory ... pen, pen, pen. Now tell me what word is still on the blackboard?"

"Pen," he quickly responded.

"Can you tell me what other words were written there before you erased them?" I asked. Larry struggled with his memory and finally admitted that he couldn't.

"The last time that you were here, we explored your youth. Do you remember how we did that?" I asked.

"Yes," he replied. "I looked at a movie screen and saw pictures." His response was encouraging.

"Will you go back to the age of five years, when you had Mrs. ____?"

"Yes, I can," he claimed.

"Good, tell me about her," I asked.

"I didn't like her ... she was old and she hollered all the time."

"Why was she hollering at you?" I asked.

"For talking," he admitted.

"What else did she do to you that you didn't like?" I asked.

"She put me under the desk and I didn't like that," he replied in his most fretful five year old voice.

"Why not?" I inquired.

"It was dark under there," he replied.

"What could you see?" I continued.

"Her feet," he answered in a very disgusted tone of voice.

"How about her stockings?"

"She wears long dresses that come down to her shoes ... she is old ... most old people wear long dresses."

He was returned to his present age and we discussed old people. "Why do old people bother you, Larry?" I asked.

"They are always nagging," he replied.

"Do all old people nag?" I persisted. There was no response. "How about your grandfather?"

Larry took time before finally replying, "Grandfather is nice ... He is seventy something."

I made a direct counselling statement to the effect that there must be a great many old people just as nice as his grandfather, and then we returned to age regression. "Will you go back in time again . . . back . . . back to the age of four?" Larry didn't speak. Finally, I asked again, "What about the age of four, can't you tell me about it?"

Larry shook his head and began to breath hard. "I can't remember," was his only comment.

I remembered something that his mother had told me about earlier. "Tell me about the time when your father put you out of the car? I believe that it was just about the age of four, wasn't it?" Larry still remained silent. I asked, "What color is the car?"

To my surprise, he immediately replied, "Black."

"Who is in the front seat?" He replied that his mother and father were. "What are you doing?" I asked.

"I'm jumping up and down," he answered.

"Tell me about it," I requested.

"I want to get in the front seat."

"Go on," I encouraged.

"I want to get in the front seat so that I can see," he answered. (But also to get between your mother and your father, I wondered?)

"What are you doing now?"

"I'm climbing over," he answered.

"Tell me about it." I have to continue to prod for every answer.

"He yells at me to get back . . . I get mad and start bouncing up and down on the seat . . . he stops the car and puts me out and drives away . . . I'm on the side of the road crying . . . I wanted them to come back . . . I just stay there and cry . . . I thought they had gone away for good . . . I couldn't see them. After a long time, they came back and he asked, if I am through playing. I said yes, so they let me in. My father tells me that if I fool again like that, then the next time they will drive away and leave me for good. I believe him, so I sit still."

"You are doing well," I commended. "Would you go back to the age of three?" Larry was breathing very hard and didn't reply. "Does your father hit you when you are three?" I persisted.

Larry continued to breathe very hard and murmured, "I can't remember."

"Perhaps you can do better at the age of two." I wanted to go back, but he wouldn't speak of whatever was there. He wouldn't be pushed but suddenly he brightened, "Coming home," and stopped.

I thought we had come upon something, "Tell me about it."

"It was fun, my mother is pushing me along in a carriage . . . it had handles on it," and he stopped.

I asked, "Why is this so much fun?"

"I hadn't been in a carriage before, it's fun." That is all he could tell me about the incident. Larry couldn't tell me anything more so he was returned to his present age.

"Tonight you are going to read without stuttering, just as you have done before." I handed him a third grade reader. He was told to remain hypnotized and open his eyes. "The tensions that have blocked your tongue are going to leave you, so relax and read." Larry read from the book without any difficulty. He stopped half way down the page and was told, "You will read more, just as you have been doing but this time, while you are reading, I am going to count to ten. When I get to ten you will awaken, as usual, but you are to keep on reading. You are to read just as well while you are awake, as you have been doing while under hypnosis." It would have been nice to say that this was exactly what happened, but it was not the case. Larry read well under hypnosis. He woke up just as he was supposed to while reading. He continued to read and for a short while, immediately upon awakening, he read without stuttering but soon relapsed into stuttering. Larry was rehypnotized and the whole process was repeated with the same results. Again, we repeated the process and again we had the same degree of success. Under hypnosis, he could do a good job, but when he was awake it was a different story.

Larry was given a copy of the Lord's Prayer and told to read it without stuttering. He read beautifully while under hypnosis but while awake it was the same old story. Some progress was evident, but not very much. I continued, but I was discouraged.

"As you know, you have been stuttering all of your life . . . you are going to break the habit, but it will not be easy. Begin with the Lord's Prayer, and practice it each day until at last you can say it without stuttering. This will lead you into perfect speech. Your success will come when you believe in it."

From this, I went into his educative therapy. "You must remember that as one of God's sons, you are equal to any of us . . . relax in that knowledge. Try hard in school and the opportunities will open for you; career, jobs, your own independence. You know that you are intelligent. Use your ability to get along well in school.

Pay attention in class and do your homework faithfully and you will get the good marks that you fully deserve. Remember, you have done nothing wrong. Therefore, you have nothing to feel guilty about. All of your reactions are normal ones. You are not responsible for the actions of others. Birth makes no difference to you or anyone else of any importance to you. You are growing into full manhood, nothing can stop you. You will feel better and better all of the time. Relax, have faith in yourself, and your stuttering will cease to bother you."—I had begun to think that I would be unable to stop him from stuttering—perhaps, shift the attack onto the tensions.

## SIXTH SESSION
## INTRODUCTION TO SELF-HYPNOSIS

Larry was developing into a conversationalist. He seemed anxious to talk for a while before beginning the hypnotic work.

"I told my mother about the episode of the car back when I was a kid ... when my father put me out. She said that she didn't want him to do it. She started to get out herself and had the door open to get out when he drove off. She argued with him and made him come back to get me."

What he told me could have been true, but it also could have been a message to me from his mother saying that she really wouldn't have gone off to leave her son by the side of the road.

Larry told me about one of his friends. "He is just like me, he doesn't have a real father either. When his mother married his stepfather, they had a son. Every time 'their' son did something, his stepfather would beat my friend. Sometimes, my father would watch him do this and then do the same thing to me. My father and his father used to be friends. I was glad when they finally moved away. I don't know where they are now. One day, I was playing with my friend, I think that we were wrestling, and we made some noise. His father came in and grabbed him and made him sit on a kitchen chair for three hours before taking him into the bathroom to beat him up. He had to sit in that chair and wait for the beating that he knew was coming."

He continued to talk. "I think that my father put me back about five lessons last week, when he came upstairs to get me up and started yelling, 'Get up! Get up!' He kept yelling at me all the way downstairs. Even when I got down he kept on yelling. I got real mad. When I got back to my room, I said over and over, I hate you . . . I hate you, hoping that this would make me feel better."

"Did it make you feel better?" I asked.

"Not really," he replied and restated, "but I think that he put me back at least five lessons with you."

Larry's speech occasionally broke into bad stuttering. At other times he wouldn't stutter at all. "Have you tried to hypnotize yourself to overcome the tension that bother you after these unpleasant encounters?" I asked, thinking that he had. Larry admitted that he had tried but without success. "I get a feeling around my eyes, but it isn't like when you do it."

"Tonight, I will give you a post-hypnotic suggestion, one that should enable you to not only put yourself to sleep, but also to awaken you at your own wish. You can set a time limit for the sleep two minutes, five minutes or more. You can determine this before putting yourself to sleep. Perhaps you will want to use this new power to help with your work at school. You know that your stuttering results from tensions that affect some of the muscles you use in speech. Sometimes these tensions interrupt your speech and create difficulty for you. These tensions must be released if your muscles are to be free to do the job that you want them to do. If you will relax mentally and physically, you will be able to speak perfectly. You know that you do a good job of relaxing under hypnosis. You have been doing this once each week for some time now. You know that you can speak clearly under hypnosis, there is nothing physically wrong. You can use self-hypnosis to build up your self confidence and to become calm and relaxed after an unpleasant encounter. When you can do this well, you will be free of the thing that has plagued you for so long."

The boy passed gently into the hypnotic trance and I gave him a copy of the Lord's Prayer.

"You can say this prayer without tension and, therefore without stuttering. When you come to the word 'Amen,' you will go into light hypnosis. When you go into this state, you will be under your own influence. You can then make suggestions to yourself."

As a result of the previous conditioning, Larry had reached a state where he could quickly enter the trance by listening to the soft gong together with a few simple suggestions.

Upon awakening, he read the prayer as directed, without stuttering, but when he came to the word "Amen," he did not automatically fall into a trance. I touched the gong softly and said one word, "sleep." Larry's eyes closed and he went into a trance. "You did well," I praised. "Now let's do it again, only this time, you must do it all by yourself." He was awakened by the usual ten count.

Again, Larry read the prayer, and this time when he came to the ending he said "Amen" with finality, sank back in the chair, and went into the hypnotic trance we sought. "You did a good job," I praised. "When you are ready, why don't you count to ten and awaken yourself?"

Soon, his eyes opened and he broke into a wide smile. He was obviously pleased with himself. I congratulated him. "It looks as if you can now take care of yourself . . . I'm wondering if you really need me any more." Once more, he practiced self-hypnosis with the same successful results.

The primary vehicle that conditioned Larry to go into self-hypnosis was the post-hypnotic suggestion given earlier in the evening. The secondary vehicle that enabled him to go into the trance when he wanted to was the Lord's Prayer. The final trigger for his trance was the key word, "Amen." I was also hoping for some secondary gains by using that particular prayer for the inducement of self-hypnosis.

Again, we probed into his earlier years. The Japanese gong helped him enter hypnosis so well that I didn't feel the need for a trance test.

"Just as you have done before, please go back to an earlier age and tell me of the important events that have affected your life. Start with age four," I requested. During the previous session, I had experienced unusual resistance to remembering those things that occurred at ages three and four.

When he was pressed for memories, his face turned red and jerked as though he had just been struck in the face. When his mother saw him later, she told him that his face had been twitching where his father had struck him when he was only four years old. She remembered the incident well, but the boy could or would not speak of it but his physical symptoms, red face, hyperventilation, and facial movement reflected the incident and was visible to his mother several hours later.

In an effort to start him talking, I reminded him of his stepfather's black car and the incident of his temporary abandonment on the lonely road many years before. He began a long discourse, that was essentially the same as he had reported during the previous session. No additional memories could be elicited. From time to time, his lips appeared about to speak, but even with the most positive support, he would not yet his thoughts seemed close to the surface. We went to the age of three where his memories remained the same as previously reported. He saw himself coming home but couldn't remember from where he was coming. It was fun going home, bouncing about in the baby carriage.

During an earlier session, he admitted that he wasn't able to get a girl friend. "They don't care for me," he explained.

"Tell me why the girls don't date you," I requested.

"Maybe it is because of my pimples," he replied.

"Do you think that there is any other reason?" I asked.

"Maybe because I stutter," he added.

I wondered if the boy was just so insecure that he was afraid to ask a girl for a date. Later, if his self-confidence firmed up, I resolved to encourage him to ask a girl for a date. The reeducative suggestions given to him were almost the same as those previously given. I also suggested that he work to develop his newly acquired skill in autohypnotics.

"You can use self-hypnosis to help you relax and overcome your speech problem. Use it to get a good night's rest and as you go to sleep say to yourself, 'I will feel better and better and in the morning I will go to school and do a good job of it.'"

The self devaluating life that he had lived for so long seemed to be negating all my efforts. I hoped that he would use self-hypnosis to overcome some of his problems at home.

### SEVENTH SESSION

Larry had improved and he knew it. His self-confidence was growing. There has been a reduction in anxiety. Along with this improvement there was a decrease in stuttering. When I commented upon these observations, Larry smiled and remarked, "It's going better in school too. I don't stutter as much there, and I'm getting the math." He went into details explaining that the homework he was now doing was equal to a test mark. It seemed that his teacher has eased the pressure by assuring him that even if he should fail to pass a test, his completed homework will even the score. Larry felt that it was necessary to explain his absences from school in detail. He explained that he had been sick, which was entirely possible, for one day the past week and one day prior to that, he had stayed home to help his mother who had been sick in bed. She had a new baby as well as a two-year-old child. I accepted his excuses and noted with interest, his need to explain the reasons behind the absences that I didn't know anything about anyway.

Larry's life was drab. He had never been to a party and only to a few movies. When asked about these things, he always seemed amused as if to say that I should know better than to think that these pleasantries are a part of his life. He had only one friend, one who collected records. The two boys enjoy listening to them. When they tired of that, they would go outside and walk around for a while and then return to the apartment.

Larry's stepfather still "bugged" him, but now, "It just goes in one ear and out the other," he commented with a smile.

"What he says to you doesn't seem to affect you," I added.

He replied, "No, I try not to let him bother me anymore . . ."

"Does your mother get to you?" I asked.

"She hollers, but not always at me . . . the other children don't mind her when she speaks to them so she hollers at them. When I try to help her out, she says that I'm louder than they are, so she hollers at me, but I don't mind that."

"Do you sometimes feel trapped with no way out?" I asked.

"No, there is a way out, but I'm not old enough to take it," he replied.

I was glad to hear his answers because his thoughts were some of the goals of my hypnotic suggestions. He was now able to see an eventual way out of his present way of life. He only had to wait for the right time to come. There was no hopelessness to his situation anymore.

"What have you done with self-hypnosis?" I eagerly asked.

He replied, "I haven't tried it for a week and a half."

"Why not?" I asked.

"I don't know why," he answered. "It worked the first night, although I don't bother with the card you gave me because I could remember the Lord's Prayer. I didn't use it for the stuttering." It developed that all he had done with this marvelous power was to put himself to sleep one night . . . Well, that was a beginning.

He volunteered, "I have to go to the dentist tomorrow, and I'm worried about it. I hate to go to the dentist."

He wondered if hypnosis could help. I knew that he was a Catholic so I placed a small crucifix in his hand and said, "Hold this, and when we go into hypnosis, I'll give you a post-hypnotic suggestion about pain and the nervousness that you normally have when you go to the dentist. Place yourself in a hypnotic trance and should it become necessary, I'll strengthen your trance."

Larry's lips moved silently as he invoked the ritual. Soon his eyes were tightly closed with absolutely no help from me.

I asked, "Are you in the first, second, or third stage of hypnosis?"

He waited a few moments before replying, "The first stage."

With this admission, I proceeded to take him into a deeper stage. I used the penlight and the now familiar technique of piling hypnosis upon hypnosis. He rapidly passed into one of the deeper stages of hypnosis.

The first post-hypnotic suggestion that Larry received centered about the coming visit to his dentist. "When you sit in the dentist's chair, you will be able to close your hand around the crucifix, and, as you do, your pain and fear, as well as your tension will disappear. You will not appear to go into a sleep or in any way seem to be under hypnosis, but the unpleasantness will leave you just the same."

I had hoped that he would make more use of self-hypnosis and perhaps help free himself of stuttering, but apparently he didn't feel confident enough of his own abilities to fully utilize this tool, or was he too lazy to be bothered to try? Did he need reassurance as part of the self-hypnosis package? Perhaps, he needed to have the suggestions written down. I typed the following on a card:

For self-hypnosis, you are to:
1. Say the Lord's Prayer.
2. After "Amen," you must enter a suggestible trance.
3. Read these suggestions to yourself.
   I will relax and sleep well this night.
   I will do well in school the next day.
   I will speak easily and without any tension from now on.
4. Go immediately into regular sleep.

I continued to address the sleeping boy. "In a moment, you will be awakened from the hypnosis that you are now in, but soon after awakening, you will put yourself back into hypnosis following the outline that I am now placing in your hand. Remember that you can awaken yourself any time you wish, but more than that, should any emergency arise while you are under your own hypnosis, you will always immediately awaken. You would also awaken should anyone speak to you."

Larry was awakened from his sleep in my usual manner of ten counts. He immediately examined the paper that I had placed in his hand. After a few moments, I suggested he read and follow the instructions on the paper. He read them silently and then went into the hypnotic trance.

Once more, he received his now familiar reeducative suggestion, "Remember, you are one of God's children, equal to anyone. You will do well in school knowing that education will open many doors . . . a job, perhaps your own apartment, and the things that money will buy. You are an intelligent boy; and, if you do your work faithfully in school, you will find it interesting and do well . . . You have nothing to feel guilty about. Your reactions are perfectly normal. Remember you are not responsible for the errors of someone else. You are growing up and nothing, nobody can stop you from becoming a man in every sense of the word. Your fears and tensions will fade away." Larry woke himself and went his way feeling fine.

## EIGHTH SESSION

It had been almost a month since our last meeting, and so I was very interested to talk with Larry and find out about his visits to his dentist. With anticipation, I asked, "What happened when you visited the dentist last month?"

With a sheepish grin, he replied, "I didn't go."

"Why not?" I asked.

"I went home from here and took a nap . . . my cousin was supposed to wake me in time to go, but she didn't do it."

I was disappointed, not only with the fact that he had failed to keep his appointment, but that he felt that his cousin was to blame for his failure.

"It is too bad you missed the opportunity," I continued smoothly. "You will probably have to pay for the appointment that you missed since your dentist could have seen another patient during the time he waited for you."

"No, we won't have to pay for it," he replied nonchalantly. "We are under Medicare." . . . So much for responsibility.

My first inquiry led to such a frustrating response that I hesitated to ask. "Tell me about your experiences with the post-hypnotic suggestion we practiced together last time. Did you practice each night?"

"I did it for about a week, but it wasn't the same as when you do it."

I had hoped to hear about a faithful, dedicated effort to rid himself of stuttering, but this wasn't the case. Still he had made an effort to help himself before giving up. That was something positive. I continued, "You felt that you were more successful here with me than when you tried it alone."

"Yes," he repeated, "it was not the same as when you do it."

I hoped that he didn't expect me step into his life and remove his stuttering without much effort on his part. Was he like some people who want to play a piano but are unwilling to put in the hours of practice necessary to master the instrument?

"Let's get on with hypnosis," I commented. With this, Larry leaned back expectantly, and I put out most of the lights and swung the crystal ball back and forth in front of his eyes. His eyes followed the gently swinging ball that seemed to glow in the soft yellow light. His eyes soon closed and he entered the hypnotic trance. I asked, "What stage of hypnosis do you feel that you are in?"

Very softly, as though from a long way off, he replied, "One."

"That's wonderful," I answered. "Open your eyes now and look at the penlight and travel into a deeper stage." Larry obediently opened his eyes and followed the movement of my light back and forth . . . back and forth. He was given a few suggestions and again, his eyes closed, and this time, he went into much deeper hypnosis.

Again, we went over the same suggestions that I had made during earlier sessions, although I added another suggestion to the battery of suggestions that he had been receiving. In spite of my best efforts, the boy continued to stutter. His stuttering was greatly reduced, and at times, he spoke without stuttering at all. When he was under hypnosis there was absolutely no stuttering. I wondered if stuttering was a crutch that he was clinging to and, if so, why not give him a less objectionable one.

"I'm placing two pennies in your hand. Keep them in your pocket and rattle them whenever you are about to stutter."

Larry's mother believed that he spent too much of his time sleeping. He slept well at night, but also napped during the afternoon. If he stayed home from school he would spend most of that day in bed. He has few friends with whom to associate. He didn't dance or socialize with girl friends as most boys his age did. He had been isolated for so long that he found it difficult to interact with others, so he slept. A suggestion made under hypnosis might be helpful so I commented, "You can get along nicely with less sleep, therefore, you will spend less time in bed and more time doing things like studying or socializing with people your own age. You will require less sleep and will want to get out and lead a more active life."

After the boy received this suggestion, he was awakened in the usual manner by counting to ten and giving him a few well-feeling suggestions. Larry opened his eyes but did not respond well. "I feel funny. I can't seem to get up." This was the first time that he had shown any resistance to awakening. He was tightly clutching the two pennies. Could the post-hypnotic suggestion have this effect? He had been told to give up stuttering, that rattling two pennies would take the tensions away from his tongue so that he would speak without stuttering. This was the only new suggestion. Could this be the reason why he resisted awakening? Could it be that he subconsciously wanted to hang on to his bad speech habit as an excuse for not doing well in school . . . for not socializing?

"Relax," I said, "Close your eyes and rest for a few minutes and then you will awaken completely."

Once more, I counted to ten, only this time, more slowly. Each count was followed by a well-being suggestion as well as a direct statement that he would awaken feeling wide awake and want to get up to tell me about his problems. At the count of ten, his eyes were wide apart and he got up to follow me into the waiting room where we visited for a few minutes.

"Why didn't you get up as you usually do when first awakened?" I asked.

"I felt funny . . . real weird . . . my eyes just wouldn't seem to move . . . it was like when your legs or hands go to sleep, and it seems like there are thousands of little needles sticking in you . . . I'm all right now," he hastened to reassure me.

### NINTH SESSION

Larry's mother greeted me with the pleasing assurance that her son was overcoming his stuttering.

"There are times when he doesn't have any trouble at all, when he is singing as he now sometimes does when he takes his bath, and when he is arguing with his younger brother." Larry was able to relax in the tub, where he wasn't trying to communicate with somebody and when he was arguing with his brother who was small and of little threat.

Again he was asked if he had been using his recently acquired skill in self-hypnosis.

"I've been using it every night," he replied, "just as you told me to."

"What effect has it had upon you?" I asked.

"It helps me get to sleep," he replied.

"I was thinking about the penny idea. Did it help you with your stuttering?" I asked.

"It didn't seem to make any difference," he replied.

"Perhaps you would just as soon drop the idea. It really is just another crutch."

Larry agreed. At best, swapping one symptom for another was a poor solution to a problem. My only excuse for suggesting it in the first place was that it would be the lesser of two evils. Faced with one or the other, it seemed better to rattle two coins together than to stutter.

"At the last meeting I also suggested you should find things to do. Were you able to follow this suggestion?" Larry claimed he had spent less time in bed as a result of the suggestion. It was interesting for me to note that he accepted the suggestion about less time in bed but rejected the suggestion that he substitute rattling two coins for stuttering. He was being selective in accepting suggestions.

Larry was asked to think about the reasons why he stuttered. He was unable to think of anything, stating "I can't think of any special thing."

"How do you feel when you stutter?" I asked.

"All I know is that I don't like it."

At this point he was placed in a medium trance and again asked, "Why do you stutter?"

There was a long silence. Finally, his lips moved, but the words were not audible. He was asked to repeat the words and make them louder. Finally, after additional prompting, I could detect the boy's words, "I don't know . . . I don't know."

We would try a new technique and hopefully get somewhere with it. "Tonight, I would like you to try and dream about the first time you stuttered and after you do this, wake up and write about the dream. Provide yourself with pencil and paper just before you go to sleep. When you dream about the first time that you stuttered, wake up and write about the experience using the pencil and paper that you provided for yourself just before going to sleep."

This post-hypnotic suggestion was repeated several times, hoping to reinforce it. If he would follow through with this post-hypnotic suggestion, it would provide me with additional information, even though there was very little doubt why he stuttered. This technique was not new and had been used with rewarding results.

Again, Larry was given the same reeducative suggestions that he had received many times before. These suggestions were designed to make him feel valuable and intelligent, to enable him to overcome his fears and tensions. I again directed him to continue with the self-hypnosis formula, because it seemed to be effective.

## TENTH SESSION

Larry came back a week later to report somewhat light-heartedly that he couldn't remember his dream about which I had asked. I asked him if he had provided himself with the pencil and paper. He passed off my disappointment, "It didn't really matter."

The boy was a good subject for hypnosis. I had penetrated enough so I decided upon a technique that might belong more in a fortune teller's office. I didn't get the dream information and wondered if he might see something in a crystal ball. Something that might provide better insight.

"Let's talk about stuttering. During the past nine sessions, we had improvement, but not enough to satisfy either of us. Up to now, we had been inclined to attribute your stuttering to the feeling that you have for your father. Perhaps we should look in another direction. Possibly your speech problem is more clearly connected with your mother than with your father. When your new father came into your life, did you feel that he had come between you and your mother?"

Larry listened intently. "Possibly you feared your mother was, in this way, being separated from you (distance anxiety). When you realized that your mother had taken a husband with which to sleep. A man much larger than yourself, you began to worry about your place in her life. If we assume that you were upset because of this, you would have been further frustrated because of your size. As a young child, there was nothing that you could do about this relationship, other than to 'act up.' This would get you scolded by both of them, your mother who you loved, and the man who had just come into your life, the man who had just separated you from your mother. Have you considered that your problems might have grown out of a jealous or lost feeling involving your mother?"

Larry replied to this, "What you say might have been true then, but it is not true now." He went on to explain how he wanted so much to get away from his home. Only last week, he considered joining the armed forces because his mother had annoyed him. He explained that some of his neighbors had told her that he had been looking at his half sisters and brother in a threatening manner, "as though he wanted to do them in."

She had told him about this, crying as she spoke. He became disgusted upon hearing this story and sad to think that his mother could believe any part of such a story, so much that all he could think of was to get away from everyone, especially his mother.

I explained that just now, his recent disappointment in his mother may have caused him to want to run away from her, however, this was not really what he felt now and certainly was not what he felt when he was a young boy and when he would have been most fearful of losing close access to his mother. The fact that this mother/son relationship was disturbed at a critical time of his life, just as he was learning how to talk could be the very thing that prevented him from speaking well. "It would seem that your speech problem could be a defense against an earlier fear, that of losing access to your mother, and something that was not established, as a habit.

"If we can assume that your mother was the object of your love when you were a young child and that this relationship was upset by the addition of a stepfather, it is, as we have pointed out, the cause of your stuttering. When your mother took another male into her life you had to helplessly watch this new relationship of a man and wife in marriage. You had experienced more the feeling of loss of a mother, rather than a feeling of gain as you acquired a father. If this is what really happened to you, there is little doubt that your loss and bewilderment turned into anger that was really directed toward your mother. Children don't want to hate their mothers, in fact, they really can't. Hating their mothers would give them greater problem than stuttering so their feelings may be displaced and, as in your case, directed upon someone else. The object of your displaced anger could be your stepfather. It might be added that this displacement of

# STUTTERING

anger also could have protected you from permanently losing your love object. Stuttering may have become a cry for affection from you to your mother."

I asked the boy, "Is it possible that your stuttering is a remnant of an early anxiety anger directed towards your mother when you felt that you were losing her to your stepfather?"

Larry had something new to think about and he showed the effect. He demurred but admitted again that the idea could have had some truth in the beginning but was hardly the cause of his trouble now. He again protested and as a kind of proof, restated his desire to run away to the armed services.

"There is little doubt that you can handle yourself emotionally now," I pleasantly lied, "but, then we are not strictly talking about today. We are talking about how you might have felt when you were young and just beginning to form your speech patterns. Most of your habits, as well as the way you think about things, are the result of early 'conditioning' or early training. We all think and react to things as a result of past experiences."

I went on to explain about Pavlov's dog and the 'little Richard' experiments of Dr. Watson. "We are aware that you stutter today and also know that there is no physical reason for your doing it. You don't stutter under hypnosis and this tells us that there is nothing wrong with those parts of the body that create the sounds for speech. Your present problem results from some past experience. You are bothered by some ghost from out of your past. It would seem that once you find and understand the past event responsible then it seems likely that your problem will be relieved. From that point on, it will be just a matter of overcoming a bad habit."

Larry was placed under hypnosis and directed to look into the crystal ball. He did as he was directed. He opened his eyes while 'asleep' and looked intently into the ball, but was unable to hallucinate. He was placed into a deeper trance, but to no avail. I tried a still deeper trance, but, again, he could not hallucinate any definite forms. He could see something in the ball but it would not come into focus. We ended this technique that had proved to be successful with other clients with a post-hypnotic suggestion calling for greater success should we try it the next time. We continued on under hypnosis.

"Why are you afraid?" I suddenly asked.

"I'm not afraid," he indignantly replied.

"When did you begin to be afraid?" I asked again.

"I don't know," he softly replied.

"What were you most afraid of when you were ten years old?" I asked.

"Of getting hit," he quickly admitted.

"Did you get hit very often?" I questioned, going to the present tense.

"No," he reluctantly admitted.

"What are you afraid of now that you are nine years old?" I persisted. The young man remained silent until I asked another question, "Are you afraid of your mother?"

He quickly answered this, "No."

"Then you are afraid of your father," I stated, but in a questioning manner.

He replied, in a childish petulant voice and manner, "I don't like him."

"What do you want from him?" I replied.

Again, in a most childish and even more petulant voice, "What I want." This answer was not a restatement of my question but a statement emphasizing that at nine years, he didn't need to specify a particular want but expected to get what he just "wanted."

He could not designate any particular want. He was asked a question with a predictable answer, "Are you afraid of him?"

"Yes," he responded, "I don't like him . . . he might hit me."

"You are eight years old . . . are you afraid of him?" I asked.

"Yes, I don't like him."

"Does he hit you?" I asked.

"I don't know," he softly replied.

"Do you look forward to seeing him after he goes away from you?" I inquired.

"No," and he repeated his statement, "I don't like him."

"Tell me Larry," I asked softly, "Has he ever really beaten you?"

In a voice that implied that this was the first time that he had really considered the question, he replied quickly, "No."

"Does he take care of you when you are sick?"

"No," the boy replied in a manner suggesting that he misunderstood the point of my question and therefore considered it stupid.

"Who does then?" I continued.

"My mother does."

"And who calls the doctor?"

# STUTTERING

"My mother calls the doctor," he seemed to be annoyed.

This part of our dialogue ended with just one more question, "And who pays the doctor's bills?"

After a few moments, he seemed to have absorbed the object of my questioning. He replied, "My father."

The lesson under hypnosis ended with one final thought, "Remember the episode of the car, when you were left beside the road?"

He made it plain that he most certainly remembered the episode.

"Now that you are grown up, you now must realize that they would never have gone off and really left you stranded there, don't you?"

The boy admitted that he realized that now.

Our visit together had at last taken on a new proportion. During the previous nine sessions he had emphasized his bad relations with his father. It seemed that I had at last raised some doubts about the validity of so much hostility. It seemed to me that neither the stepson nor the stepfather ever understood the roles assigned to them by circumstances.

In general, my post-hypnotic suggestions for the evening were repetitions of the previous session. He didn't like his math teacher who was always 'yelling' at him. As a result of this alleged 'yelling' the boy had refused to do his homework in math. He had told me this story while speaking almost as petulantly as he had while regressed to 9 years old.

"I won't do the homework."—I thought to myself—that this was a new excuse for not doing homework but I suggested to the 'sleeping' boy, "You must understand that homework is designed to help you master a subject, not to help the teacher. It is nothing to the teacher should you choose to fail in class. The teacher will continue on with his work should you do your homework or not. The only one hurt by your childish attitude is yourself. Homework is for your own benefit and therefore you will want to do this work each night ... to help yourself." The session ended after this with the usual awakening technique.

## ELEVENTH SESSION

The lessons that I had with Larry together with additional information provided by his school had given me ample evidence of his poor social and personal adjustment. His attitude was very negative and he seemed to have lived under the negative feelings of hatred, guilt and fear almost all of his life. It was no wonder that he stuttered and exhibited other non-physical manifestations of his faulty emotional conditioning. These conclusions were subjective so I decided to give the boy the CALIFORNIA TEST of PERSONALITY to obtain a more objective view of his personality.

This test has been discussed earlier in this book. You may remember that there are two main groupings for this test; PERSONAL ADJUSTMENT and SOCIAL ADJUSTMENT and that these two main groups are broken down into several subgroups.

I. PERSONAL ADJUSTMENT
   A. *Self-reliance*—Larry scored highest in this group. It was also his only area of strength. Even here, he only received a 50 percentile. He did feel that he could do things independently of others and could rely upon himself but just to the degree at which half of his peer group are.
   B. *Sense of Personal Worth*—He dropped to one percentile. In other words, 99 percent of his peers were better adjusted in this area than he was. Larry felt that people held him in very little regard, that he was not as worthy as they.
   C. *Sense of Personal Worth*—He rose in rank but only to the five percentile. Possibly his feeling of constriction was a result of economic deprivation. He seldom had any spending money of his own.
   D. *Feeling of Belonging*—He rose this time to the ten percentile. As an illegitimate member of the family, it was especially hard for him to make a healthy adjustment. The boy's environment had added to this handicap. He had to worry about if the other members of his family, 'really want him.'
   E. *Withdrawing Tendencies*—The boy dropped to a low two percentile. This was a lonely boy who lacked any success. It had been easy for him to withdraw into a world of fantasy and to occupy himself with self-pity.
   F. *Nervous Symptoms*—He gained a better score but only to to the twenty percentile. He stuttered, had nightmares, and was tired much of the time. He also had trouble sleeping.

Larry's total PERSONALITY ADJUSTMENT score came to 43 or the fifth percentile. According to this test 95 percent of his peers had better adjusted personalities.

## II. SOCIAL STANDARDS
  A. *Social Standards*—He received only a twenty percentile for his efforts. Even so, it was the highest score that he obtained in this section. His sense of integrity was as poor as was his understanding of common courtesy.
  B. *Social Skills*—He dropped to a fifth percentile. Larry had trouble meeting people and socializing with groups. He never attended parties.
  C. *Antisocial Tendencies*—He dropped to the lowest percentile one percent. Many of his problems in this area could be attributed to his self-concern and his constant criticism of others. He was willing to lie and to swear and felt that this was all right to do if other people provoked him into it. It was others who were always at fault.
  D. *Family Relations*—He made absolutely no acceptable response in this area. It wasn't possible to assign him a percentile. There was nothing right with his relations with his family. He felt unloved and unwanted at home. He was lacking in self-respect.
  E. *School Relations*—Larry came up to the ten percentile. Possibly there was some strength in this area although he had a long way to go if he was to achieve a satisfactory adjustment. The prognosis was poor.
  F. *Community Relations*—He scored a ten percentile in this area. He didn't go to church where he could meet and perhaps make a few friends. He claimed that there was no church near him to attend. There was one very close to him with an active youth group, but this church was of a different denomination, but I don't think that was a problem. The community held teenage dances in the nearby school. Larry didn't attend them.

His total score under the second heading of SOCIAL ADJUSTMENT was just one percentile. The total combined score was just two percentile. How could the boy overcome his background? His conditioning was deeprooted and resisted change. It seemed that stuttering might have been just one adjustment to his unfavorable environment. Larry was a student who could be labeled as having more than just superficial problems. Fortunately such children are a minority of the large numbers of children needing help.

We talked for a while before going into hypnosis. During this discussion it was interesting to note that he did not stutter and I commented. "You seem to have lost something . . . are you sorry to lose it?"

He knew just what I meant. "I have been practicing what you said and hardly stutter at all anymore."

When we talked about his relationship with his father, the stuttering returned, but to a much less degree than it had been before.

"Have you accepted the idea that your speech problem began during that time when you were learning to speak and at the same time experiencing an emotional difficulty . . . a displaced anger from your mother to your father because you felt that you were losing her?"

Larry was quiet for some time and he appeared to be evaluating the thought. He did not speak. Finally to break the reverie I asked, "How many times has he actually hit you?"

"He hasn't hit me very much," he reluctantly admitted in a far away voice . . . "Some of what you say makes sense, but I'm not sure of all of it."

"You accept some of this theory but also reject some of it."

"No, it isn't that I reject some of it," he astutely answered, "It is that I'm not sure of it at all."

"Tell me again what it is that you are not sure of."

"That he ever loved me."

"Is it important to know that he loved you?"

"Yes," he answered, but then went on to explain, or to cover up his emotions, about the lack of good food in his house, "About all we ever get is hamburger, and I have to buy my own clothes . . . my mother hasn't had a new dress in years." The boy was anxious to defend his long lasting hatred, but did so without much enthusiasm, perhaps out of habit.

Larry went into hypnosis confidently and was again given the suggestion that had been a part of his reeducation for the past several sessions, but with one important addition. I added the new explanation for his speech problem.

We went through the usual ten count awakening process, but the boy failed to wake up. If anything he had passed into a deeper sleep state. I went through the process again and told him aggressively to awaken at the ten count as he had done many times before and this time with each count I moved his head gently from side to side. This time he awoke on schedule.

## TWELFTH SESSION

Larry came and spoke with a remarkable improvement. "You realize that you are speaking well this evening," I offered.

"Sometimes I stutter."

"It doesn't matter," I cheerfully responded, "If you can speak a little, well then there is nothing to really stop you from speaking as much as you want and in the same great way."

"Yeah," he replied in a tone that was close to being disagreeable.

I used up most of this hour discussing the personality test that revealed so much the week before. "You feel that you are often treated poorly by many people."

"Yes, I do."

"I would like to hear about some of these unpleasant things that have been done to you."

Larry held his head in his hands and seemed upset, "I have a headache and can't think."

It seemed that the boy was trying to evade. "All I want to know is in what way have you been treated badly by people?"

Larry blurted out defensively, "I don't know . . . It is just a feeling that I have . . . I don't have any proof if that is what you mean . . . My head is killing me, my eyes hurt and I'm having trouble breathing through my nose and throat." He didn't like to have his old antagonism destroyed.

"It seems that you have a cold but don't worry . . . you will soon get over it." I returned to our dialogue and ignored his physical symptoms.

"You say that you have a general feeling that people often treat you badly, but you can't think of any examples. Is it possible that you haven't been treated as badly as you think that you have?"

He refused to reply to this question so I struggled on to another. "You feel that very few of your classmates ever do any nice things for you?"

Larry seemed to be happy at the change of subject. He began another discourse, but, unhappily, his stuttering returned. "Only one kid has ever done anything for me and he is using me . . . When he wants me around, then he comes out but when he doesn't, well, he doesn't, that's all."

"You have trouble making and keeping your friends. Do you feel that you need help in this area?"

"No, I know how to make friends. They just don't seem to like me. When I find some kid that I like I try to hang around with him. That's how I make friends."

"Do you feel sensitive or worry whether they like you or not?" I inquired.

The boy began to hold his head. He was reluctant to continue the discussion, even so, I continued for a while longer, "Have you heard that you have to be a friend in order to have a friend?"

"I'm lost," he replied, "I just don't know what to think."

We passed on to still another question. "You feel that there are many people who are willing to take advantage of you. What has happened to cause you to feel this way?"

The boy stuttered pitifully, "I don't know."

"Just who are some of the people who take advantage of you?" I persisted.

"My father and . . . everybody."

"Just what is it that you have that all these people want from you so much that they are willing to take advantage of you?" I demanded.

The boy didn't seem to understand the question, or else he chose to ignore it, so I restated it.

"What they need," he stuttered angrily.

"Can you explain just how your father takes advantage of you?"

The boy seemed to relent. "He is nice to the other kids on the block . . . Now and then he is nice to me."

"You still haven't told me just how he takes advantage of you," I persisted.

In a surly, defiant tone he replied, but not to the point, "He does dumb things like waking me up on weekends at 8:30 or 9:00 and then going back to bed himself."

"What do you feel would be a better time for you to get up on weekends?" I asked.

"About 11 or 11:30," the boy offered in an explanatory tone.

"Why does he want you to get up as early as he does?" I returned.

"He says that I'm lazy . . . but I know that he leans on a broom handle all night." His father was a night custodian in a large plant. Larry continued, "I'm cranky all week long because of being woken up. I just have to sit and hang around doing nothing because I can't get back to sleep . . . It's boring."

Changing the conversation a bit I asked, "Are you sometimes lonesome even when you are with people?"

"Yes," he admitted. "But only in one way. I have no girl friend." We discussed this problem at length during which he revealed his simple, succinct feeling. He cannot see why the girls haven't appreciated him. 'They' are at fault, not him, for the problem he has in this area.

"There are dances held by the community near your home. Maybe you could find a girl there just looking for someone like you."

"I know about those dances," he returned, "They are sickening."

"I went to one and watched. The bands are no good."

"You went to just one dance and then only watched and as a result of this one visit you decided that none of the dances are any good. Not only that but all of the bands are bad."

Larry again seemed confused and could only reply, "Yeah, but . . ."

"Is it possible that your attitude towards almost everything is negative . . . that is you tend to look for the worst instead of the best in people."

"I don't know what you mean . . ." he insisted.

We went around this theme again, but he was unable to accept the idea that his own attitude was defeating him . . . The world was wrong.

Many psychologists have been profoundly influenced by the creative ideas of Andrew Salter. He has explained that psychotherapy is on the threshhold of becoming a true science, and this rests upon the conditioned reflex theory.[1]

Larry had an extremely low adjustment personality factor. His attitude was that there is nothing that can be done about it. The boy and I talked on about Salter's theories explaining that his attitudes were the result of his past experiences, that all the mechanisms for reconditioning are within him so that there were good reasons to believe that he could change if he was willing to put forth the effort.

The boy had a low self-sufficiency and wanted someone else to do the work for him. If he could just be handed a new personality he

[1] *Conditioned Reflex Therapy*, Andrew Salter; Capricorn Books. New York

would accept the gift, but would work for one only if it was not too much trouble. It was much easier to withdraw and to feel sorry that the world is such a miserable place in which to live.

"Can you still use self-hypnosis?" I asked.

"I don't know. I haven't tried it in a long time," he replied.

He was again instructed through the steps of self-hypnosis. When he reached a trance he was handed some written suggestions to read for himself:

> I will awaken free of tension and anxiety . . . I will want to be able to enjoy the company of others . . . I don't need to blame myself or others for the problems that I am now going to work out.

Larry awakened himself as he had done before. He left the office without comment. In fact, he appeared glad to depart. This session had not been to his liking.

## THIRTEENTH SESSION

Larry seemed to be a different boy this evening. He was more self-assured than I had ever seen before. He stuttered, but not greatly. He didn't seem to mind the fact that he still stuttered somewhat.

"I'm rather tired tonight," he commented.

"You have been tired all of your life . . . What is so different about this night?" I returned, but not as unkindly as it sounds.

"I've been working," he returned proudly.

"I want to hear all about it, but not if you insist upon stuttering while you tell me about it. Let me hypnotize and make you stop . . . at least while you are here with me."

He leaned back in the chair, and with just a few simple suggestions he entered a good trance. "You will remain in this state but with your eyes open so that we can see each other as we speak."

Larry opened his eyes, but looked straight ahead. "You should look at me if we are going to have a conversation," I insisted.

This time he looked straight at me and again we discussed his recently acquired job. He washed windows for a neighbor who was in the window-washing business. He stammered on a word that began with "S." He was corrected, "Please say that word again and then don't do that again because we both know that you no longer need to stutter or stammer."

An obstacle that occurred in my work with clients was time. The time that elapses between visits. For this reason, self-hypnosis has much to offer, but only if the client is sufficiently motivated to use this skill. Larry wasn't too interested and I could only see him about once a week. In the intervening time, the power of the post-hypnotic suggestion diminished. Had I been able to see the boy twice a week our results might have been successfully finalized. Our hour together passed quickly and mostly in pleasant conversation.

## FOURTEENTH SESSION

Larry came to our last session looking rather pleased with himself. He was speaking very well although he appeared to be carefully picking his words and seemed interested in avoiding a long conversation. "Did you practice self-hypnotherapy as I asked you to do last week?" I inquired . . . He didn't want any criticism.

"No," he returned, "I didn't find the time."

"What were you doing that kept you so busy?" I inquired.

"I was out," he returned rather shortly.

"That doesn't tell me very much . . ." I pressed, "Where is out?"

"Just out with my friends," he replied, somewhat annoyed.

I wondered, "Is some of his hostility now being directed at me . . . Perhaps that would be good."

"I've been coming here for a long time and I'm losing interest . . . Maybe if I stopped for a while and came back some time later . . ." he commented.

"Perhaps you would like to contact me sometime in the fall," I replied . . . He looked a little less confident upon receiving my quick acquiesence.

He stumbled a little as he left the office saying, "Thanks a lot for seeing me."

Larry was a much more confident boy as a result of his hypnotherapy. He had acquired a few more friends. He still stuttered at times, but this habit was greatly improved. Possibly with another hypnotherapist or with a greater effort on his part he might have lost this disability altogether. He hadn't put as much personal effort into his therapy as I would have liked. He shunned personal responsibility. He was a neurotic person. He resented a statement that he would be all right. His viewpoint was masochistic, possibly acquired by mistreatment. He was afraid to change. He had a good excuse to feel sorry for himself. This short course in hypnotherapy had made some improvement but, I had to work against a personality that preferred to lash itself with self-reproach.

His self-contempt appeared to have been modified. He was going "out" with friends.

Larry was a weak, lazy individual. He couldn't be depended upon. Every personal item that had been loaned to him had not been returned. His home environment was poor and had produced the disturbances in his relationships with others. This was his "basic anxiety." To cope with his environment he had taken on neurotic defenses or at least tendencies towards them. His most obvious defense was hostility, especially towards his stepfather, who may not have deserved it at all.

I helped him and in so doing took on some of the hostility that the boy had reserved for his stepfather. He had been faithfully hating this man for years, but was helpless in resolving his hatred. This helplessness was important to his "basic hostility." We have been only partly successful with the boy. Perhaps someday he will drop his physical manifestation of the adverse psychic energy with which he abounds, stammering . . . he had been partly turned around and about to head in the right direction. I never saw him again.

# CHAPTER FIVE
# BILLY: SIBLING RIVALRY

The oldest child in a family is very apt to have a feeling of hostility directed at the yonger brothers and sisters. The oldest child was the first born child and for a while enjoyed the privileges of being the only child in the family, and then he had to face his rivals.

Jealousy is a normal reaction for the older child to exhibit toward the new baby. It should be expected. The older child needs to be convinced again and again of his parents' love. As the family looks forward to the coming of a new baby it would help the older child if the parents avoided long anticipatory discussions about the new baby but simply told their oldest child that the new baby would be a nuisance for everybody for a while and would necessarily take up a lot of mother's time and that this was an unavoidable family matter but eventually the whole family would benefit from the new arrival.

The oldest child's jealous feelings should be expected and allowed to be expressed, but they should be directed against inanimate objects. Billy needed his hockey games for they afforded him the chance to work out some of his hostilities and a time-out from the family. He also needed to spend more time alone with his father, doing some things together.

### BILLY
### FIRST SESSION

Billy is a good-looking teenage boy who admits having a few problems that centered around his home. He is the oldest of three boys and is frequently involved with them in some kind of fracas that left them crying. He also has an older sister and he has trouble getting along with her as well, but most importantly Billy cannot get along with his father for any length of time. Meal times are particularly difficult. Billy had been banned from eating with the family for weeks at a time.

Several years before, Billy did well in school and his father would say with pride, "At least he does get good grades." His grades have fallen in school. He claimed that he once liked to read but now was no longer interested in reading. He would rather go out and socialize with his friends. Billy was a junior in the college preparatory division in his high school. He spent very little time with his homework.

Billy admitted that his father was the boss of the family, and that he was sure that his father loved him, but he also felt that his father picked on him. He belived that his father might like the two younger boys a little better than either he or his older sister, "She and I are in the same position." He expanded with what appeared to be satisfaction saying that his father "has no sense of value."

"I can always talk him into something that costs more, but my mother always buys the cheapest. She is stupid about things and I always correct her."

"Do you mean that she is less educated than you?" I asked.

"I guess so, probably the schools were no good where she lived," he added.

Billy liked his mother more than he did his father. "She doesn't always favor the younger kids, but she does tell my father if I do anything so that he can yell at me."

Billy thought that his parents took advantage of him. He appeared to have a feeling of superiority over his parents. There were times when he felt that he hated his father. I explained that this was somewhat normal for a teenage boy who must live with parents who also must restrict their teenager's activities. He need not feel guilty about his feelings.

"You seem to get along with your personal friends?" I inquired.

"I have a few good friends," he replied, and listed the names of some of his neighborhood chums. "By now the kids know me. I guess I have a good personality with friends ... I've just recently learned how to make friends. When I got good grades I didn't socialize and my brothers and sister used to say that I didn't have any friends. Now I have a lot of friends to hang around with so that I don't have time for studying. I think that having friends is more important than getting good marks."

Billy was concerned about the problem that he had in relating to his father. He was concerned but seemed unable to do anything about improving this relationship. The younger boys would go outside to shovel snow in the winter to make some money and also to earn their father's approval but Billy preferred to stay inside and watch T.V. Their father felt that the other sons were industrious and that Billy was lazy. Billy rationalized his inactivity as a difference in viewpoint. He resented the approval that the younger boys obtained for being industrious but not enough to make him go out and do likewise. At one time Billy had a paper route but intentionally or otherwise failed to properly manage the finances of the route and was forced to give it up. His father had to pay his debt to the newspaper company.

Billy believes that his parents didn't understand him. "My father is always trying to analyze me. He claims that the reason why I do some of the 'things' that I do is just to annoy him. He is wrong. I don't try to annoy him. I don't know why I do the things that I do."

He believed that his public school teachers were inadequate. "Kids in private schools have a better chance of going to college. I wanted to take the exams for," and he named a local private high school, "but my parents wouldn't let me ... I hate my teachers in the high school. They don't talk to you. They are too busy to be bothered with you."

He later qualified this accusation by indicating that his English teacher and his math teacher weren't too bad. During the entire interview, Billy squirmed and fidgeted about in the chair. He constantly raised his hand to his face and brushed his hair. He seemed to be unable to sit still.

The boy was nervous. He worried about being admitted to a college although he lacked a definite career goal. He worried but not to the point where he was willing to work hard to prepare himself for college admission. His fears appeared to be real but lacked definition. He was worried about almost everything. He was concerned about the future of his country thinking that so much of the nation's manpower was being wasted away in small parts of the earth when a major conflagration is in the offing. We do live in an age of anxiety because we live in the age of instant communication. Some individuals, like Billy, have a hard time handling the wonders of modern T.V. and radio communication.

The boy's earliest school impression occurred during his second year in school. He liked his teacher. She was Chinese and he believed that this teacher also liked him. She encouraged him to draw. He felt that he could draw well then but had since lost the talent. He couldn't remember having any significant trouble with strangers. He admitted to being in a few fights, winning some and losing some. He was looking forward to that day he would be able to 'take' his father. "He used to beat me when I was in the seventh and eighth grade . . . He doesn't do it much any more."

Billy examined the following list of items and selected those that he was most afraid of: father, mother, brothers and sisters, men, women, dark, school, food.

I had expected him to select 'father' as his first fear but to my surprise he selected 'woman.' Later, just before I was about to hypnotize him, he again spoke of his fear of women. I asked him if he had been bothered by an older girl when he was a young boy . . . perhaps by a babysitter. "No," he couldn't remember this happening to him.

"Were you masturbating with a girl and got caught?" I asked.

"No," but he could remember as a boy of 4 or 5 years having his pants off to urinate when a girl was with him. He thinks that they did something but can't remember what it was.

He was assured that I wasn't interested in what they did but would like to know if they were caught and yelled at. He didn't think so. He seemed surprised to find that he could talk about such things, especially masturbating. He admitted that he had done this, but assured me that it would never happen again, never. I told him that he needn't make such a promise. He had only done what just about everyone else had done at one time or another and would most likely do again, even so he should try to avoid making a habit of it.

Billy's second fear was school. He spoke again of the future. Would he be able to get into a college? He wondered if his hocky playing would help him get into some school that offered a hockey scholarship.

We changed the conversation. "What do you know about hypnosis?"

"Nothing . . . I don't know if it works or if it is true," he replied.

"How do you feel about my hypnotizing you?" I inquired.

"If it can work then I would like to use it," he answered.

"Then let's find out just how well it does work," I added, and moved the boy to the leather hassock just in front of the drafting table. The soft sound machine was turned on and the door closed to the outer office. The small weight was placed upon his finger. His attention was directed to the Moire patterns. I explained about his hand becoming heavy and how the weight would sink to the table. In just a matter of a few moments Billy was under light hypnosis. His head rested upon my hand that cushioned the hard table.

Billy was directed to remain in the light hypnosis but to open his eyes to see the leather chair where he was to move and be more comfortable. When this was done I used the penlight technique to pile additional hypnosis on top of the light stage that he was already in. This hypnotic procedure was repeated several times until at last, he appeared to be in one of the deeper stages. I asked him if he could open his eyes and he replied that he could not.

Billy had reached a suggestible stage and received the following suggestion: "You will discover that when you go to bed this evening as soon as your head reaches the pillow you will sink into the most restful sleep imaginable and in the morning when you awaken you will feel refreshed. Your tensions will have gone away during the night leaving you happy and contented to feel secure in the love you have from your devoted parents and loving brothers and sister."

## SECOND SESSION

Billy was confused about selecting a career. "I think that I would like to take up journalism although I don't know if that is the right thing."

To help him settle upon a career I brought out Dr. John C. Flannagan's Aptitude Classification Test. This instrument is a foremost tool of its kind. Dr. Flannagan directed the Army Air Force Aviation Psychology Program that, among other things, developed the procedures for selecting air crew members during World War II. Sometime after the war, Dr. Flannagan developed his famous FACT battery for civilian occupations.

This battery of tests is based upon elements of a large number of jobs. The job element is a "specific" found in a job that is unique to the job. Obtaining these elements required an extensive analysis of many different kinds of occupations. There are other career prediction tests but most of them lack the depth of the FACT. Many of these other tests are of the preference type. The Flannagan approach required his test developers to examine occupations for the yet unlearned specifics that a person must possess in order to be successful later on in a particular job. The Flannagan test consists of 18 separate job element tests:

1. Inspection
2. Mechanics
3. Tables
4. Vocabulary
5. Assembly
6. Judgement/Comprehension
7. Components
8. Planning
9. Arithmetic
10. Ingenuity
11. Scales
12. Expression
13. Precision
14. Alertness
15. Coordination
16. Patterns
17. Coding
18. Memory

This battery of tests has been standardized upon thousands of high school students located throughout the country. It appears to test what it is supposed to test with a great amount of success. This session with Billy was taken up mostly with the FACT Battery.

Billy had complained about stomach cramps when he arrived at the office, in fact he complained about them all during the testing session. He even found it necessary to open the top of his pants to relieve the pressure on his stomach. He joked, "I think that I've been poisoned." But there was no joke about his illness. He was distressed.

The boy went quickly into hypnosis. He looked steadily at the small neon light and listened to the steady drone of suggestions that directed his attention to every part of his body. "I will relax the muscles and nerves in my arm," etc.

I closed his eyes with my fingers while saying, "I cannot open my eyes..."

He passed several tests of hypnosis before receiving the following suggestions that had a three-way direction. He was told that his power of concentration would improve, that his tensions would leave him, and that his self-confidence would develop. To help him overcome his tensions I asked him on this occasion, to think of himself as possessing a balloon and to see himself filling it up with air from his tensions. Perhaps even the tension that may have caused his stomachache might be inside the balloon. I asked him to release this balloon and watch it soar away into the heavens to be lost forever in the sky. I told him that these lost tensions would be replaced with self-confidence in himself as a young man, as a hocky player, and as a student.

I had the boy repeat the words of Emile Coue. "Day after day I am getting better in every way." All of the suggestions were given to him in the first person. He repeated them many times for extra emphasis. When he was awakened in the usual manner he smiled with some amazement. "Hey my stomachache is gone . . . do you suppose that it was caused by nerves?"

### THIRD SESSION

Billy had some good news to relate. "I got a 90 on my chemistry test, the teacher thought that I had cheated." This was especially interesting news because just two weeks earlier he had brought home a deficiency report in chemistry indicating that he was failing the subject. That was one of the reasons for visiting me.

"How do you account for the fact that you did so well on that test?" I asked.

"I don't know . . . I just knew the stuff and I was so relaxed when I took the test," he replied, somehow skirting around the fact that he had received hypnotic suggestions directing the results that he had just described.

"Did the hypnotic suggestions about relaxing and feeling confident that you had received here last week stay with you during the week?" I asked.

"They did for about three days and then I was about the same as I was before," he answered.

"That is to be expected. It was the first time you had heard the suggestions under hypnosis. The more that you hear them the longer they will stay with you until at last they will become a part of your outlook," I reassured him.

The boy was again placed under hypnosis, only this time we did not use the relaxation technique. Instead he looked directly at a penlight that is capped with glass fibers causing the light to shine through in many different colors. For some reason he failed to respond as well to this technique although he did enter into a trance and successfully passed the eye closure, hand fastening and arm stiffening tests. He received essentially the same suggestions that he had heard the week before although this time I made more of the visual imagery.

To help him develop confidence I suggested, "See yourself in a classroom taking a test. You are prefectly relaxed and confident of yourself. See how relaxed you are. You have studied the material the day before and have listened to your teacher. See yourself writing the answers upon the paper. You are perfectly at ease."

Billy was a member of the high school hockey team. He loved the game and dreamt of winning a college scholarship through this sport. "See yourself dressed in your hockey uniform. You are out on the ice, skating confidently. You are in a game and you are playing well. You know that you are a good player, as good if not better than any other boy on the ice. See how skillfully you weave in and out, outplaying your opponents. You are a good athlete and you are aware of this . . . see yourself making another goal . . ."

To help him relax I suggested, "See yourself as having bottled up all of your tensions inside of a balloon. See yourself making a sign that reads, 'Inside are all of my tensions and anxieties.' Now you let the balloon go and up it rises . . . it travels high up into the sky to disappear forever . . . your tensions are gone now. See yourself as a wax doll sitting out in the summer sun. As this wax doll melts so do you relaxing down completely." With this Billy could be observed becoming more physically relaxed. His body slumped down into the chair.

To help him concentrate I suggested, "Your ability to concentrate upon things taught in school will increase as your interest grows. You will find less interference from distracting thoughts. Think of your mind as though it were going down a road, not an old-fashioned road with many sideroads and flashing signs that distract attention. Think of this road as a new superhighway. There is nothing to interfere with your attention to business. Nothing is allowed upon the road that will distract you or disturb your thinking. Because you are able to devote all of your attention to the task of studying you will be able to retain the material that you want to learn, you will be able to accurately recall the material studied."

Billy was awakened from his light hypnosis in the usual way. He actually opened his eyes before the final number had been called but he seemed to do so more to view the small neon light that always shines in the office rather than to test his ability to open his eyes.

### FOURTH SESSION

Billy was again eager to talk about some of the good things that had happened to him since he began this series of lessons. "I feel much more relaxed in class." He explained that he had just received a 94 in a French examination, "I never do that well."

"Didn't you play a hockey game the other day?" I inquired.

"Yes," he answered, "and I got two goals . . . another boy got three goals. Together we made the only goals our team scored." Billy was proud of himself and for good reason. The boy who made the other goals was a senior.

"Do you credit hypnosis for any of these successes?" I asked.

"I don't know," he returned but with a nod added, "I think that it's good."

Billy entered hypnosis through the somewhat lengthy process of looking at the small neon light and concentrating upon parts of his body. When he had successfully passed the arm stiffening test he received exactly the same suggestions that he had received the week before. Part of his procedure is to repeat after me the Coue formula. "Day after day I am getting better and better." It would seem that repeating this in the trance state should be much more effective than in the waking state.

He had to be spoken to several times before he would respond and repeat Coue words. After he had been brought out of the trance he was asked if he had experienced any particular difficulty in this. He explained that he thought that there were other people in the room and he was embarrassed. There were, of course, no other people present . . . I don't know why he thought that others were present.

## FIFTH SESSION

Once again he was happy to be here, perhaps especially this time because he had to face an examination in chemistry the next day. He was hoping to achieve the kind of successful results that he had enjoyed on some exams that had followed his previous sessions.

He again looked at the small neon light and quickly passed into a light hypnosis that was immediately deepened through the recount method described earlier in this book. This method is exceptional because it introduces an element of self-hypnosis. Part of the success of this technique in trance induction rests with the subject. He is required to count and follow simple directions during the count. After three or four recounts Billy was asked to see if he could succeed with the arm and leg stiffening tests. He found that he could not move them until this rigidity was removed from him. "When I count to three and snap my fingers you will pass into a deeper hypnosis and at the same time your body will completely relax and all stiffness will be gone." I have found it well to suggest that the removal of a hypnotic phenomenon will not cause the subject to awaken but if anything lead him to a deeper state of hypnosis—if that is what I want."

The suggestions that I have to the boy were about the same as those given the previous week except that the tone of the suggestions were commanding rather than suggesting. "Tomorrow when you pick up the paper that the teacher will give you to write upon you will relax completely and the studying that you are going to do tonight will reveal itself through your answers. See yourself picking up the paper, putting it down, and preparing to write upon it. See how completely relaxed you are. This relaxation will completely open up your memory cells."

To emphasize these commands he was reminded of how completely his body had obeyed my commands just a few moments earlier. "You will again be reminded of the power of these suggestions when, post-hypnotically, you will respond to these suggestions tomorrow and so do well on your chemistry test.

Billy was awakened a few moments later with the usual suggestions for feeling well. He was quiet upon awakening. He seemed to be impressed with the power of hypnotic suggestion although he made no comment to that effect.

## SIXTH SESSION

During the previous session Billy had been given post-hypnotic suggestions to help him prepare for a test to be given the next day. I was extremely interested and asked him to report. Came as a breeze," he went on, "I felt as relaxed as a lark."

He had, that day, received the results of the test—100 percent. It was the first 100 he had received during the year in that subject. Needless to say he was pleased with himself but placed the reason for his success upon his own natural ability—and that was consistent with his personality.

Once again Billy easily entered into a good hypnotic trance that might be labeled a medium trance. As before, I used the recount method to deepen this trance. The results of the recount method were plainly evident. As his trance deepened it became harder for him to open his eyes and his pauses between the recounts grew longer and longer. I suggested that his body would become stiff. On this single command his body took on a rigidity that he could not break. Every part of his body assumed a stiffness that extended from his toes to his head. He readily relaxed and may have entered an even deeper hypnosis had I not counted to three and snapped my finger, to break his rigidity and release his body from the stiffening command.

My therapeutic suggestions were the same as before. I told him to visualize himself in the several different situations. It was interesting to watch his body move as he visualized himself skating. "Feel the strength of your hands as they grip the hockey stick." As I said this his hands moved.

"You are skating confidently upon the ice . . . see how well you more upon the puck. Feel the impact as your stick strikes the puck and drives it accurately into the net." I observed his whole body experience the effect of his visualization. "As you see yourself playing a great game of hockey so it will be when you are out there in reality."

As he continued to work toward the release of his tensions, I asked him again to visualize a balloon filled with all of his tensions and anxieties and to see it rise to be lost in the heavens. When he left the office he was a completely relaxed and confident boy.

He had been playing football prior to coming to my office and as a result complained of minor aches and pains. No specific mention was made of this during the hypnosis, but he was reminded of the great power that the human body possesses to repair and to restore itself. I told him, "You will find that your body will be completely restored physically as well as mentally upon awakening." It seems that this is exactly what happened for he had no complaint to offer upon awakening.

Dr. Maxwell Maltz writes in his book, *Psycho Cybernetics,* about our success mechanism. This was something that seemed to be deficient in Billy. The visualization exercises may have helped him to obtain a new success orientation. I had tried to help him use a visualization technique to obtain a successful orientation. Dr. Maltz has pointed out in his book that the nervous system of an individual cannot tell the difference between a real or an imagined experience. The brain reacts to information and doesn't distinguish the difference.

The situations that we created for Billy, under hypnosis, were real to his mind so that his body moved appreciably and appropriately. He experienced a success situation as close to reality as possible. He saw himself as a successful hockey player on the ice and in the classroom he saw himself successfully passing tests.

Dr. Maltz states that we can picture ourselves performing a task and make this experience almost real. Mental practice does help and he offers examples of successful people who have done exactly that. He writes of a great chess champion who visualized himself being in his matches before the events. This champion mentally played his moves weeks, even months, before the game.

"Skull practice" is standard for athletic coaches and for the army rifle instructors who have recruits go through many dry runs with their weapons before firing live ammunition. This can be likened to what we have done with Billy but because of the peculiar benefits of hypnosis his visualization experiences are magnified and have the additional advantage of being augmented with a post-hypnotic suggestion that commands him to go forth and repeat the experience.

I only saw Billy six times in hypnotherapy. While he never succeeded in becoming a big-time hockey player, he did go on to success in college. He eventually obtained a degree in business administration and is operating a small business.

# CHAPTER SIX
# TIMOTHY: SCHIZOPHRENIA

Schizophrenia (Dementia praecox) is a functional psychosis that causes gross personality, social character and intellectual maladjustments. The maladjustments can develop to the extent that the individual becomes a menace or a liability to society. He is then considered to be criminally insane. Occasionally there is personality splitting.

Schizophrenia can take many forms of motor and intellectual disorders and there are many theories concerning the causes of schizophrenia. The prognosis for treatment is rather poor. Timothy was schizophrenic.

### TIMOTHY

Timothy is a new student in one of our local parochial schools. He had upset his teacher so much that she contacted me to see if there was anything that I could do for her student.

"He needs a lot more help than I can give him," she admitted. "He is doing nothing for me in class and frankly the other pupils are beginning to make fun of him," she confided. "He stays to himself ... he talks so funny that most of the time I can't understand him. Actually the only time this year that he spoke so that I really knew what he was talking about was the time that he got angry with me."

"How was that?" I asked.

"I made a reference to the fact that he had spent much of his life in the South. After school he came up to me and angrily wanted to know what made me think that he was from the South."

"You must have touched some raw nerve that he is very defensive about," I replied and agreed to see the boy but suggested that she first ask the boy's mother to get in touch with me. She did and I was able to obtain a few facts from the boy's school record.

Timmy's health record was good. There were no particular problems indicated by his physician. He had been examined by a doctor during each grade level. Two years ago it was recommended that the boy obtain eyeglasses since one eye tested 30/20 and the other eye tested 20/20.

The boy's cumulative record told me that he was not born in the South but in the midwestern part of the United States. He was born January 3, 1955, and that made him 13 years old. He had repeated the first grade. His reading mark for the first year was F but for some reason that was not mentioned on his school records. He was absent from school many times. When his attendance at school improved, so did his marks. His reading improved to B in the previous year's fifth grade. These marks were not very meaningful because I didn't know at what level he was reading in order to obtain his marks. If he were in a low reading group, perhaps working in a fourth grade book, then his B at that level would indicate a low level of accomplishment.

Someone had given him an intelligence test (Otis Quick Scoring) and the boy had obtained an I.Q. of 85. If this score turned out to be valid it would determine that the boy probably was a slow learner with subnormal intelligence. He could hardly be expected to do well in school.

The year before I saw Timothy he was promoted from the fifth grade to the sixth where his final average marks for the fifth grade were as follows: Social Studies, D; Spelling, B; Reading, B; Grammar, D; Penmanship, C; Math, D; Science, D; Music, A.

The boy did poorly in some of the academic areas; social studies, science, and math, and these subjects require independent reading. It should follow that he could have been expected to do poorly in reading but this subject was the one where he obtained one of his highest marks. I thought that was strange.

Timothy had two younger brothers. His teachers indicated that he was not only the oldest but also the slowest. Some of their comments had been abstracted under the following headings: *Social and Personal Adjustments:* Very introverted ... seems to have a great deal of pressure toward perfection ... few friends among the boys and is unable to compete with them on a personal basis ... longs to have friends but must learn to relax first ... seldom does anything in the room ... seems quite shy with the other children ... dreads being criticized or being called out in class.

*Academic Adjustment, Work Habits, and Attitudes:* Becomes confused ... tries to please ... doesn't always complete assignments ... seems withdrawn and afraid ... intensely afraid of failure ... proud of successes ... difficulty in concentrating ... escapes from his frustration by daydreaming ... usually has his homework done but is always the last one to complete his classwork, tests, etc.

After I had examined the records, Timothy's mother brought the boy to see me.

## FIRST SESSION

Timothy came with his mother. While he waited in another room she provided some material that could be described as being opposite to that provided by his teacher. Although the mother was soft-spoken, she left little doubt that she strongly disapproved of some of the teacher's remarks toward the boy. These remarks had been made during the several Parent/Teacher conferences that had occurred before I saw the child. According to Mrs. ———, Timothy's teacher had called her and said that her son was emotionally disturbed and that their home was somehow responsible for his disability. This had upset the parents. They were aware that their son had some kind of difficulty but didn't feel that he was a "disturbed" youngster.

One remark that the boy's teacher was supposed to have made consisted of a threat to return him to the fifth grade for failing to do some of his work. The mother felt that the teacher should have used more tact with her son. The boy later added the comment that his teacher made him feel different from the other boys. When I later saw Timothy and his mother together, I observed that during the time that his mother was talking and even while he contributed to the conversation he occupied himself with seeking and picking small bits of lint from the dark socks that he was wearing. Timothy was a good looking boy, perhaps a little small for his age. His dress and appearance seemed very neat. His teeth sparkled with such brightness that he could have been used as a model for any good leading toothpaste. I wondered if he was always this neat or if he especially cleaned up for this interview.

Timothy's younger brothers were in school with him and to his apparent dismay the next youngest (ten years old) had grown to almost his size. Timothy claimed to love his brothers and his parents. He felt that they also loved him. "Of course they love me," he affirmed.

His younger brothers were more athletic. "They climb trees and do things like that, but I don't. I can't seem to do it." Timothy was not involved with any sports. He felt that he was different and unable to participate with the other boys in baseball, etc. When his brothers were out in the street playing "stick hockey" Timothy would not join them. He continually referred to the things that he did "back home" in the midwest. There was more room in which to play. Things weren't so crowded. There was more room between houses.

Timothy and I left his mother in the waiting room and settled down in the small private inner office. "I'm trying to put my finger on something that we might call a problem for you. Perhaps you can help me? Do you feel that you have any special problem that I can help you with?" I asked.

Timmy explained that his problem was with his teacher. "She said that she was going to put me back in the fifth grade. I was worried that the other children would hear her say it." The boy was very concerned about the opinions of his peers and his teacher. While talking with me he again began to remove small bits of lint from his dark stockings.

"Tell me more about the problem that you seem to be having with your teacher," I requested.

The boy went on. "She doesn't understand me and I don't know what's wrong with her. I can't talk with her. Sometimes when I have tried to do some work, like some kind of homework, she thinks that I haven't done it and won't listen to me or believe me when I try to explain it, she doesn't give me a chance."

I asked Timothy about his physical health. "I sometimes get stomachaches," he explained. "I get nervous. Last year the doctor gave me some pills to take when I get nervous. I don't know what they were except that they were small dark ones. They had a bad taste if you didn't get them down fast ... Sometimes when I get home from school I have a headache."

He showed an unusual interest in the elimination of waste from his body. "Sometimes I can't go to the bathroom," he carefully evaded certain words, "so my mother has to give me some prune juice."

"Does this happen very often?" I inquired.

"Not too much," he replied. "I keep track when it does and make marks on a piece of paper ... sometimes it goes two or three days."

"Who punishes you when you act up?" I asked. Timothy skirted around this question for some time before answering. He wanted me to believe that no one punished him . . . that he never really needed such a thing. He finally admitted that occasionally his mother cuffed him, but his father would only yell at him. It seemed that his father's yelling continued as a lecture for five minutes. "Who do you ask for money when you need something?" I asked.

"My mother," he readily admitted. "My father leaves all those things up to my mother."

"Would you say then, that she is the boss of the family?" I asked. Timmy explained that she was the boss in the household more so than his father because his father was out working most of the time. I wondered with which parent the boy was beginning to identify.

I asked Timothy to tell me what he hated most in the world. This question had to be explained several times before he seemed ready to accept the fact that I wanted him to name an object subject to his hatred.

He evaded this issue. "I hate some kinds of music." Timothy talked on and on explaining the type of music he hated. The boy was very talkative almost to the point where it appeared to be a defense. When he started discussing a point, he seemed reluctant to stop. Parts of his conversation seemed irrelevant to the point under discussion.

Timothy hadn't encountered any great difficulty with any member of his family or with strangers. At least if he had, he was not ready to talk about it except one safe exception. "There were some strange kids that bothered me once . . ." Timothy went on to tell me in great detail a story about some boys who took candy away from him. I wondered about his submission to older boys.

I asked Timothy to select his fears from my list; father, mother, brothers, men, women, dark, school, and food. He selected food.

"I throw up when I eat sweet potatoes." He explained how he did like regular potatoes. He seemed almost apologetic to admit that he wanted to have nothing to do with lobsters. Now that he was living in New England he might think that it was heretical to admit to a New Englander that lobsters are loathsome. "I saw some in a tank and they had pieces of wood in their claws. I'm afraid of the claws."

The interview seemed to indicate that Timothy was a submissive boy but when I tried to place him under hypnosis he was just the opposite. Timothy was seated behind the unlighted drafting table that had proved so effective in the past. A string with a small weight was fastened to one of his fingers. He was asked to look down the string to the middle of the Moire pattern resting on the table. He asked if this was some way to test his eyes. It was not, I explained, but an instrument to test suggestibility. I dimmed the lights and turned the hush sound machine on. The weight seemed to get heavier, just as I suggested and it actually appeared to get so heavy that it was "pulled" down to the table where it remained. His hand followed the object down to the table and also remained upon it. I should have ended the session at that point. Timothy's eyes opened and closed ... it was obvious that he didn't intend to enter a trance without a struggle. When I gently placed my hand upon the back of his neck he moved his head backwards and stiffened up to prevent any forward movement of his head. Timothy was pushing backwards against my hand. Touching him was a mistake. After a few minutes I decided to recline him and try another device.

Timothy moved readily to the reclining chair and leaned back obediently. The penlight which had by now assumed a soft yellow glow as its power declined from much use, was placed in front of his eyes. This action precipitated the greated resistance that I have ever encountered with a child. As his eyes closed he gathered his forces, screwed up his face and forced his eyes back open. His hands rubbed his eyes open until I clasped them together in mine. I suggested that he would be unable to pull his hands apart. He seemed unable to do so a while and then he quieted down.

Then the boy began to move his body in a strange effort to resist. His hands came apart and moved to his penis where he pulled at his pants. He appeared to have an erection. His hips moved from side to side and up and down. His legs worked back and forth in almost venereal excitement. Was he having some kind of orgasm? Did hypnosis represent a kind of excitement or assault? I took one of his hands in mine and held it tightly. I had only seen such a reaction to the induction of hypnosis in just one other case—that of an adult female. The attempt to induce hypnosis was terminated, much to the boy's apparent relief.

"What are you thinking about?" I asked.

"I was wondering when it would stop," he replied.

"You resisted my attempts to place you under hypnosis, didn't you?" I questioned. The boy admitted that he had. When asked for an explanation for his resistance he replied that he was different from other boys. I told him that I hadn't noticed any difference and let the matter drop.

Was his lint picking just as simple as doodling? Was his interest in keeping track of his days of constipation significant? Is that action 'withholding'? What caused him to be so nervous that he required pills? Are the stomachaches and the headaches only a result of nervousness? Had he identified more with his mother than with his father and in doing so acquired some feminine attributes? What did he really hate? Why did he talk so much? Was his talking a cover-up, a camouflage made up of hundreds of words? Was he submissive to other boys? Especially older boys? Had he been used for sexual experimentation by older boys? Does his fear of lobster claws have any special significance? What about his most unusual resistance to hypnosis? Does he fear that under hypnosis he will be stripped of his power to withhold information of all his secrets? Did the movement of his body during the attempt of introduction of the hypnotic trance indicate that there was some kind of sexual interaction going on?

## SECOND SESSION

I wondered if Timothy would return for another session because we seemed to have had such a rough experience during the hypnotic part of his first visit. "Did you really want to see me this week?" I asked.

"Yes," he answered. "I felt like coming back over here and looking at some of the things." The waiting room is a kind of museum of articles picked up during my travels to other countries.

"I'm glad that you did," I replied.

"Tell me about your latest school experiences," I requested.

"The school is O.K.," he appeared eager to report. "I'm getting along better with my teacher. I don't know why, maybe it was something you did . . ."

"I have an interesting test for you to do today," I continued. "It isn't a test with right or wrong answers like those you are accustomed to taking. It is just a yes or no kind of thing. If a test question should ask, 'Do you have a dog?' Then you would answer yes or no." This activity appealed to the boy so he sat down and did the Elementary Form of the CALIFORNIA TEST OF PERSONALITY. (This has already been explained in an earlier part of this book.) The results were as follows:

| Personal Adjustment | Percentile | Social Adjustment | Percentile |
|---|---|---|---|
| Self-Reliance | 30 | Social Standards | 10 |
| Sense of Personal Worth | 20 | Social Skills | 10 |
| Sense of Personal Freedom | 90 | Anti-Social Tendencies | 50 |
| Feeling of Belonging | 30 | Family Relationships | 60 |
| Withdrawing Tendencies | 10 | Community Relationships | 50 |
| Nervous Symptoms | 50 | | |

His total percentile under this second general grouping was 40 percentile. I made a profile of all of the tested scales and found that his responses skewed rather remarkably to both sides of the median. His greatest indicated area of maladjustment under the first heading was withdrawal. This sadly enough is the area that was daily demonstrated. There was little doubt that he was a lonely boy. He seemed ready to give up and giving up would lead to the most serious consequences for the boy. A referral to a psychiatrist was indicated and I would have recommended that action if there was no early improvement in this important facet of his personality. He was a discouraged boy who worried about his failures. His feelings were hurt by others. There were times when his classmates would, as all children do, deliberately hurt his feelings, but if it should develop that he was imagining some of this, then his maladjustment would be substantial.

Under the heading of social adjustment, Timothy dropped to the tenth percentile in the subgroup—social skills. His withdrawal tendencies must have interefered with the development of social skills. Instead of becoming actively involved with his classmates he was actively withdrawing from them. He didn't care to play games or to learn new ones. He didn't meet new people well.

There were some strong points brought out by this test. One strong point was his good relationship with his family. It appeared he felt loved by his parents, was well treated by them and enjoyed a sense of security. He had some high social standards. These good points are first acquired in the home.

Timothy's overall adjustment was not a dismal failure. He was in the 30th percentile. Had it not been for the two very low scores in withdrawal and social skills he might have come close to being an average child of his age group.

It seemed prudent to begin the second attempt at hypnosis with more salesmanship than I had used before. This time I explained the nature of hypnosis. "Don't expect to lose all control of yourself . . . it just doesn't work that way at all. In fact, you actually hypnotize yourself." He didn't seem to be impressed and he made no move towards the reclining chair. I physically nudged him toward it just a little but he resisted so I continued. "Hypnosis is really the basis of the work that we are doing here. The reason that I use it at all is due to its effectiveness in helping boys just like you learn to concentrate in school . . . should I say to you while you are awake, 'You will not daydream in school,' the chances are that you would continue to do so, but should I say the same thing to you when you are under hypnosis the chances are that you would not . . . In this way you would be able to concentrate upon what your teacher is doing or is saying." He still didn't seem to be convinced. "You can find out for yourself if you will go into hypnosis. Let me show you how easy it is. I proceeded to place myself under a light hypnosis. Timothy watched with interest but still there was no sale, so I resorted to adult authority. "You sit in this chair and try it." Timothy submitted to the procedures but would not be hypnotized.

I tried and his eyes would close but then he would struggle mightily and finally open them again. My hypnotic suggestions were put to him as though he were hypnotizing himself. "My eyelids are getting so heavy that I cannot hold them open." His eyes would come together until at last there would be just the smallest slit for him to see through, but by great effort that involved his whole body moving about, he would pull them apart again. There seemed to be an improvement over last time because his body movements were less pronounced. His hands didn't move to his penis as he had before, instead they were rubbing each other. His body moved but not as before, it was more of a constant squirming motion. His eyes would leave the object of fascination to dart about the room in spite of my instructions to desist. It was obvious that he was not looking at the light but to one side or the other. He just didn't want to be hypnotized and saw determined to avoid it. What was it about hypnotism that frightened him?

### THIRD SESSION

When Timothy came to me I thought that I had never seen a boy so nervous and disorganized. I had planned to go over the California

Personality Test with him thinking to use some of his answers to the test as part of a reeducative effort. This obviously wasn't the day for that.

"Everything went wrong this week," he blurted out along with other things that were not understandable.

"I want to hear all about it," I answered, "but let's get your coat off first and maybe if you relax upon the couch you might be better able to tell me . . ."

The boy sat upon the very edge of a chair as far away from me as he could get, he moved constantly. His hands were never still. One minute he was picking lint from his socks and another moment he would find something else to do with them.

He began to talk and continued for some time but in such a disconcerted fashion that it was almost impossible to understand his points.

"Could you talk slower and perhaps more carefully. I'm having some trouble understanding you," I implored. This criticism only succeeded in raising a wall. He tried to follow my request but only became more confused and began an even more disjointed pattern of conversation.

After about 45 minutes of listening to his disorganized thoughts, I was able to detect a few points. His teacher had asked the class if there were any questions with reference to a class assignment. Timothy had a question and raised his hand for permission to ask it. The teacher responded, "Yes, Ma'am." The boy felt that his masculinity had been questioned and went into a panic. He was unable to ask the question. He looked about the room to see if the other children were laughing at the teacher's little joke. He tried to get the question out but he was in such a nervous panic he was unable to ask it. His teacher, unable to understand him, asked a girl who sat next to him if she could interpret his question. The girl apparently wasn't much help.

The situation was an awful experience. The boy's masculinity had been questioned in front of the class and so he went into a panic. He seemed to have a problem in sexual identity but where did it start? His anxiety over this must be very great. The boy felt that he had been held up for ridicule in front of the entire class. Another child with no sex identity problem would have laughed at the teacher's cruel remark thinking it was a joke. This was no joke to Timothy. His problem and her careless remark triggered his panic.

He wanted to talk more and so he talked on, but lost me because he went from one thing to another. There could have been a relationship between everything that he was saying, but he was unable to communicate their relationship to me. Somehow another unhappy experience was related to a friend, Keith, but Timmy was having trouble verbalizing it.

"Why don't you try ... it doesn't really matter what it is ... you can tell me knowing that it cannot bother me or change my opinion in any way. I like you just as you are and there is nothing that you can say that will change that fact."

My efforts seemed to be in vain. Timothy had a problem with his friend Keith or at least thought that he did, and the latter is just as effective. He could not put into words what bothered him.

Two of my young friends who were about the same age as Timothy had been invited to drop by this evening. These boys were intelligent and sympathetic to the needs of others. I had informed them that I wanted them to meet Timothy and to appreciate the fact that he had a problem. It was good to see them arrive after about an hour of sparring with Timothy. Timothy was apprehensive, and appeared a little frightened at the aggressiveness of these two healthy young males. These boys know me very well and we engaged in some physical 'horse play' and joked and laughed together. Timothy replied to some of the boys' overtures and smiled at the roughhouse. He looked a little shocked when I seemingly admonished one of the boys for hiding a copy of a *Playboy* magazine under the cushion of an easy chair. I said that he could have found a better hiding place had he felt secrecy was necessary, but in no way did I chastise the boys for showing an interest in the pictures.

I addressed a few remarks about hypnotism to all three boys.

"You have been hypnotized before by me, Eddie ... and when you were in the trance did you feel that you had lost control of yourself?"

Eddie thought that this was ridiculous, "Of course not."

"Were you unconscious at any time while in the hypnotic trance?" I asked.

Eddie answered, "No, it's more like you were half asleep ... you know what is going on all the time ... I know that it has helped me with my work at school." Eddie responded beautifully, almost as though he was on cue.

"I'm glad to hear that," I replied. "Do you think that it can be just as helpful with Timothy?"

"Of course," was his optimistic answer.

"Let's all go back to the office," (the next room) "and Eddie, would you be willing to demonstrate just exactly how we go into hypnosis?" I asked, just as though the whole thing had not been previously arranged.

Eddie reclined in the chair and was soon under the hypnotic trance. He was given a few suggestions designed to help him relax and be relieved of tensions that generally negate school progress. The other boy wanted his turn at the reclining chair, in fact there was some rivalry between the two boys as to which one would be hypnotized first. Bobby relaxed and followed the example set by Eddie. He too was given a few helpful suggestions. Timothy watched the demonstrations with great interest. At one time it seemed that Timothy was experimenting with hypnosis on the sidelines.

When my two young friends said goodbye, I turned to Timothy, "In spite of what you have been trying to tell me I know that you are no different than the fine boys that you met tonight. Bobby had been having a terrible time with one of his teachers who had been completely unreasonable and Eddie flunked his first year in school and as a result of that felt that he was a poor student. Did you think that you can go into hypnosis just as they did?" Timothy seemed a little hesitant but was willing to try.

Not only did he try but also he succeeded to a modest degree. On this third attempt at hypnosis he became still and appeared relaxed. His hands no longer sought something to do—instead they were still even without my suggesting that they be. His body rested and he lay quietly for the first time. I knew that he may not have been under hypnosis. He may have been acting so I dared not try any of the tests, instead I congratulated him for having achieved a light hypnosis. While he was resting, I made a few hopeful suggestions.

"You will feel relaxed and free of tension . . . the events of your school room will no longer be of concern to you as you realize now that these events were of no real importance. Relax and feel free of tension, tonight you will sleep well and have sweet dreams. In the morning you will awaken completely refreshed and look forward to the day."

Timothy was aroused from his trance looking and acting like a new boy. His speech was understandable and he was smiling. He invited me to visit with him some day in his own home.

## FOURTH SESSION

After two weeks of absence, Timothy bounded in glad to see

me and to talk about his teacher who had obtained a copy of a letter that I had sent to his principal. The letter asked the principal to see if the boy's teacher had used sarcasm detrimental to the child. The teacher had not only berated the boy, but she had called me to say, "I've taught mentally disturbed boys and I know one when I see one. If you knew what you were doing then you would know that this boy is mentally disturbed. He doesn't belong in a school like this. He belongs in a classroom for people like him . . . etc."

The teacher continued. "Yes, I said 'yes Ma'am' to him but that is my way of breaking down the ice in the classroom. The students think that it is very funny and he knows that. You are only hearing one side of the story. I've worked hard with him. I'm the only one of his teachers who is giving him a grade. Just a little for his work. The others aren't giving him anything. I'm the one who has fought to get him some help . . . but that stupid kid etc."

When she had finished with her defensive comments I thanked her for giving me this additional information about herself and we both hung up. She felt much better.

I was surprised to discover that this teacher had examined my letter that was addressed to her principal in confidence. The teacher had even talked about this letter with Timothy. He asked me, "Why did you tell Mrs. ——— that I was upset when she said, 'Yes Ma'am' to me?" He rambled trying to tell me of his troubles in communicating with people. He struggled on with disjointed sentences that seemed to camouflage the point he wanted to make. Helping this unfortunate boy was like flying in a fog without the proper instruments. How could I have told the child that I wrote to his principal hoping that in turn she would supervise the teacher and ensure that he would no longer be ridiculed in class . . . that his teacher was inadvertently adding to his problems.

I decided to give Timothy the Michigan Picture Test. This is a true projective test that consists of pictures. It is similar to the TED in that the child is instructed to make up a story about the pictures and to tell how the people in the pictures feel about what they are dong. The purpose of the test is to investigate and measure the emotional reactions of the child to the special situations in the picture stimuli. Timothy was inflicted with deep inner conflicts. Hopefully the picture stimuli would enable him to verbalize and describe his emotional problems. There was an analysis sheet with the test that aids in scoring the student's responses. This scoring breaks down into the following categories:

1. *Tension Index*—Love, Extrapunitiveness, Submission, Personal Adequacy
2. *Tense*—References to the past or to the future
3. *Direction of the Forces*—If the forces acting upon the child are outward, inward, or neutral with no specific direction
4. *Interpersonal Relations*—Relationship between the number of persons present in the story
5. *Personal Pronouns*—If the story is in the first, second, or third person
6. *Psychosexual Level*—Oral Passive References, Oral Sadistic references, Anal References, Oedipal References, Masturbatory References, Castration References, Poet-oedipal Reference

The test had been well researched and the scoring was objective. Hopefully the test would give the boy an opportunity to unleash his feelings by telling me a story seemingly unrelated to him, and perhaps this would reveal his basic anxiety that had been elusive so far.

Timothy received the first picture from my female assistant. The boy seemed puzzled by the picture. We waited a while for him to begin. I repeated the simple directions that were intended to get him going with his story, but the boy asked, "What are these pictures for . . . some kind of a joke?"

Again, I explained that the stories were to help me understand him and I asked him to cooperate and make up a story about the picture. "Tell me what they are doing, how are they feeling, and how the story ends."

Because he took more than the two or three minutes with the picture I should have followed the test instructions and taken the picture away and not scored it. An unusually long reaction time indicates a blocking around the picture stimulus. I continued to wait until he finally said the picture looked like a typical family having breakfast. That was all that he would volunteer.

"How does this family feel about this typical breakfast scene?" I asked. He replied, "How would you feel?" He had told me something.

We went on to the second picture consisting of a young boy and a young girl looking at the ground. This time the boy volunteered readily, "They look like they feel depressed."

"Tell me about it," I asked, feeling encouraged.

There was another long pause that he eventually broke. "Oh hogwash . . . you can't talk about it in public."

Now we were getting somewhere and I dismissed my female assistant.

"Now that there is no one here but us perhaps you will feel freer to speak. Now tell me about your story."

Timothy reddened and seemed to lose his calm. "You are here," he protested.

"Yes, but I hope that you don't think of me as the public," and went on to explain why he should feel free to discuss anything with me that he wanted to. It did no good. He just wouldn't talk about the picture.

There was no use in continuing with the Michigan Picture Test.

"You seem to be having some difficulty making up stories today. Perhaps you will have better luck another day. Perhaps you have something that you want to tell me," and then I wainted.

The boy finally spoke. "I keep trying to tell you but you don't understand ..." He talked aimlessly using many words, but failed to make a point that I could understand.

"You are talking around a bush ... what is it that you wish to tell me?" I asked.

The boy talked on but seemed less sure of himself. I had said the wrong thing.

"You don't understand ... she doesn't understand," he cried.

"Maybe I would understand if you told me what it is that you want to understand," I pressed on. We continued fencing until it was time to send him home.

Perhaps by now the reader may agree with Timothy's teacher, who has worked with abnormal children, was correct in assuming he was emotionally disturbed.

It seemed wise to refer Timothy to a medical doctor specializing in psychiatry and that is what I eventually did with the boy.

I have tried to emphasize the boy's confused thought patterns. The boy was trying to communicate with his teacher, parents and me, but was afraid to say what he meant. In simple everyday language ... he just couldn't communicate his thoughts in understandable language no matter how hard he tried. Was some kind of subconscious barrier sparing his conscious feelings with a smokescreen?

There had been times when Timothy could converse with me without his self imposed barrier of words. Those conversations were the simple ones that did not threaten him in any way. He could discuss my boat without any trouble because my boat had no personal significance to him. His language became disorganized when he was involved in a way that seemed to challenge or threaten him. In a way, Timothy's schizophrenic-like reactions were similar to those of some stutterers. Both reactions keep people away.

Timothy's pattern of disturbed communication was a standout schizophrenic reaction and it alone was enough to warrant his referral to an M.D., but the boy also had some other reactions that are indicative of the more serious mental disturbances than I am prepared to ameliorate. His scores on the California Test of Personality were highly skewed to an alarming ten percentile in withdrawal tendencies. As had already been explained, his score on the social skills was also just ten percentile. The boy's test results together with his teacher's comments about his inability to relate with others were also indicative that the boy should be referred to a psychiatrist. There was an apparently obsessive search for lint on his immaculate clothing . . . also suggestive of schizophrenia.

There were many different types of schizophrenic reactions. Some adult reactions were very severe but hopefully Timothy's problem would be solved long before his symptoms became seriously ingrained. If he was schizophrenic at all his reactions would be labeled, "Childhood Type." Because I intended to place him under the care of an M.D. who specialized in such problems, the boy will hopefully resolve his difficulties and make an adequate adjustment to life.

## FIFTH SESSION

Timothy's difficulties indicated that a medicine prescribed by an M.D. could slow the child down long enough for a therapist to begin the search for his basic anxiety. He had been unable to evolve picture stories or even to answer my questions. He was so concerned about concealing his basic conflicts that he was unable or unwilling to cooperate with me in solving these conflicts. He may have wanted help but wasn't able to admit me into his innermost thoughts. He appeared clever enough to realize that should he evolve imaginary stories about children in the picture situations I would use his stories to find out some of his carefully concealed secrets. He didn't want this to happen.

I permitted this session to pass with no attempt to accomplish any of my preplanned activities hoping that if we just talked he might be able to relax. We talked on in much the same way that we have done before.

"You know that you are just wasting your time as well as mine," I finally remarked. "Why do we continue to see each other if you have so little trust in me that you conceal your thoughts by beating around the bush all the time?"

Timothy protested and admitted that he did have two problems. "I'm shy and have trouble meeting people." He then rambled on in the same old way until I stopped him.

"Let's go back to the problems that you say that you have. Can you tell me about these two problems?" Timothy again talked on until I asked, "Are you trying to tell me that you don't know why you are shy?"

Timothy said nothing but looked at me for a while as though he hated me.

"Why don't we try to find out just why you have these two problems," I continued.

Once more I attempted to put the boy into a hypnotic trance and there seemed to be some success even though the boy did put up a resistance. He looked into a penlight equipped with optic fibers of varying lengths and saw a fascinating array of color. His eyes closed and opened again and again.

"You must cooperate and relax your body if you are to be successful in this," I remarked, and lifted his arm while speaking the word, "relax." He resisted the effort to lift up his arm. This resistance was followed by only a momentary submission.

Timothy would watch me out of half-closed eyes as I raised his arms and then lowered them. At times his eyes would close tightly to give the outward appearance of a person under trance. Even though at times he seemed to acquire eye closure, his body remained rigid. His arms never fully yielded themselves. He appeared to fear that something would happen to him should he relax his guard. There seemed to be just an element of a trance so he received some suggestions, "You will learn to relax your body more and more each day. You will find that you have nothing to fear. That you can have complete trust in your therapist and in this way you will see how quickly your fears and anxious moments will disappear." Timothy was allowed to "officially" open his eyes but without any of the special awakening processes. He was not hypnotized ... even so I said, "We seemed to have had some success this evening. That is a good sign. I think that you will feel much better because of this success." When the boy left, he was quieter and actually seemed relieved of some tensions. He spoke better. His sentences made sense. Maybe it was only because we were through for the evening.

## SIXTH SESSION

Timothy arrived a little late for his appointment. He felt guilty and peeked around the corner into my office before really showing himself. "I just wanted to see if you were with someone else," he explained. So far the boy had resisted all efforts to help himself, and he had used a great deal of ingenuity and determination. The only I.Q. score I had for him was from an old Otis Quick Scoring Test administered to him by someone else. His score on that test was 85. He must be more intelligent than that I reasoned to have evaded all my efforts so well. So I gave him the Otis Lennon Mental Ability Test.

Surprisingly the boy settled down to the task and worked diligently for the required 40 minutes. He did very well on the first part of the test answering most of that section correctly. Towards the end he did very little. I think that if we had used two sessions he would have scored better. As it was he obtained 50 correct responses out of the 80 possibilities. This gave him an I.Q. close to normal. If he could overcome his learning and emotional blocks he should have been able to perform well.

During a previous lesson I had attempted to give him the Michigan Picture Story Test, but he was unable to get started with the stories. I had thought that we would return to that test some other day, but in the meantime why not try to get his reaction to the Bender Gestalt. This is a test that can be used to explore many things. It is such an interesting and "harmless" appearing test that the boy might accept it as such.

The test consists of plates upon which are printed various shapes. Each plate provides a stimuli for the integrated human organism hences its name "Gestalt." Some of the plates offer possibilities in exploring retardation, brain defects as well as personality deviations. The Western Psychological Services publish a complete package that includes a children's record form conveniently arranged by Dr. Aileen Clawson to facilitate the scoring of a child's responses.

Timothy's figures were examined according to the standards of Bender's twenty initial categories:
    1. Distortion of Shape. Timothy's shapes were not distorted at all.

2. Rotation. Every one of the boy's figures was rotated 90 degrees.
3. Erasures. Timothy made two erasures. He erased part of an overlong tail on his copy of Plate No. 6 and also erased and enlarged his copy of Plate No. 8.
4. Parts Missing. There were no parts missing from any of the boy's pictures.
5. Confused Order. Timothy's figures followed an orderly arrangement.
6. Overlapping of Figures. There was no overlapping of his figures.
7. Compression. Timothy's figures occupied most of the page. There was no compression of his figures.
8. Second Attempt. Timothy erased and redrew Plate No. 8 and in doing so made a larger or more nearly exact copy of the original.
9. Perseveration. There was none. The boy counted the dots and reproduced the exact number.
10. Circles or Dashes for Dots. He reproduced the dots and small circles faithfully.
11. Wavy Line. There was no gross deviation from the straight lines.
12. Shape of Circles. His circles were more than adequate.
13. Deviation of Slant. Plate No. 6 showed a slant deviation of about ten degrees.
14. Dots or Dashes for Circles. Timothy made no substitutes for the appropriate dot or dash in the stimulus picture.
15. Blunting. There was none. (Obliterating point of arrow)
16. Incorrect number of dots. The boy was accurate. He took care to count the dots before he reproduced the plate.
17. Square and curve not joined. They were properly joined together.
18. Angles in Curve. Plate No. 4 should have been more curvacious.
19. Extra or missing angles. There was no problem in this area.
20. Boxes. The boy did not box in any of his drawings.

It would seem that Timothy had developed an adequate visual-motor perception. He was able to see the designs as a whole and to copy them correctly. He integrated the parts into a whole Gestalt but with some variations. The boy did redraw Plate No. 8 and made some erasure of an extra-long wavy line on his version of Plate No. 6. Elizabeth M. Koppitz[1] writes that these erasures and redrawing suggests tension and anxiety. Of this there was no doubt at all. I have mentioned several times that the boy counted the dots very carefully. Koppitz suggests that the examiner *might* have informed the subject that it was not necessary to count the dots. I didn't do this, but I watched him count. Koppitz writes that his actions did suggest a perfectionistic behavior of a compulsive nature.

Koppitz mentions a study by E. Byrd[2] in which he indicates that the rotation of the designs is useful in identifying children with emotional problems. Another study making reference to rotation of designs is by G. Baroff (1957), C. G. Bensberg (1952), and I. Feldman (1953). They suggest that institutionalized patients of an exogenous nature are apt to rotate their designs. Their research suggests that patients who grow by adding to themselves from without, layers covering their inner-selves as opposed to the patients who do grow from within have a greater problem. This problem is sometimes identifiable through the Bender Gestalt Test.

An interesting study of the relationships between Rotation and brain injury is suggested by C. J. Bensberg (1952) and L. Hanvick (1953). There would appear to be diagnostically significant correlation between the two. There could be a correlation between a patient with a permanent brain injury or with one who is suffering with a temporary brain disease.* There also seems to be a relationship between Rotation and reading disability suggesting that good reading skills is dependent upon the ability to correctly see the shapes and directions of the letters and words of a printed page.

It seemed that the most significant point brought out by Tim-

---

[1] Koppitz, Elizabeth M., The Bender Gestalt Test for Young Children Grune & Stratton, N.Y., London.

[2] Byrd, E., The Clinical Validity of the Bender Gestalt Test with Young Children, J. Proj. Tech. 20: 198-206, 1956.

*The following Bender deviations have been mentioned as being diagnostically significant for brain injury: Rotation or the disorientation of the whole figure or part of it on the background was suggested by Bensberg and Hanvick" ... The Bender Gestalt Test for Young Children pg. 72 Grune & Stratton Publisher N.Y. 1963.

othy's response to the Bender Gestalt was the fact that he rotated his drawings. This fact indicated that he may have had an emotional problem. This was more clearly observable by his actions and his conversations. But more than that, the test indicated that there could be brain damage. If this was so then his problems in school were readily explained as well as his failure to achieve any significant success in hypnosis. The reason that I say that there has been no "significant success" with an emphasis upon the word "significant" is because there seemed to have been some. The boy had learned to relax and stop the body contortions that were once so evident. He relaxed almost to the point of hypnosis.

## SEVENTH SESSION

This session was devoted entirely to testing. When Timothy came into the office he carefully walked around the reclining chair used by clients seeking help through hypnosis.

"I'm going to let you look at some pictures today," I stated. Why don't you sit in the comfortable chair?"

He smilingly answered, "I like to sit on the stool."

"Well, if you are not going to sit there then I will," and I adjusted the chair to a comfortable adult angle.

Again I brought out the Michigan Picture Test that had been discontinued rather miserably several weeks ago. I was interested to see if some of the testing that had gone on since had changed his attitude toward this test.

This time we were able to go through all twelve pictures and he made up sketchy stories for each of them. He required prompting for every picture. He rarely mentioned how the subjects felt in the stories unless he was directly questioned about their feelings. It seemed that the boy was tyring to tell me as little as possible in his stories. Perhaps he lacked imagination or he wanted to withhold information that he thought might reveal something of himself. During all our sessions he seemed to be matching wits with me and it could be that he was doing that again with his responses to the pictures.

Of the twelve pictures, four of them have been described as core pictures. These four are scored in accordance with standardized procedures worked out by the Michigan Department of Mental Health.

The results appear to be subjective. This apparently was recognized by the authors as they suggest several ways that "clues" might be derived and used by the clinician to understand the subject. The authors provide seven scoring areas in the analysis sheet but stress the importance of only three of them—Tension Index, Tense, and Direction of Forces as being the most successful in discriminating between the well-adjusted and the poorly-adjusted child.

The importance of the tension index is based upon the assumption that the subject is reflecting his own needs through the stories about someone else. In trying to assess Timothy's physic tension, I was confronted with a near absence of scoreable points. His story was dull, unimaginative and offered little chance for assessment. The emphasis upon his tension maladjustment seemed to be *extrapunitive*. This finding was based upon scant material. I had not expeted to find a *submission* resultant and was not disappointed. Timothy showed no evidence of a *submission* problem.

Another important variable in this test is TENSE. The authors of the test feel that poorly-adjusted children use the past tense as a means of resolving their difficulties. There is no doubt, based upon the strength of Timothy's teacher's comments that he was not adjusting well to the classroom situation, but this teacher assessment was not supported by the test. The boy made absolutely no reference to the past and only a slight reference to the future tense. Each of the boy's stories were based upon the *present*. I can only say from this that if the boy was poorly-adjusted he was not using the past tense as a means of escape.

The third variable that is supposed to significantly discriminate between poorly- and well-adjusted children is the DIRECTION OF THE FORCES working upon the child. Do the forces act inwardly and indicate withdrawal tendencies or do they act outwardly and demonstrate a healthy sign. The Michigan Test also scores a neutral force that is neither centripetal or centrifugal. This is the area of force that is most indicative of a poorly-adjusted individual. Again Timothy appeared to confound his teacher's evaluation. The forces acting upon the individuals in Timothy's stories were predominantly either centrifugal or centripetal. The weighted scores gave a ratio of one to five in favor of the non-neutral forces.

Of the three most important variables only one gave any indication of a poorly-integrated boy. Other variables indicated a possibility of deviation but these variables had not been classified by the test authors, and so they could not be described as significant.

On the psychosexual level, there seemed to be some indication of an Oral Sadistic* problem but only because there seemed to be so little emphasis in any other psychosexual area. The overall picture seemed to be only of withholding with an inability to express his aggression. He failed to respond to the blank card indicating a very restrictive imagination. While he could not fantasize a story around a blank card he did spot two specks of dirt. This was supposed to be an anal reference. It did tie in with his history.

"Sometimes I can't go to the bathroom ... my mother has to give me prune juice ... I keep track of it when it does ... and make marks on a piece of paper ... sometimes it goes on two or three days."

Under the heading of POPULAR OBJECTS, Timothy referred to seven of the possible nine references. He omitted the girl in the first picture and didn't mention the boys in the twelfth picture. This emphasis on objects may be one more indication of a compulsive nature. This indication was correlated by his straightening of objects around the office. A picture left askew was apt to be put in order by the boy.

The Michigan Picture Test gave me a little more to think about. Timothy might have a problem centering around extra-punitiveness. The forces working on the boy were both inward and outward acting and therefore seemed to be perfectly normal. He was compulsive in nature and restricted in making responses to questions of any kind.

## EIGHTH SESSION

During the boy's previous work with the Bender Gestalt text, I observed that he rotated his copy of each of the nine plates exactly 90 degrees. The other scoreable possibilities were in order. This particular variation suggested the possibility of brain injury or brain disease, so it seemed prudent to retest the child. This time I noted that he picked up the first plate offered to him and turned it around so that the rectangular plate was in the same relationship with the rectangular blank sheet of paper. As a result of this, the design that he copied was 90 degrees off from the original angle. Timothy

---

*The oral erotic and oral sadistic phases of infantile psychosexual development lasting from birth to twelve months or longer. The oral erotic phase is the initial pleasurable experience of nursing. The oral sadistic phase is the aggressive biting phase. Oral erotism and oral sadism may continue in later life in disguised and sublimated forms.

started to pick up the second picture and I assumed that he intended to rotate it in the same manner. But this time I rested my finger upon the plate, thereby preventing him from picking it up. He made no further attempt to pick up that plate or any of those that followed. That drawing as well as the rest that followed were not rotated. I assumed that the Bender did not suggest that he had a brain injury but did have a compulsive and perfectionist nature. There were many erasures made before the boy was satisfied with his efforts.

It was interesting to again watch how carefully Timothy skirted around the reclining chair. He chose to sit upon an uncomfortable hassock rather than the comfortable chair connected with hypnosis. This chair naturally faced some of the gadgets that I use in hypnosis including the little neon light that is constantly lighted.

"Why don't you sit in the reclining chair?" I asked.

"The hassock is more comfortable," he pleasantly lied.

"You know that I'm not going to attempt hypnosis with you unless you ask me to," I reassured.

He was not to be tempted, he sat upon the chair when told to do so. He sat upon the very edge of the chair, stiffly and fearfully.

"Why don't you lean back and relax?" I asked. He seemed uncertain as to what he should do and remained alert to the possibility that he might be tricked into being hypnotized.

There had been little, if any, hypnosis with this boy. He steadfastly resisted all of my efforts. He appeared fearful that he might talk about things while hypnotized . . . things that he didn't want me to know about. This boy was either unable to go very far into hypnosis or refused to. The results were the same in either case. He was tense and full of anxiety. His schoolwork and his social life were suffering as a result.

Somehow Timothy had received the idea that he was different from the other boys. He didn't participate with them in their usual roughhouse activities. He could be described as a "sissy" and might have been considered as such by the other boys.

He had a great deal of trouble communicating with others, especially when things did not go the way he felt that they should. He was opinionated. At one time it seemed that he had feminine characteristics but later this didn't seem to be the case. He was at a critical crossroads and could possible develop abnormal sexuality. Great care had to be exercised by his parents to see that he correctly identified with his father.

His self-concept had been devaluated. He lacked the social skills that would enable him to become a part of his peer group even if he wanted to do so. He was concerned about himself and was critical of others. Most importantly, he had strong withdrawal tendencies.

There seemed at one time during our diagnostic sessions a possibility of brain damage, but even this as an explanation for his problems was ruled out. At times there seemed to be an unresolved sexual conflict, but I had not been able to find out what it was. I was inclined to believe that this was at least one facet of his anxieties.

Timothy felt that he was not understood. He admired the hippie whom he thought had something in common with him. Unless his outlook changed, he may join that interesting group someday.

He had a tendency to be a perfectionist although he lacked the mental capacity to do perfect work. He knew that and was frustrated by the confliction. For some reason he had been trying to match wits with me throughout the testing sessions. He had tried to give me answers or stories that would protect his secrets, perhaps his ego. He wanted help but only on his own terms and he was perfectly willing to tell me just how his therapy should go. When first confronted with the revealing Michigan Picture Test, he was unable to make up stories to accompany the pictures but when faced with the pictures again he was able to develop bland, unimaginative stories. There seems little reason to doubt that he had spent some of the intervening time between the first and the second testing session trying to analyze my motives for giving him the pictures in the first place. Perhaps having come to some satisfactory conclusions about this "problem" he felt ready to "cooperate" and create some stories. I wondered just how valid his responses were to the Michigan Test.

## CONCLUSIONS

Hypnotherapy with Timothy had not worked for the very simple reason that the boy was unable to enter the hypnotic trance. He either would not enter into hypnosis or was unable to. He just could not relax sufficiently to hear and to accept the soothing balm of the suggestions made under hypnosis.

There was another recent breakthrough in psychological therapy that might help him. Pharmacology has helped some patients and it might be the answer to Timothy's problem. Pharmacology, like hypnotherapy, also cuts through the time barrier, but it may only mask symptoms. Still this masking effect could be effective and allow other more lasting therapy to be realized. It seemed to me that this boy should receive medication from a physician and then he might be receptive to hypnotherapy. Timothy appeared to be both anxious and depressed at the same time. In his case, the depression might be feeding upon an anxiety that he was unable to share with me.

Chemotherapy might be just the right kind of therapy to alleviate the symptoms troubling Timothy. Physicians have found certain psychotopic drugs that can mysteriously reduce anxiety and depression. These drugs can alleviate psychic pain but there is the problem of drug addiction. I wondered if chemotherapy was the answer. Only a physician can prescribe drugs. I can not.

The drugs that are used in chemotherapy are referred to as the CNS drugs as they are used to affect the brain and the spinal cord. These two intelligence centers are referred to as the central nervous system. The drugs that are available to act upon this center can cheer, excite, depress, calm, blunt the thinking, twist the thinking or stupefy the individual. These psychotopic drugs have a special ability to be selective in their effect even to the point of distinguishing between the normal and the psychotic individual.

It is possible that, in time, Timothy would come to a successful experience in hypnotherapy but at the cost of more time than I wanted to spend. The boy's best interest was to find a shorter treatment and a more successful one. Timothy returned to his school with the suggestion that he see a psychiatrist who could prescribe chemicals should he feel as I did that this was the way to quicken alleviation of Timothy's anxiety and fears.

A few months after Timothy and I parted company, his father called to inquire what schizophrenic meant. He was upset because he had just been informed by Timothy's psychiatrist that his son suffered from this problem. Also this doctor had prescribed some drugs for the boy who refused to take them saying that he didn't need them. Several months later, still wondering about my young friend, I called his school to inquire and discovered that the family had returned to the beloved midwest, so favored by Timothy. Hopefully this move "back home" was the change that Timothy needed.

# CHAPTER SEVEN
# MICHAEL: RESISTANCE TO HYPNOSIS

I don't really know why some individuals are not amenable to hypnosis. Unfortunately, for them, they are apt to be the ones who could best benefit from it. The hypnotic resistant individual seems to try hard to become hypnotized and his very effort might be the thing that defeats him. The fact that he is trying so hard may indicate that he expects to fail or really wants to fail hypnosis.

Hypnosis is a teaching procedure that begins with a familiar idea that builds upon an active imagination. If there is an absence of imagination or an imagination that is present but resisting the induction then hypnosis may elude the subject. Michael successfully eluded hypnosis and I don't know why, but I suppose that he really wanted to.

## MICHAEL

Michael is eleven years old, he is next to the youngest of five children. He is in good health although he squints a little as he reads. I wondered why. He is an attractive boy with a good personality. He claims to get along well with his siblings but with one exception. He scraps with his oldest brother. He likes to go to school but only because there is nothing else to do. He loves baseball and is on a little league team. During the winter, he enjoys bowling and hockey. He has nothing to do with girls older than the three in his own family. He doesn't have anything against girls—it is just that he prefers to be with the boys.

The greatest personal happiness that he can remember was a gift from his parents. They gave him a "stingray" bike for one Christmas.

Michael believes that his friends, family and his teachers understand him. When I asked him about his greatest success he wasn't able to remember anything successful. This response seemed significant and I marked it down as such. When I asked him about failures he mentioned one that stood out interestingly. He failed a special spelling test when he was in the third grade. "I knew the words but I still got them wrong."

When I asked him if he hated anything he was slow to answer but he admitted he hated getting a haircut. This admission was made with a smile. His earliest childhood impression was centered around a piece of glass that entered his eye when he was only four years old. This possibly accounted for his squint.

Michael had not encountered any special trouble with his parents or with his brothers and sisters, but he could remember a stranger who once followed him as he was doing his paper route. The stranger asked for his name and also wanted to know if the boy's dog always followed him around. Michael's mother later verified this. She had watched for the stranger and accosted him. He never returned to the neighborhood.

Michael trusted his friends and indicated that they would lend him some money should he need any. A willingness to lend money appears a test of friendship between many boys. He likes all of his present school teachers but hated the third grade teacher because she held him back.

"Not just because she held me back," he explained. "I didn't like her before that." I wondered if he was being honest with himself.

Michael was asked to select something that he feared from the following list; father, mother, sister, men, women, dark, school, food. He selected "Men, for what they can do to you."

Next he selected, father. "When I do something bad he hits me, but I'm not afraid of him all the time." He hastened to assure me, "Just when he is going to hit me."

He also admitted that he was afraid of the dark. "I'm scared of the graveyard because there are no people living there and sometimes I hear sounds. I've seen bats flying there." The boy's home is almost adjacent to a graveyard.

I asked him if he had any special problems concerning this school.

"Yes, when the teacher talks I dream . . . I just can't seem to pay attention or listen to her . . . I try but when she talks I can't pay attention."

He also has a problem in math. "I don't understand the big numbers, I know about carrying and borrowing but I forget about them when I need them."

In another area of thought, Mike reluctantly recalled having some trouble over a bike that he "found" in a swamp. He explained, "We thought that it was no good so we wrecked it but the kid's father who claimed the bike called up my father and we had to pay for it."

When I asked him if he had any knowledge of hypnosis he replied, "Not until you said it." We agreed to try hypnosis upon the next visit, but perhaps we shouldn't have waited.

On this first visit I gave Michael the *Iowa Every Pupil Test of Work Study Skills Form L,* the elementary battery for grades 3-4-5. The results are as follows:

| Subject | Amount | Correct for Score of |
| --- | --- | --- |
| Map Reading | 4 out of 16 | Third grade |
| Use of References | 4 out of 21 | Second grade, seven months |
| Use of Index | 4 out of 11 | Third grade, four months |
| Use of Dictionary | 3 out of 13 | Second grade, seven months |
| Alphabetization | 10 out of 20 | Fourth grade, two months |

Michael obtained a total of 25 correct responses out of a possible total of 81. This gave him a total score of third grade plus two months. In these tested skills Michael was one year and eight months behind the fifth grade level where he was located. He had also repeated a grade.

## SECOND SESSION

Mike reported with more confidence than he had exhibited upon his first visit. Even so it seemed that he was holding something back—perhaps I would find out later. I immediately gave him the *Otis-Lennon Mental Ability Test,* Elementary 11 Level, Form J, 1967 Edition. Out of the possible 80 correct answers he got only 30 correct. The test was administered at the onset of the session hoping to eliminate any fatigue factor that could adversely affect his score.

The raw score of 30 gave Michael an I.Q. of only 87, with a percentile rank of only 18. This meant that he was better than just 18 percent of all the children upon whom this test had been standardized. Unless this boy had a severe reading handicap it was reasonable to believe that his performance in school was due in part to a limited ability to do the work. We have also indicated elsewhere in this book that subjects with low intelligence are hard to hypnotize. Possibly we should have ended our work with him at this point.

During Michael's first attempt to gain hypnosis, he became concerned about his eye. I asked him to look at patterns that became optical illusions. As soon as he objected to this I changed the induction technique. I then asked him to look at a soft flashing light and to listen to the soft sound machine.

The room was darkened and Mike apparently began to show the effects of the procedure. He seemed to enter the first stage but resisted going beyond that stage. He resisted mightily. I thought that it might be possible to hypnotize him, if he would allow himself to be hypnotized. Michael's eyes would close and then he would begin a struggle to reopen them. His eyebrows would arch and the strain of his struggle was plainly visible.

During the history taking, he spoke of a stranger who followed him and frightened him. Later when he was asked to identify some of his known fears he listed "men" as his first fear. Were these two associations being connected with me? Was he afraid to go to sleep, for what I "might do to him"? I had determined that Mike was a slow learner. Could he concentrate long enough to enter into a hypnotic trance? It seemed that he could but was resisting for reasons of his own. Hopefully, he would come to trust me and enter a trance long enough to receive suggestions that would be helpful to his education.

### THIRD SESSION

The first thing that Mike did upon entering the office was to assume a comfortable position in the soft leather chair used by most of the subjects going into hypnosis. He had used the chair before. He had seen the reading test waiting for him upon the desk. It didn't interest him so he passed it by. Children always like to fool adults. I wondered if Mike had the idea that he could and would play the role of the hypnotized subject or did he want to test his resistance.

"Aren't you going to hypnotize me tonight?" he asked.

"Sure," I replied, "but I would like to get you started on this reading test unless you are really anxious to get going with the hypnosis first."

He looked rather disappointed. "No, I'll do whatever you want to do." Mike got behind the desk and sneaked a look inside of the covers of the *Scott Foresman Reading Inventory Survey Test,* Form A for grades 4-5-6. Sneaking a look was of no importance as this is a power test without any time limit. This is a long, time consuming test and must be administered in parts over several sessions. After an hour, I stopped him and asked him to relax in the soft leather chair.

He appeared to listen intently. "The last time we used hypnotism you did not go into it as deeply as you could have. Maybe you were holding back. If you want me to help you with your education then you will have to let me guide you into hypnosis. Maybe you are thinking that you will go into this sleep and lose control over yourself. Well, this sleep is not like the sleep that you enjoy at night. It is more like "half-sleep." Something like the state that you are in when you awaken in the morning from what may sometimes seem to be a long way off. Perhaps then you heard your mother calling you to get up. Remember how lovely that kind of half-sleep was? Well, hypnosis can be just like that. You will always hear my voice and you will always be able to talk to me. As a matter of fact, I want you to talk to me while you are hypnotized. Last week you gave me some word associations while awake. Now I would like to have you repeat the associations while hypnotized. Remember you will always know what is going on and can always wake yourself should you feel the need to do it. At no time will you surrender all control to me. In fact you will be in control at all times, but you've got to give me your trust."

I continued to reassure the boy and continued to explain carefully just what we would do.

"The first time that we used hypnosis we used this instrument. (I indicated the drafting device.) "You will recall how well everything went . . . your arm got heavy just as I said it would and your head became tired and so heavy that I had to guide it to the table. You then enjoyed a pleasant and most relaxing form of hypnosis."

I tried to remind the boy of what I hoped had been a previously successful hypnotic session, trusting that remembrance might lead him into another one. I said before that success is the father of success . . . but had I really been successful?

"Last week we used several devices to help lead you into hypnosis. Which one was the most successful?" I asked.

Michael really didn't seem to care. "Whatever you want to do," he agreeably replied.

I decided to use the blinking light machine. I measured his pulse beat before setting the metronome and then carefully set the machine to blink in time with his pulse. Some therapists believe there is a connection between the beat of the heart and a flashing light that facilitates hypnosis. This may be so although I doubt it. However, there is something to be said for the showmanship involved. This is important, whenever it is possible to set the subject's imagination to work, it is always a good idea to do so. Maybe that is the connection. I placed the instrument carefully in his lap and instructed him to keep his eyes on the blinking light at all times. I told him that under no circumstances should he take his eyes from the light. To augment this procedure, the hush sound machine was turned on to create a soft, soothing murmur and then the lights of the office were turned down.

His eyes half closed quickly and it appeared that he was entering a light stage of hypnosis. "Remember, hypnosis can help you in many ways, but you've got to trust me if I am to lead you all the way into this." I repeated this several times.

His eyes were about three-quarters closed when he began to repeat his performance of the week before. Michael screwed up his face and struggled to keep his eyes open. His effort to resist was mighty and successful. His eyes opened wider and he looked about the room and at me to see if I was watching his efforts.

"You should try to cooperate with me and follow my instructions if you want this to work. I asked you to keep your eyes upon the flashing light. And you needn't have tried so hard to open your eyes ... if I am to help you, then you must keep your eyes upon the flashing light and wait for me to ask you to open your eyes, just relax and you will be helped."

I continued with hypnotic suggestion and when his eyes were almost completely closed I used the recount method.

"When your eyes close at the count of ten you must not open them again until I tell you to do so."

I continued to make suggestions of trust and confidence and tried to avoid any form of challenge but without success. He again arched his eyebrows and screwed up his face and forced his eyes open.

"You must not try to open your eyes until I ask you to ... I will count to five and then you may open your eyes, but only to look at the flashing light. I will continue counting to ten and then your eyes will again close and they are to remain closed."

We recounted in this way until he could hardly open his eyes at the number of five. It would seem that his struggle to resist had vanished. At least there was no more effort to open his eyes. I persisted with additional hypnosis and placed my hand upon his head.

"My hand will feel warm and comfortable and will help you to relax and go deeper into this pleasant sleep." His brow began to sweat, perhaps from the suggestion that my hand was warm, but maybe not. He made no more struggle to open his eyes and it seemed at the time that he had entered a light hypnosis.

While under hypnosis, Michael responded to the word association as follows:

| Stimulus Word | Awake Association | Sleep Association (One week later) |
| --- | --- | --- |
| Dark | Light | Day |
| Sickness | Good | Good |
| Mountain | River | River |
| Girl | Boy | Boy |
| Beautiful | Ugly | Ugly |
| Smoth | Snow | Rough |
| Big | Small | Small |
| Slow | Fast | Fast |
| Man | Woman | Tall |
| Brave | Strong | Fast |
| School | Hate it | Principal |
| Woman | Man | Man |
| Ruler | Hungry | Pencil |

The similarity was striking although there were some interesting variations. Michael associated opposites in some instances, dark being associated with light. The fact that I am a tall man could have inspired that association with the word man. The association of the word pencil with ruler might have been sexual connotations for those who see a penis involvement whenever the word "pencil" is used.

He stated his feelings towards school very strongly by his awake association to that word but didn't carry this association through the following week when he was apparently under hypnosis.

Because some subjects have a tendency to awaken during an activity such as a word association, I immediately attempted to deepen his hypnosis before making the following suggestions, "You are an intelligent boy, there is no reason why you can't remember the things taught to you in school ... some time ago you told me about a spelling test ... you explained about knowing the words, but you couldn't say them correctly. This never need happen again. You will pay attention to what your teacher is talking about."

Michael spent about a half-hour under the hypnosis with much of the time devoted to deepening the trance. The ten count method of awakening with each count brought him closer to awakening. As usual suggestions for well being were made during the count to ten. "You will feel good upon awakening having had a pleasing sleep experience."

Michael opened his eyes and continued to remain still for several minutes. In answer to my inquiry he replied, "I feel good."

It did appear that the boy had a successful hypnotic experience and was pleased with it because he remarked upon leaving, "When do I come again?"

## FOURTH SESSION

Instead of having Michael complete the Reading Inventory Test he had started the previous week, I decided to change the pace. The reading test was reminiscent of school and he claimed to hate school so why not go into the TED test *Tasks of Emotional Development.* Here he would make up his own stories to go along with the pictures of the TED. Hopefully it would be fun and allow him to use his imagination. I was wrong. What appeared to be an interesting task turned out to be a chore. He even remarked that he would have preferred to have finished the reading test rather than to have to make up stories.

The regular standardized tests require little or no imagination. Usually the student has to plod on through the tests. Rarely was the student required to imagine. It is hard for Michael to "make up" stories requiring the use of imagination.

I should not have been surprised. Dr. Bernard Gindes in his book, *New Concepts in Hypnosis,* states that imagination is a vital factor in hypnosis and hypnotizing this boy was a struggle. At best, it had been only a touch and go situation.

Michael took the TED test twice, while in the waking state and again under the best hypnotic state that we could obtain. In both instances the responses were about the same. The interesting thing about the two performances was the boy's ability to relate the stories twice in pretty much the same manner. The tests were given on the same visit with about one-half hour separating the effort—was he hypnotized?

*Picture No. 1:* The Task of Learning to Socialize

The boy scored a "one" in each of the areas. He immediately perceived that there was a game between some boys and that another boy was coming to join them. The outcome of his story was scored a "one" as the boy did join the group. He had simply arrived late but upon arrival joined his friends without any trouble. He was happy to be with them—"He felt normal."

*Picture No. 2:* The Task of Developmental Trust

Again, he scored a "one" in all areas; perception, affect, outcome and motivation. Michael saw a mother handing some cookies to a boy who had just come into the house. The mother gave the cookies to her son because the "kid was nice."

The boy felt good because the cookies were being handed to him. To get this story out of Michael it was necessary to use many neutral probes. Sometimes when asked for "feelings" he would look as if to say, "What a foolish question to ask."

*Picture No. 3:* The Task of Handling Aggression

Once again Mike scored "ones" for his responses. He explained that the two boys, in this picture, had just had a fight and that the kid with his arms up was telling the other kid to get out of his yard. The boys had fought because, "They were mad at each other."

The neutral boy was ordered out of the yard by the aggressor.

*Picture No. 4:* Task of Developing Learning

The boy's responses were all scored "ones" from the perceptual dimension through the motivation dimension. His response to the learning motivation could have been scored less generously because he didn't see a student studying for the sake of gaining knowledge, but then very few boys really study from that dimension. Most of them study because they have to. Michael saw a boy studying because he had been assigned some work by his teacher. The boy remained at his task until it was finished and then he was allowed to watch TV. "At least that is what I do," he said.

*Picture No. 5:* The Task of Developing a Conscience

We unfortunately found a problem area and one that may have been substantiated by the version given under hypnosis:

PERCEPTION—Michael readily perceived a wallet with money protruding out of it on a table with a boy standing close by looking at it. He saw that the boy was in a position to take something that did not belong to him. Michael received a "one" for perception.

OUTCOME—Michael scored a "three" for his response to this as he had his boy taking the money.

AFFECT—Here Michael dropped into an even lower response, "The boy took the dollar and felt sneaky."

I asked, "What do you mean 'sneaky'?"

He replied, "You know," and he reemphasized the word "sneaky."

MOTIVATION—Once again Michael indicated his problem in this area and in doing so received a higher number.

"He took the money to buy something for himself."

"What did he buy?" I asked.

"Candy," he answered.

Michael had a problem in this important area of growing up healthy emotionally. I also recalled something from his history that seemed to bother him. It was the story of a bike that was broken up. He had passed over the episode as trivial and seemed to bring it up only for its historical significance as it involved some man calling his father to complain.

*Picture No. 6:* Task of Separating from the Mother Figure

As in most of the other tasks, Mike scored a "one" in all areas. He saw a boy going out to play with his friends. The mother was reminding her son not to be late for supper. This small hesitation didn't lower the score, in my opinion, as most mothers do the same thing. Mike's make believe boy was happy to go out and to play and he left the mother without any hesitation.

Placing this boy into a hypnotic trance was a problem. It appeared that he could go readily into a very light trance, but put up a great amount of resistance to going beyond that state. He resisted hypnosis so much that I had become carefully alert to observe any activity that seemed designed to avert hypnosis.

Again, the lights in my office were dimmed and I held a small penlight a foot or so away from his face. Gradually, I lowered this light, originally held above his eye level until it was below. While doing this, he received the usual suggestions and his eyes were forced to close somewhat because they had to follow the light. His response to this induction was negative. I finally turned up the office lights, "to see what to write," I explained.

I decided to give up the penlight technique and try the flashing metronome again. I carefully placed this machinery in his lap and advised him to keep his eyes steadfast on the light. The proper suggestions were made and soon his eyelids closed to the extent that he was looking out under his eyelids which were hardly opened at all. At that point, he screwed up his face and forced wider openings. Again and again I asked him to keep his eyes upon the flashing light. This required constant vigil.

I said, "You are to think sleep, sleep, sleep every time the light blinks." For a while I said the words in unison with the flashing light. Perhaps he reached a slight state of hypnosis. I wasn't sure, but it seemed I had done the best that I could that evening so I gave him the following message. "You will find that school will become interesting and you will not want to spend time in useless daydreaming." I reminded him of how valuable school would some day become for him.

Hopefully this helped him to remember better than he had been doing.

"As you become interested in doing well in school, you will find that the things taught to you there will remain with you . . . during tests information that you learned before will come back to you."

We talked for a while about reading.

"Reading is fun and as you master the words, as you are going to do, you will come to love to do it. You will find that words are easy to understand . . . it will be easy for you and you will love doing it."

I wanted to try a test of the hypnotic state and used an experiment with amnesia.

"I'm going to do something now, but you are not to remember anything about it after you wake up . . ." With this I took a piece of paper and slipped it into his shirt pocket.

When I asked him about this action upon waking up, he replied, "I could feel the paper being slipped into my pocket." I wondered if he opened his eyes a little to peak. Hypnosis was obviously very slght, if at all.

I had decided that this boy was unimaginative and he had a limited amount of intelligence. Hypnosis had been hard to achieve with him. He appeared to be a child that may not benefit from this type of therapy. If he did at all, it will be minimal. There seemed to be little real hope from any other sources. Normally, a boy of this type would be expected to remain dull and unimaginative.

## FIFTH SESSION

Michael worked on the reading test but was unable to complete it in the time available. This is a power test with no time limits. He could take all the time he wanted or needed to complete the work. It did drag out the interview.

We returned to the drafting device, having failed to get very far with the other techniques. It seemed that we were somewhat successful during our first interview when I first used this device. He objected to this type of induction. "Do we have to do it that way again?"

"No, I replied, "but it seems that we were successful and you may remember that we used the drafting tool . . . I know that you want to succeed, so why not?" I asked.

Michael sat on the stool beside the drafting device. The small weight was placed upon his index finger. He fumbled it off. It was replaced more securely. He rested his elbow upon the table.

"You are supposed to hold your arm up," I reminded.

He steadied his hand against his forehead.

"You are to look down the thread towards the target so you will have to hold your hand in front of your eyes," I added.

Finally, he got in position for this technique to be used, but this didn't last long. I was hardly able to say that the weight was drawn down to the target when he dropped it. Suddenly, his hand followed the weight to the table and his eyes began to close.

It was obvious that the boy was going to really fake hypnosis this time. Children can and frequently do simulate hypnosis with much realism. Michael was going to fake hypnosis before he could be brought into it.

I was in no mood to play games with him. "It's getting late, Michael, and we both have much to do." With this, the boy got up and left quietly.

Why was I really failing with this boy? Was it just for the reasons that I have already suggested? Had I really listened to all that the boy tried to tell me about his fears and hates, etc. He had told me in several ways of his fears of men. Why had he done this? Could hypnosis and I represent a form of assault that the boy was reacting to as best he could?

## SIXTH SESSION

Michael came full of vigor, for some reason. He rapidly finished the reading test that he started several weeks before. The results of his efforts were as follows:

| Category | Correct Responses | Grade Score |
| --- | --- | --- |
| Word Meaning | 17 out of 25 | 3.2 |
| Sentence Meaning | 9 out of 25 | 2.9 |
| Total Meaning | 23 out of 50 | 4.4 |
| Word Analysis | 33 out of 35 | 3.5 |
| Dictionary Skills | 18 out of 35 | 4.5 |

The boy's total score for the test came to 3.9. This score was similar to the score obtained in the *Iowa Word Study Skills Test* where he obtained a total score of 3.2. These two low scores presented a boy with great limitations and predicted a very limited success for this kind of therapy and that is why I have inserted this study.

We tried something new. I removed the black cover from the spinning disk machine and asked Michael to fasten his eyes upon the hypno-disk. He did so with interest. While the boy watched the spinning disk, I again talked about the aims of our work together. It seemed that we had established a new rapport and he appeared to relax and his eyes closed. It appeared that we had reached a true hypnotic state.

Thinking to deepen this probable light hypnotic state, I began a rehypnotization and repeated the formula several times until at last it seemed that he could no longer open his eyes. I explained something about the several stages of hypnosis and asked him, "What stage do you feel that you have entered?"

"Stage two," he promptly answered.

"In that case you soon won't feel a thing in this finger."

With this preamble, I proceeded to the anesthesia induction procedure following the steps described elsewhere. I picked up his hand and felt no resistance. I coated the tip of his finger with an antiseptic and gently pricked his finger with a needle. I felt a slight reaction in his hand that was nestled in mine. I pricked his finger again but a little more firmly and watched the expression of his face change as well as a more noticeable twitch in his hand.

"What's the matter, Mike?" I asked.

"You stuck me with that pin," he answered with what appeared to be surprise as well as anger in his voice.

"But you assured me that you were in the second stage of hypnosis . . . I didn't expect you to feel anything," I lied.

He looked rather foolish and for a while it seemed that he would cry.

"You are a good faker," I continued, "I thought that we were going to be honest with each other . . . have you been honest with me through this project?"

We talked for some time now, mostly about the events of the past several weeks and the boy admitted that he had never really been hypnotized.

"Perhaps I'm one of those that you can't do it to," he remarked with a smile that appeared to reflect some satisfaction.

"Perhaps you are right," I admitted, "but this doesn't mean that we can't work together in another way."

He left the office in a friendly fashion but never to return.

# CHAPTER EIGHT
# EDWARD: POOR SELF-CONCEPT

Edward has a good home situation. It is conductive to the development of a healthy self-esteem but unfortunately the school he attended is not. Edward's negative self-concept developed from failing in school. His desirable accomplishments were undramatic, but his failures stood out in contrast, and they were brought to his attention by his family and his teachers. That is when things went down hill for Edward. The adults he looked up to, his teachers and his parents, should have been reinforcing all of his desirable qualities and accomplishments.

Fortunately, Edward was not an emotionally upset child. He suffered no real learning difficulties. All Edward needed was some self-confidence. He needed support and many successful experiences. His areas of strengths needed to be highly commended. The elevation of his low self-esteem was imperative. Edward entered hypnotherapy—just in time.

## EDWARD

Edward is 12 years old, and gives the impression of being a very independent boy. He is the youngest of six children. There are two older brothers and three older sisters. His father was a successful businessman but had retired. Eddie's mother and father appeared to share the leadership of the household . . . a partnership.

Edward had an "awful" lot of friends but admits that only five or six of them could be called real friends and all are boys. He likes girls but feels that his mother might not understand this and suggests that it shouldn't be mentioned to his mother.

He likes football, baseball, and hockey, in fact all sports. He is well-built and is probably a good athlete. He experiences his greatest happiness when he is engaged in sports.

Eddie believes that his friends understand him all of the time; that his parents understand him most of the time; and that his teachers (parochial school) understand him least of all.

"They think that if you did something wrong once that you might do it all the time and they don't understand how it is if you stick up for your friends."

Like most young people Eddie sides with his friends his age and not adults who are all too frequently considered by many youth as unfair.

He admitted that he had an emotional problem when he once failed to get promoted. He hated letting the others in his class get ahead of him. He claimed that this feeling no longer bothers him. He was quick to point out that it was his mother who decided to hold him back when he was in the first grade. He was suggesting that he really could have gone on . . . and that his mother was responsible for his failure. When I asked him about his health he replied that it was pretty good but at times his iron would become low and he would then take some pills. He seemed to place no special importance on his occasional iron deficiency.

When I asked him to talk about his greatest success he couldn't think of a thing, but when I asked him to tell of his greatest "flop" he quickly replied, "When I repeated the first grade." His response to these associations were significant. There had been no real success story for him to remember, but he had an impressive failure. Was this a key to his academic future? Had Eddie been conditioned to think failure, rather than success? When I asked him to talk about his earliest memory he told about an incident that occured when he was two years old. One of his friends had a birthday party and around his friend's neck was a sign that said "I am two years old." He admitted that someone told him what the sign read . . . that he couldn't read it by himself.

The only trouble that he remembered having to do with strangers was an episode with some unknown older boys who stopped him and then without apparent reason beat him up.

There was trouble in his home which may prove significant. When he was only three or four years old, he set his mother's bedspread on fire. The fire got out of control.

He was quick to add that the fire was eventually extinguished by the fire fighters with no real trouble. Why did he set his mother's bedspread on fire? How much guilt did he have from the incident? Can we abreact the episode or is this technique necessary?

While the boy felt that he was misunderstood by his teachers he did like them. He also liked his friends and neighbors. When he examined the eight associative words and was asked if he had any fear around them he bravely claimed that he wasn't really afraid of anything, but if he "had" to make choices then he would first select dark and then men, "for what they can do." Perhaps he could have been asked what did he think that they could do ... but I really wasn't ready yet to find out. Most likely he was reflecting the advice of his school and maybe parents, to watch out for strange men for "what they can do."

Eddie didn't appear to have any problems with his school beyond those aleady mentioned. He only had the "normal" arguments" with his friends and occasionally liked to slug it out with his next older brother, something that is not out of the ordinary.

When I questioned him about hypnosis he confidently replied, "It works if it is applied right. It feels good in that you can forget the things that hurt you." Where did he get that information I wondered, but I saw no reason to seek it out.

## SECOND SESSION

Eddie's second session was a test experience. He completed the *Iowa Every Pupil* test of work study skills, Form L. He was behind in most of the areas covered by this comprehensive test. His scores were as follows:

| Part | Subject | Possible Score | Raw Score | Grade Equivalent |
|---|---|---|---|---|
| 1 | Maps | 47 | 12 | 6.3 |
| 2 | References | 21 | 7 | 4.3 |
| 3 | Index | 22 | 3 | 3.3 |
| 4 | Dictionary | 23 | 6 | 4.0 |
| 5 | Graphs/Charts | 25 | 10 | 5.4 |
|   | TOTAL | 138 | 38 | 4.6 |

Eddie's chronological age at the time of the test was 12 years 5 months. On this test, his age equivalent score was 10 years 4 months. He also completed the 1967 edition of the *Otis Lennon Mental*

*Ability Test,* Elementary II Level, Form J and did not do as well as I expected. I had been told that several years before, he had been tested with the Stanford Binet. The specialist who tested him reported that the boy was very bright. He was described as well above average in intelligence. The same specialist tested his performance on an achievement battery and reported his achievement as well below average. The Otis Lennon Score follows:

Out of a total of 80 possible responses, he obtained 53 correct ones to give him a derived intelligence quotient of 96. This score of 96 gave the boy a percentile rank of 33 meaning that he is only ahead of 33 percent of others the same age.

One answer regarding this difference in opinion of the boy's I.Q. is that two different types of tests were used. The Binet was almost a true performance test while the Otis Lennon was a paper and pencil test that depends upon a pupil's ability to read and interpret what he reads ... I assumed that both tests were given properly and that the boy had a reading problem ... and was bright.

## THIRD SESSION

I decided to check out the boy's reading accomplishments so he started working on the comprehensive Scott Foresman Inventory Survey Reading Test Form A for grades 4, 5, and 6. This is a power type test with no time limits. There are five parts to the test:

1. Word Meaning
2. Sentence Meaning
3. Total Meaning
4. Word Analysis
5. Dictionary Skills

This is not a regular standardized test but is exceptionally thorough in its coverage of reading skills. Eddie worked an hour and reached the end of a section of the test. The test would be completed during his next visit. Eddie was pleased to start a more interesting activity. I wanted the boy to examine word associations, first in the waking stage and then in the hypnotic stage. He was quickly hypnotized. He watched the flashing object that was timed to flash in synchronization with his heart beat. He held the flashing object and the lights in the office were reduced. I told him what we were going to do, how his eyes would presently close and how he would drift off into the most pleasant kind of sleep imaginable and tht a happy warm feeling would come over him as he began to relax. His eyes closed. Gordon

# POOR SELF-CONCEPT

Ambrose's* pre-count method, that is described in this book, was used several times to deepen the hypnosis. In this state he again examined the word list. The results were as follows:

| Stimulus Word | Awake Association | Sleep Association |
| --- | --- | --- |
| Dark | Light | Light |
| Sickness | Ill | Ill |
| Mountain | Hill | Climbing** |
| Girl | Boy | Boy |
| Boy | Girl | Girl |
| Beautiful | Pretty | Ugly** |
| Smooth | Rough | Rough |
| Round | Square | Diameter** |
| Big | Tall | Small** |
| Small | Big | Big |
| Slow | Fast | Fast |
| Man | Women | Women |
| Brave | Hero | Fearless** |
| School | Teacher | Teacher |
| Woman | Man | Man |
| Ruler | Leader | Dictator** |

The responses given under hypnosis that vary from those given while awake have been marked with a double asterisk. There is some difference in the two responses, but they may be of no great importance although his response to the stimulus word, beautiful, was interesting. Awake he responded with "pretty" but asleep he responded with "ugly." I wondered about the word Dictator . . . what did that signify?

While he was hypnotized, Eddie received the following suggestions. Because I wanted to increase his ability to remember, I told him, "You are an intelligent boy and will have no trouble remembering things taught to you in school. Tests will be easier for you because you will be able to remember the things that go into the school tests."

He needed to pay better attention to his teacher, so I suggested, "Your ability to pay attention to the teacher will get better and

---

*Ambrose, Gordon, M.D. *Hypnotherapy with Children*, Staples Press London, England better all the time. You will do less daydreaming and will pay greater attention to the important things going on in your class room."

Perhaps, like most youngsters, he didn't fully appreciate the opportunity to receive an education, so I added, "You understand the importance of getting a good education and you will want to go to school and will learn to like being able to be there. You know it is a good thing for you."

During a previous test on study skills, he did very poorly. I decided to offer a suggestion for improvement in this area. A suggestion could have been better formulated. I told him to use his family, friends, teachers and any other source of instruction that would help him gain a better knowledge in the use of dictionaries, reference material, maps and globes.

The hypnotic part of the lesson lasted for only 15 minutes and was terminated in the most gentle manner. The awakening from hypnosis should always be gentle and all suggestions made to a hypnotized subject should be carefully considered. Hypnotists who use the art to make an entertaining fool out of a subject may harm him. Hypnosis is a way to go past the normal guardians of the subconscious. Careless suggestions could be shocking to the hypnotized subject. Every effort must be made to protect the subject from thoughtless suggestions.

Eddie was told during the awakening count that he would feel very well upon awakening; that he would begin to awaken during the count.

"With each number you will begin to leave the very pleasant sleep state that you are now in. Finally, at ten you will be wide awake, and feel better than ever.

Even though his eyes opened at the count of six, the counting continued to ten. Eddie smiled, stretched and looked about with complete confidence.

## FOURTH SESSION

Eddie completed the Scott Foresman Reading Inventory Test that he started the week before and did better than expected on dictionary skill, an area covered by another test taken several weeks before.

The results of the Inventory Test were as follows:

| Part | Subject | Possible Correct | Actual Correct | Grade Equivalent |
|---|---|---|---|---|
| 1 | Word Meaning | 25 | 17 | 6.0 |
| 2 | Sentence Meaning | 25 | 17 | 5.0 |
| 3 | Total Meaning | 50 | 31 | 5.2 |
| 4 | Word Analysis | 65 | 53 | 5.2 |
| 5 | Dictionary Skills | 35 | 26 | 6.0 |

He obtained a total of 144 points for a grade equivalent of 5.5. This score was not too far below the actual grade in which he was, but it must be remembered that he repeated the first grade.

Several years ago, I worked with members of the staff of Boston Children's Hospital to try a test developed there that pinpoints some of the problems children may have in developing properly. The test contains pictures of children in varying situations. Each situation represents one task they encounter in growing up. Their response to a task is interpreted by the counsellor with reference to guidelines prepared by the hospital's staff. This examination is called the Tasks of Emotional Development, or (TED). There are sets of pictures of boys as well as girls in their latent period and in their adolescent period. Of the many pictures available, the first six are the most significant. For this study, these are the ones used.

Eddie examined the pictures and responded as follows:
*Picture No. 1:* Learning to Socialize

Eddie failed this task. He looked and acted as though he had absolutely no problem with this task, but his responses indicated that he did. In his story, Eddie perceived a boy who wanted to join a group of children but failed.

"He is new in the neighborhood so they would not let him join."

"How does he feel about this?" I asked.

"He feels sad because they won't let him play," the boy continued.

In this picture, as in all of them, Eddie had to make up a story about the children he saw there. He could be asked certain questions should he fail to answer adequately, but these questions had to be neutral, "neutral probes." Eddie's responses to the first picture indicated that he had a problem in socialization. Each story was examined and scored in several dimensions.

Eddie scored well in perceiving the situation but failed the outcome and the effect dimensions.

*Picture No. 2:* Trust

In this picture, there was a situation between an adult and a boy. Eddie did well. He saw the situation and explained, "The boy has just come home from school, he did bad in school, so his mother is going to give him some cookies; she is also going to give him some milk. She wants him to feel better."

Eddie saw a normal situation and went on to tell how much better the boy felt after receiving food from his mother. The food that he saw the boy receive from the adult in the picture represented the love that a mother normally gives to her child.

*Picture No. 3:* Aggression

Here were two boys, one with his hands raised in a threatening gesture. Eddie scored well for perception because he immediately saw the impending fight, but he did poorly with the outcome aspect of the picture. Eddie said, "Jim" the neutral one, "doesn't want to fight." "Tom," the agressor, "punches him. Jim feels bad being punched but he just stands there."

This picture was a revelation as was the first one. Eddie was a robust individual and should be able to take care of himself well. His outward appearance was of a boy who was able to handle aggression.

*Picture No. 4:* Learning

There was a boy seated behind a desk looking at a book. Eddie immediately perceived, "This boy is trying to get through his homework, fast. He has some records that he wants to listen to. He is unhappy about the homework, but he will be happy when he finishes it . . . his mother makes sure that he does the homework."

In all dimensions perception, outcome, affect and motivation, Eddie scored well. He recognized the learning responsibility and had his boy meet it.

*Picture No. 5:* Conscience

There was a picture of a wallet lying upon a table with a boy looking at it. Eddie responded, "The boy wants to go to the movies, but his mother would not let him . . . she feels that the movie is no good. The mother left her wallet upon the table (it was a man's wallet) and the boy saw it . . . He feels like taking the money so that he can go to the show anyhow, but doesn't because it wouldn't be honest."

"How does he feel about it?" I probed.

"Sad because he didn't get the money to go to the show, but glad because he knew it was not right to take it."

Again, Eddie scored well in all four dimensions. He saw that the situation and the motivations for his successful outcome were acceptable. The word "mother" came up often in his stories.

*Picture No. 6:* Separation

In this picture, there was a woman and a boy. The boy had one hand upon the knob of a door leading outside. I wanted to know if Eddie saw the boy separating from the mother or mother substitute. Eddie began, "This looks like the same boy in the picture before . . . the mother had found out that the boy didn't take the money that she left lying on the table. Both the boy and the mother are happy. She is happy because he is honest and he feels good too. She is telling him to go out and play with his friends. He feels good about this because he likes to go out and have fun."

Eddie scored high in all four of the areas. He saw the boy leaving his mother to go outside to play with friends. From this it can be assumed that Eddie had no problems in separating from his mother.

The TED test indicated that Eddie may have had problems with two areas of emotional development. He was a boy unsuccessful in joining a group and unhappy about it. This reflected his own difficulties. He may also have had a problem in handling aggression. Although the neutral boy in Eddie's story was unhappy about the situation, he stood still and allowed the aggressor to hit him.

The time for the hypnotic part of the session came so the lights were turned off in the office, but some light came in around the edges of the almost closed door.

Eddie remarked, "I can still see some light."

The door was then completely closed. It was pitch black.

"We are going to use a different hypnotic procedure tonight."

I held a dim penlight about two feet directly in front of his eyes and asked him to look at it. I had not found it desirable to tire a subject's optic nerve by causing him to stare at a bright light from an uncomfortable position . . . though I know that some hypnotists do.

We engaged in casual conversation about some early work with hypnosis and I told him that his eyes would quickly close and that it would be pleasant to again drift into the helpful sleep of hypnosis.

Within moments, he was fast into hypnosis. The lights were turned on without disturbing his sleep. I told him ahead of time, "In just a moment I'm going to turn on the lights . . . you won't notice it . . . you will not awaken." I always tell the subject what I'm going to do ahead of the act so as not to startle him.

Again I made positive suggestions to him to improve his ability to recall and to concentrate on his school work. I also told him that he would experience a feeling of success . . . that he was intelligent and there was no reason why he would not become very successful. He was again awakened by counting to awakeness. Although his eyes opened at the count of six, I continued to count to ten when he smiled and stretched.

## FIFTH SESSION

Edward's mother came with him. It was time to explain what we had been doing for the past month. She was interested and concerned about the progress of her boy in school . . . and perhaps in therapy as well.

We discussed in detail the tests that Eddie had taken. We became so engrossed in our conversation that much of the time allocated to the boy was gone. The discussion had excluded Eddie and may have contributed to his headache. He admitted to this when I observed that he looked distressed and was leaning forward with his head in his hands. I guess that we had bored him with our talk . . . and if we had, it wasn't surprising that he had developed a headache. I told him that he needn't be concerned about his headache because if it had developed as a result of boredom it would disappear under the influence of hypnosis. Eddie went readily to sleep with only a few side glances toward his mother.

I gave him the following suggestions: "You will continue to bear down upon your study skills. You did well to come up on dictionary skills. Your tests of intelligence have proved that you are a very intelligent boy . . . but for some reason you haven't used your great ability . . . but you are going to do so." Returning to problem task as pinpointed by the TED test it was suggested, "You have always liked people and you know that they like you . . . as a result of your ability to mix with people you are popular with your friends . . . in fact your friendliness will grow and grow."

He was reminded, "You know how important school is to you . . . as you do better and better with your school work you will like it all the more."

In conclusion, I told him that he would become so interested in his school work that he would have no time for daydreaming . . . that all of his attention would be focused upon his teacher and the work that she was doing with the class. Remembering his headaches, I said, "When you are awakened from this pleasing sleep, you will be completely refreshed."

He was awakened by the ten count method interspersed with suggestions of well-being and of the coming awakeness. As usual, with Ed, at about the six count, he opened his eyes and at ten he was wide awake. After a few moments of casual conversation, Eddie remarked with a grin, "Hey, my headache is gone."

## SIXTH SESSION

Once again I used a penlight to put the boy into hypnosis. He was simply told, "Tonight you are going into the deep stages of hypnosis so that you will be able to go back into time to the very day that you were born."

He was no sooner hypnotized when I told him to open his eyes while remaining in his present sleep state. As soon as his eyes opened, he was rehypnotized in the same way. His eyes soon closed again and I continued to repeat the procedure until it seemed that he must be in one of the deeper stages. What stage was he in? Why not ask him?

"Eddie, as you know there are several stages of hypnosis . . . first stage, second stage, third stage, and maybe much more. Perhaps you can tell me the number of the stage you are now in."

He hesitated for a while and then replied surprisingly firm, "The second stage."

"That's wonderful," I answered, but how could he really know? "Tonight I want you to go back in time to the very day that you were born. We will do this by having your life flash backwards as though it were on a movie screen. In a moment you will open your eyes and before you there will appear to be a movie screen. On it will be the story of your life. You will see important parts of your life at each stage . . . naturally we can't take the time to see every small detail so let's look at the important ones. Remain in hypnosis but open your eyes now. Can you see the screen?" I asked.

Edward opened his eyes and nodded, "Yes," he could see the screen. "You are now eleven years old going on twelve. What do you see yourself doing?" I asked.

"I had a big birthday party this year . . . a lot of fun."

"Go on," I insisted.

"I joined the little league and was happy because my brother thought that I couldn't make it."

"What else do you see?" I asked.

"I first started playing hockey ... I didn't know a thing about it but Mr. ——— showed me everything ... I got so I could do it ..."

There were moments of silence. He needed prompting.

"You are now ten years old going on eleven, what do you see now?"

"I won the city 50 yard dash for the city championships at the school ... somehow I got my sneakers wet and thought that maybe I couldn't run fast wearing wet shoes ... I was worried but still I won."

"What else do you see?" I asked.

"I'm not sure that I will make the fourth grade ... I have some bad marks in reading ... a couple of F's." A long silence followed this admission. His fear of failure had already appeared four times.

"All right, Eddie, you are now nine years old going on ten, what do you see?" I questioned.

"This was the year we went to New York for the Easter Parade ... we went to St. Patrick's Cathedral. My father took a picture of Cardinal Spellman when he came out on the front steps." Something amused the boy because he laughed a little and then was silent ... we will never know what it was.

"You are now eight years and you are going on nine, what do you see?" I asked him.

"I was in the second grade and had Sister ——— for my teacher ... she was nice ... she let us get away with murder."

"Who sat in front of you?" I asked.

"Anne ——— sat in front of me, but I didn't like her ... she was small and cried a lot. My sister went to San Francisco ... she used to take ... me places ... and we missed her." This was followed by silence.

"You are seven years old and you are going on eight, what do you see now?" I asked.

"I had my First Communion ... we had breakfast in church ... Peter ... was with me. Nothing much happened this year," he stated after some silence.

"You are now six years old going on seven," I informed him. "What do you see?"

"I had Miss ——— in the first grade. She was a lot of fun. We played games a lot."

"What are you doing right now?" I asked.

"We are playing Red Rover and I am running across, but I can't get through the two boys."

"Why not?" I asked.

"They are too strong," he replied.

"Who are they?" I asked.

"Tommy and Steve," he replied. "I couldn't go on with the rest of the class . . . I didn't read too good . . . the rest of the kids went on."

Eddie was breathing heavily and appeared disturbed. This memory was more than memorial.*

He continued, "That summer we couldn't play baseball . . . I was always picked on the second team . . . I was always on the poor team." This was followed by a long period of silence. The boy's self-devaluation appears throughout this story like thread weaved into a cloth.

"You are now five years old and going on six, what do you see?" I asked.

"We have a big party on the Fourth of July . . . my cousin came over and we ran around together . . . I was in kindergarten . . . Miss ——— was my teacher . . . she was a good piano player . . ."

"Who sat next to you?" I asked.

"Mark ———," he replied. "He used to pull up the girl's dresses and look under . . . the teacher caught him and he got slapped. I got a truck for Christmas . . . it was about a foot long . . . I could ride it down the driveway." Once again there was a long silence.

"You are now four years old going on five, what do you see?" I asked.

"I played a lot . . . I played trucks. I had an eye operation so that I wouldn't have to squint. My sister was in the hospital with me for the same thing. The bandage on my eye had a tiny hole in it so that I could see . . . this was my secret. I felt good because my sister couldn't see, but I could still see."

"You are now three years old and you are going on four, what do you see?" I asked.

"I set my mother's bedspread on fire . . . when the fire got

---

*Memorial—Something remembered from the *past* but evaluated in the *present*.

started I shut the door to her room so that no one could see it ... I got some water from the bathroom to put it out but I dropped it. ––– was on his way to kindergarten ... He was wearing a yellow raincoat."

"Why did you set your mother's bedspread on fire?" I asked.

"I like to play with matches because they were bright ... she had long strings on her bedspread that would burn nicely ...

"My friend Robert had a birthday party that I attended. He had a sign around his neck that said he was two years old ..." He became silent so I continued.

"You are now two years old going on three, tell me what do you see?"

"My brother Steve got a cart for Christmas and I got a fire engine ... it was a long one."

A long silence followed this statement. This was interesting. The boy's parents gave him a fire engine, then he began to play with fire resulting in a near catastrophe. The deeper symbolism of the fire was set aside. I thought that this boy's imagination had been stimulated as a result of his receiving a fire engine. I suspected that the little boy was probably considered amusing as he went about putting out imaginary fires with his very own fire engine, but then he started a real one ... not so amusing.

"You are now one year old going on two," I stated. "Tell me what you see."

"My mother is washing me in the kitchen sink ... I don't like it."

"Why don't you like it?" I asked.

"I don't like it because I get wet ... she washed me lightly," he added. "Kelly sleeps under my crib all day long ... I like having her there." Later it was determined that Kelly was a dog.

"You have just been born and you are going on one year old, can you see yourself?" I asked.

He replied, "I can see myself in a blanket with my mother ... it feels good ... I don't like the milk." This admission was followed by a long silence.

"Can you remember anything before you were born?" I asked. Eddie shook his head. Our time together was ending so I had to restore Eddie to his chronological age. We began the return, "You are now one year old and you can see yourself on a comfortable blanket where you are warm and happy. You are now going on two years old and you can see your mother washing you. She washes you gently but like most boys you are not fond of getting a bath. You are now going on three and for Christmas you receive a fire truck. Like all kids, you play with your new toy and imagine that you are putting out fires just as grownups do. You are now three years old and you accidentally set fire to your mother's bedspread. You are too young to realize the dangers of matches, you try to put it out, but are so young it gets beyond your control and firemen have to put it out for you.

"You are now four years old going on five. At this age you play with tricks. You have an eye operation and can peek out of the bandage. This was your secret. You could see through a tiny hole in the bandage, but your sister could not. You felt pretty good about this. You could do something that she couldn't do. You are five years old going on six and you have a big party on the Fourth of July. You like your kindergarten teacher. You are now six years old going on seven. You like playing Red Rover on the playground. You were not promoted this year and felt bad because the other kids that you played with went on. There was no reason for you to feel bad because you got a better foundation that will help you do a good job in school now and later.

"You are now seven years old going on eight. You received your First Communion and were very happy about this. Now you are eight and are going on nine. You miss your sister because she was so good to you. You know that this is the way of life. Loved ones must live their own lives and we love them just as much as ever when they do. You are now nine years old going on ten. You enjoy being with your father in New York where you see Cardinal Spellman at St. Patrick's Cathedral. You are now ten years old and you are going on eleven. You are a good runner and win a city wide championship in spite of having to run handicapped with wet sneakers. You are now eleven years old going on twelve and you have successfully joined the little league and have learned a lot about playing hockey . . . and now you are back to normal in this office, where you were when we started going backwards in time."

Again to test the depths of the hypnosis, I inquired, "Tell me how deep you are in hypnosis . . . did you come out of it a little as you talked?"

"Yes," he replied. "I'm now in the second stage."

This was interesting. He again stated that he was in the second stage although he also felt moved into a lighter stage . . . did I somehow suggest that he would reach the second stage? However, I answered "In that case, let us use the light and again take you deep into hypnosis." Once more I held the penlight in front of his eyes. They closed slowly and it was obvious that he had gone into a deeper level.

"Tonight we will again strengthen our faith in hypnosis by demonstration." With this preliminary, I coated a small part of his finger with iodine and then sterilized a needle. "Please recite something that you have learned and while you are reciting I shall do something to your finger that will not bother you in any way at all." Eddie responded with a prayer. As he was doing this, I pricked his finger with the needle several times. He completely ignored the needle stuck in his finger. The needle did not interrupt his recitation or change the inflection of his voice.

Again he received the suggestions that he had received before. He would like going to school. He would be able to remember the things taught there; that he would begin to enjoy reading; that he would pay attention to the teacher; his mind would not wander from the subjects as she talked about them. Added emphasis was given to the suggestions this time by the sounding of a small gong along with each suggestion . . . it may not have added anything.

He was awakened in the usual manner and said he felt fine in spite of the rather unusual experiences that had happened to him under hypnosis . . . and during a longer than usual session.

## SEVENTH SESSION

Tonight Eddie brought a "doubting Thomas," his brother, to watch us work. His brother was a high school student and believed that there is such a thing as hypnosis but doubted if it would work on him. He seemed so sure of this that I resolved to hypnotize the "doubting Thomas," as soon as Eddie's session was over.

Eddie had a request to make tonight. He had noticed the large spinning wheel device[1] mounted on the wall of the office and he wanted me to use this disc to help him achieve the trance. No device was really needed to hypnotize the boy. He was well conditioned to enter the trance, almost at my command. Eddie, like many children

---

[1] A hypnodisc from the Powers Company in California is mounted on phonograph turntable on the wall.

like gadgets and often feel that these gadgets are useful in providing them with something to focus upon and so occupy their attention while suggestions are being made—the gadgets may be useful and can serve the hypnotist in the same way a magician distracts the attention of his audience with one hand while he performs his tricks with the other. The hypnotist may use gadgets to distract the subject's attention while hypnotizing him. Catching the subject's attention and diverting it away from the real hypnotic suggestion works very well.

Eddie went to sleep nicely. He focused his attention upon the spinning disc and when he was told that it was causing his eyes to close, they did. Eddie's conditioning with the previous sessions of hypnosis helped him to go into a complete restful hypnotic state almost immediately. His brother watched every move. If hypnotism was as infectious as I had hoped, then "Thomas" was catching it. The brother, without his realizing it, was being conditioned to go to sleep.

For the brother's benefit, I remarked, "Eddie, I am going to do something that you will not remember when you wake up." I removed his watch saying, "I'm taking off your watch and will place it inside your shirt pocket, but you will not remember anything about this watch episode when you are awakened."

I gave Eddie the same helpful suggestions that I gave him the previous Monday. We returned to the fire episode. I remarked that parents sometimes buy their children fire engines and that their small boys go around putting out imaginary fires. Their young imaginations are stimulated and sometimes they will light fires in order to put them out. I reassured Eddie that it wasn't his fault that he once started a small fire. He was not guilty of any wrong thinking so he might as well forget it although if he ever has any kids of his own he might remember to buy them trucks of another nature, etc.

Throughout this session, as in all of the others, I attempted to remove any guilt feelings that he might have resulting from past mistakes. He needed to lose the tensions that resulted from his past school failures. He needed to understand that he was a bright boy capable of doing very well. He needed to feel successful rather than guilty and negative.

Eddie had been conditioned to hypnosis. His imagination had been enhanced by the use of this tool, but it now seemed prudent to begin to break him away from this conditioning. I wanted him to avoid depending upon me. He needed to learn to rely upon his own strengths.

We began the break, "It might be better for you to avoid letting others hypnotize you in the future, not that there would be anything wrong. If you want to use hypnosis then you can learn how to use it by yourself. You can use it to help commit things to memory."

With these thoughts, Eddie was brought back to the waking state in the same gentle manner that he was accustomed to ... firmly ... and slowly. He woke with a grin and looked at his brother as if to say, "See how easy it is."

The three of us talked about hypnosis and its various uses until I "noticed" Eddie's watch in his pocket and asked, "Why do you keep your watch in your shirt pocket?" Eddie looked puzzled as he put it back on his wrist.

"I don't know how it got there," he admitted. His brother was again impressed.

"How about it, Steve?" I asked. "Would you like to be tested for susceptibility ... not that I intend to hypnotize you," I pleasantly lied. The brother sat down beside the table. The weight was fastened to his finger. He aimed it at the middle of the Moire pattern I had placed on the drafting table. He looked down the thread to the target, I informed him that his hand would become heavy and pulled down to the target. I placed my left hand upon some "nerves" in the back of his neck to provide additional weight to his head that now leaned over the table. I placed my right hand on his forehead to give it "support" just in case his head should come suddenly down. As he came to rely upon the support of my right hand, his forehead was surreptitiously lowered, I made suggestions for heaviness and drowsiness. The weight soon became so burdensome that at last he couldn't support the weight or his forehead. His eyes blinked once or twice and rolled upwards. In a few minutes, all resistance passed from Steve and he was completely drawn to the table ... completely devoid of the power to resist ... completely passive.

"You will remain in the hypnotic state that you are now in but will move to the comfortable chair. You may open your eyes to see as you move from the hassock to the chair ... I'll help you move," I added. This help seemed necessary for him to move the few feet to the chair, where he completely relaxed. His eyes closed tightly and he appeared to be in deep hypnosis.

"To remove any remaining doubts from this nonbeliever, he was moved into a still deeper stage of hypnosis. "I'm going to place an object into your hands. Open your eyes and look at its flashing light, and listen to its beating sound . . . and again your eyes will close but when they do you will have reached another state of hypnosis . . . deeper than the one that you are now in."

His eyes rolled up twice before closing. During his trance he was told of the wonderful things that hypnosis could accomplish: that the pleasant relaxing sleep would remove his tensions; that headaches, tummyaches, etc. coming from tensions would completely disappear; that all heaviness in his arms and eyes would disappear.

The brother was carefully brought back to the conscious state. He felt good, completely relaxed. He wanted to know if he could be used in any hypnotic experiements or be taught to hypnotize himself as his brother had been promised. Could he use hypnosis to help commit passages of his schoolwork to memory?

## EIGHTH SESSION

Several months passed since the last visit. There seemed to be no special reason for continuing hypnotherapy with him. He was doing well in school, and was enjoying life in general. He was a completely normal, well-adjusted school boy, happy in all aspects of his life. Still, he wanted reinforcement of the suggestions given to him during his previous visits. Why not teach the boy something about self-hypnosis now.

"Eddie, tonight you will be introduced into the art of self-hypnosis. When you have mastered this new art you will be able to implant suggestions into your subconscious mind in exactly the same manner that I have been doing. Tonight I am going to talk to you in the first person singular . . . it will be just as though you were talking to yourself. When I say the words you say them again to yourself." Eddie relaxed in the easy chair and looked at a spot on the ceiling and the induction of the hypnotic state began.

Eddie repeated after me, "I will put myself into a state of hypnosis so that I will be able to implant suggestions into my subconscious mind. My rapport will be with myself. I will have complete control over myself at all times. I will begin the introduction of the trance by completely relaxing myself. I shall relax my body beginning with the top of my head, the muscles and nerves in the back of my neck will relax. The muscles and nerves in my lower jaw will be relaxed." At this, Eddie's jaw noticeably relaxed. "The muscles in my back will be relaxed along with the muscles and nerves of my chest. I am beginning to feel relaxed and comfortable all over. The muscles and nerves in my thighs are now relaxing and so are the muscles of the calves of my legs. Even the muscles of my feet are relaxed. I am beginning to slip into a comfortable lazy kind of half-sleep. The nerves of my whole body are beginning to tingle in a most pleasant fashion. I feel good all over. My legs and arms are beginning to feel heavy and so are the eyeballs. My eyelids are getting heavy and will soon close tightly together. They will not reopen until I say so." Eddie's eyelids flickered and closed slightly.

"I will now count to ten, during this count my eyelids will get very heavy and close altogether. They will stick together and remain closed until I tell them to open. One, my eyes are getting heavier and heavier. Two, my eyes are going to close tight. Three, I am relaxed and sleepy all over. Four, my eyes are now very heavy and are closing tighter and tighter. Five, I am going to be successful in putting myself into the hypnotic trance. Six, my eyes are closing tighter and tighter. Seven, I will not be able to open my eyes until I say so." Eddie's eyes were now completely closed, even so we continued to count. "Eight, my eyes will stick together and I cannot open them. Nine, I have been successful this evening, I have placed myself under my own hypnosis. Ten, I am completely under my own hypnosis. I shall check myself to see how well I have mastered the eye closure by seeing if I can open them without my telling them that they may open." Eddie's eyes moved under his lids. It was obvious he was checking his closure.

"Now that I have been successful in passing my own eye closure test, I will go on to another test of my own hypnosis. Subconsciously and without any effort on my part, I will swallow and I shall only swallow once. After this is done I shall pass into the deepest trance that is possible for me to enter on this night although I shall remember that my skill will improve with practice." Eddie's throat could be seen in the act of swallowing.

"There is just one more test that I shall check myself on tonight and that is the hand grasp. I shall clasp my hands together and hold them tightly, tightly, tightly and as I do this they will stick, stick, stick, stick together until at last they will stick so tightly together that I will be unable to pull them apart until I say that I can. My hands will stick, stick, stick, stick, stick, and I will now check to see just how well I have done with this test." Again it became apparent that Eddie was checking to see if his hands would come apart. They would not.

Eddie was given the same suggestions as received during the last session but with this new twist. Instead of my saying to him, "You will become so interested in the work that goes on in your classroom that you will not have any time to spend daydreaming, etc.," the suggestion was modified to, "I will become so interested in the work . . . etc." The boy was finally told to count to ten all by himself and at the count of ten awaken himself. He was successful in doing this.

He seemed amazed that he could awaken himself from hypnosis or that the entire first person singular approach had worked so well. He was asked to practice self-hypnosis just once, all by himself. He seemed a little dubious as he settled back in the chair and silently began. After some time had elasped, he appeared to be experiencing some difficulty with eye closure. I commented, "You will succeed in doing exactly what you wish to do." This comment was all he needed in order to overcome the last bit of resistance. Eddie went into his own self-induced trance. I asked him to repeat my suggestions again and after doing it to awaken himself. Eventually, the boy's eyes opened and he smiled, pleased with his new prowess.

## NINTH SESSION

His mother reported that for some reason while his grades were good, his effort was poor. She wanted to know how this boy could get good marks without trying. Could it be that he was remembering the material taught in class by his teachers so well that he found it unnecessary to research further into the subjects in order to pass the school's examination? Perhaps for no other reason but to please his mother we returned for one more session.

The boy passed easily into a medium trance and received suggestions based upon those previously given to him but now the element of compulsion was introduced into the suggestion.

"You will be compelled to spend the few nights that remain in the school year to examine the homework given that day . . . you will be compelled to see that it is done to the best of your ability . . . you have to do the work of the school knowing that it is in your own best interests to do it well."

Because of his previous training in self-hypnosis, Eddie was able to bring himself out of this short trance. The therapy session lasted only five minutes.

## ONE YEAR LATER

Eddie was convinced that his course in hypnotherapy was responsible for his improved school situation. He assured me that all of his work had improved and his claim was verified by his parents and his teachers. Not only did his work improve, but his expectations became positive. He had become success-oriented. His skill in reading had improved remarkably as compared with the reading test that he took one year earlier.

### SCOTT FORESMAN INVENTORY SURVEY TEST

| Reading Areas | Grade Equivalent 1965 | Grade Equivalent 1966 |
|---|---|---|
| Word Meaning | 6.0 | 8.0 |
| Sentence Meaning | 5.0 | 8.0 |
| Total Meaning | 5.2 | 6.0 |
| Word Analysis | 5.2 | 9.0 |
| Dictionary Skills | 6.0 | 6.0 |
| TOTAL | Grade 5.5 | Grade 7.0 |

It has to be noted that the boy failed to improve in the final reading skill. A possible explanation for this might be that he was allowed to take the first test in two sessions, but he had to complete the second test in one and this depressed the second scoring, but I don't really know. This particular skill was also tested at the end of the examination at a time when he would be most fatigued. Even though there was no progress in one area, the total picture improved far more than could normally be expected. The only new ingredient to Eddie's education was the hypnotherapy outlined in his case study.

It can also be added that Eddie eventually became a very successful college student—graduated with honors and obtained the fine job that he now holds.

## CHAPTER NINE
# SANDRA: SUICIDE

The suicide-risk client creates one of the most difficult situations that could possibly confront a therapist so many therapists refuse to accept one. There is always the possibility that a suicide-risk client is a psychopath or have irremediable defects in their situations. Sandra was suicidal, but I didn't know that until several weeks had passed and when that knowledge surfaced she was not the only one in a state of anxiety.

Children who are suicidal have poor self-concepts and frequently enter deep depressions. They view their environment as both hostile and non-rewarding. Their contact with the world has been a painful experience. Their parental relationship has been extremely poor.

Suicidal children can not be permanently talked out of their situations by either their parents or their teachers because these well-meaning, interacting people are unable to understand the great foreboding and anxiety that exists within the child. Sandra's pleasant physical appearance effectively masked her grave situation.

### SANDRA
### FIRST SESSION

Sandy is a good-looking, rather small 16-year-old girl with dark expressive eyes that were moist with tears many times during our hours together. She is in the eleventh grade of the local high school where she is taking a business course. Only the week before she had been suspended from school as a result of excessive absences. What a strange reason for suspension. She claims that these absences were the result of personal illnesses. "Since my tonsils have been removed I havent been absent very much, but before that I was out a lot."

Sandy was no longer living at home but was staying with a family that lived several towns distant from her own hometown. Sandy explained that she had been thrown out of her home by her stepfather yet the "aunt" with whom she was living stated that she took Sandy in because the girl's stepfather had not only abused her but boasted that he would "have" the girl as soon as she turned 16. Perhaps Sandy would have had to "consent" to his desires at that age—or had already done so? Sandy greatly appreciated living with the aunt. She hated and feared the stepfather with whom she had lived since she was a baby. Sandy had never met her real father.

She admitted to caring something about her mother but claimed that she didn't love her. The mother worked at a factory and had one other child, a boy 19 years old, before marrying her present husband. Sandy felt close to this other brother who was already married. She explained, "We were beaten together when we were kids. My brother was thrown out when he was 16 and has been on his own ever since. He is making out all right now." She felt very little kinship for her three stepsiblings. There was one ten-year-old stepbrother and two stepsisters ages thirteen and nine. She felt that these three youngsters were "their" children. Sandy seemed to feel that she didn't really belong to anyone.

Sandy liked boys as well as girls and had a special girl friend residing in her old hometown. She liked to discuss her problems with her girl friend just as they once did but now they can only write to each other. There was no telephone in her present home. Sandy dates with boy friends and even had a special boy with whom she wanted to go steady. "Boys are different from girls," she explained, "you can't talk about 'things' with a boy like you can with a girl." She believed that her friends and to some extent her teachers understood her, but her parents certainly didn't understand her. The only family member that she could relate to was her brother. "I like *my own* brother a lot." She emphasized the words "my own."

When asked about the problem that had brought her to my office she replied with some hesitation, "I have bad dreams and I wake up crying." She hastened to add, "I don't do it as much now as I used to, but I still do it sometimes."

"When did these bad dreams begin?" I asked.

"They began when he used to beat me up," she answered.

"I cried a lot in B——— (her former home) when he would holler at me ... I would try to hold it back ... I guess it really began when he threw me across the room. I still dream of that time." With assurance she added, "Yes, that is when it really began."

Sandy appeared to be physically healthy, her tonsils had been removed and this operation may have been instrumental in helping improve her attendance at school. She unfortunately couldn't remember every having been successful at anything, but she couldn't remember any particular failure. Perhaps if the question had been more carefully defined I might have found out something.

I asked Sandy to list some of the things that she hated most of all.

"I'm afraid of dogs," she answered.

"Why?" I asked.

"When I was nine or ten years old I was bitten by two German police dogs," quickly deflating the thought that raced through my mind—perhaps the dogs that frightened her represented her stepfather. But this apparently was not the case, she had a good, logical reason for hating dogs. The second item on her list of fears was, as expected, her stepfather. This fear was also understandable because her earliest childhood memory was of him hitting her. I wondered why she didn't put that fear at the top of her list—perhaps there was some symbolism with the dogs after all. I asked Sandy if she had ever had any trouble with strangers—if she had ever been molested by anybody. She replied in a very quiet voice, "No." I suspected that she would have said "No" one way or another. Sandy apparently was able to get along with her school teachers, although understandably she liked her own age friends better. Her best friend, as already mentioned was a girl who lived in her old home town. She felt that her neighborhood where she was residing, a low-cost housing project, was "O.K."

"I'm going to give you a list. Will you please select the one item from the list of which you are most afraid?" I requested. Sandy's answer was, "My stepfather." She had selected this from the following; father, mother, brother, sister, men, women, dark, school, and food.

"What would be the second thing on the list that most frightens you?" I asked.

She replied, "I'm afraid of the dark." Perhaps later we would find out what darkness really meant to this young lady.

"What do you know about hypnosis?" I asked.

"I don't know anything about it," she answered.

"Perhaps you have some feeling that it is either good or bad . . ." I continued.

"Actually I don't know anything about hypnotism, but I am interested in it, and I would like to know something about it," she returned very matter of factly.

"What do you expect hypnosis to be like?" I continued to set the stage for the trance that would hopefully soon envelop her.

She replied, "I have no idea."

The lights were extinguished until at least only a soft yellow glow came from the desk lamp. The hush machine was turned on and I explained that this mysterious setting, although maybe not necessary, could possibly help her to enter the hypnotic trance. I also explained that we would not go into hypnosis very deeply on this first occasion, but deep enough to determine how good a subject she could become.

Sandy sat down behind the drafting table and looked down upon the Moire pattern. The small weight was attached to her finger and she was directed to look down the string past the weight to the center of the pattern. I started the patter in the monotonous voice that I keep just for hypnosis. "You will find that after a while the weight will become heavier and heavier . . . the weight will be pulled down . . . down . . . down . . . down . . . to the table where it will stick . . . stick . . . stick . . . until at last you will be unable to hold it up. When this happens, your hand will also be drawn to the table, down . . . down . . . down . . . to the table. With this preamble, I placed one hand upon her forehead and another hand on the base of her neck. "The hand that is resting upon the nerves of your neck will become pleasantly warm. As it does you will want to rest your forehead upon my other hand. Just as your hand is now being pulled to the table so will your head be pulled down . . . down . . . down . . . down . . ." She then entered hypnosis.

Sandy was awakened from her trance soon after she entered it. While in it, her only hypnotic suggestions were designed to make her feel rested and free of tensions, and after she left my office she would go home and enjoy a pleasant night's rest. At the count of ten and accompanied with my usual waking up thoughts, and opened her eyes and smiled. "That was really cool."

"Would you like to come again?" I asked.

"I sure would," Sandy replied with more assurance than she had displayed all evening.

## SECOND SESSION

During this session, Sandy completed the Otis Lennon Mental Ability Test, Advanced Level, Form L. This test took 40 minutes to complete and consequently occupied the major portion of the hour. It was time well spent and it did yield a score in the shortest time. It is always desirable to get as much information about the children as possible in order to understand them. Understanding is a prerequisite to constructing reeducative or reconditioning therapy. Sandy's performance on this test was disappointing. Out of 80 possible correct responses she only obtained 29 correct ones. This raw score computed together with her age resulted to an I.Q. of 89. This was eleven points below normal. However, it had to be warily accepted in view of the girl's background. Her life had been a disturbed one. Cultural factors had been absent from her home environment. She had lived under almost constant tension and in an absence of something most important to all growing boys and girls, the feeling of being loved ... the I.Q. of 89 was probably low. It was at best only an indication. I could honestly say that her I.Q. was at least 89 and possibly much more.

The remaining twenty minutes were devoted to conditioning the girl for hypnosis. At the last session she received an introduction to the art and as a result was ready to accept the oncoming hypnotic trance. The lights were dimmed as usual and the stage set for the introduction of the trance. There are practitioners in the art of hypnosis who are critical of elaborate preparations for the trance. They feel that any form of mysticism has no place in hypnotherapy. Then there are others like myself who have, at times, even burned incense, to aid in trance induction. Why not use procedures that might be instrumental in assisting a successful inducement?

This time I swung a crystal ball gently back and forth in front of Sandy's eyes, in cadence with counting 1-2-3 etc. and between numbers, softly uttered suggestions. Sandy relaxed her body as requested and began to breathe deeply noticing that I said, "You will breathe deeply and easily ..." Her eyes closed tighter and tighter until at last she admitted that she was unable to open them. Her hands were brought together and I instructed her to grip them tightly.

"As you do this, your hands will stick together just as your eyes did."

I wanted to show her new evidence of the power of hypnosis and relate it to other evidence just demonstrated, her eye closure.

I told her, "Your hands will stick together," etc. I then asked her to try and see if she could release her hands. As she made the effort again and again I told her that she could not do it. Finally, she gave up trying and admitted that she was unable to pull her hands apart no matter how hard she tried.

Again, in another demonstration of the power of hypnosis, I took one of her hands and pulled her arm straight out in front of her and asked that she hold it that way for just a minute. My fingertips, touching lightly, passed down her arm along with the following suggestion, "Your arm will stiffen as I stroke it and soon you will be unable to move it from the position that it is now in." Her arm stiffened and assumed a complete rigidity. She was unable to move the arm at all—until at last I made suggestions that released it.

Sandy was a good subject and I believed that every successful exercise we did would strengthen her acceptance of hypnotism and her belief in the suggestions that would eventually be made to her. I asked her to visualize a blackboard. When she was able to do this I told her to imagine herself writing three words upon it: paper, pencil and pen and then to erase the first two words.

I continued, "As you erase the words from the board you will also find that you have erased them from your memory so you can now just remember one word remaining there and that word is pen. What is that word?"

Sandily readily replied. "Pen."

"Yes," I responded. "The word left on the board is pen . . . pen. You have already forgotten the other two words."

She cocked her head to one side as if this would help her bring back the forgotten words, but even this didn't help. She was asked to try very hard to remember the first two words but no matter how hard she tried she could not remember them. We had successfully induced amnesia to Sandy. Before ending the trance and the evening's session, I asked one more activity to strengthen Sandy's conditioning.

I took her two hands in mine and started rotating her hands about each other. "Continue to do this by yourself," I said, "when you hear this gong." (My small Chinese gong.) We had a demonstration and a practice lesson before continuing, "In a moment I shall awaken you from this pleasant sleep and still later you will hear this gong again and you will start rotating your hands one around the other. You may wonder why you are doing this because you will not remember being told to do it or the practice that you have just completed."

Before awakening, she received a few post-hypnotic suggestions that were based upon her first visit. She had told me about being disturbed as she slept and that sometimes she would wake up crying.

"Tonight, you will sleep easily and peacefully all through the night. You will wake up the next morning feeling refreshed, free of tensions and worry. You know that things have a way of working themselves out and this is the way it will be with you. When your head touches your pillow tonight you will immediately go into the best sleep that you've ever had. You will dream sweet dreams through the night and awaken the next morning feeling so refreshed and full of life that you will actually be anxious to get off to school."

Sandy awakened from her sleep with the usual ten count. The count was interspersed with suggestions to feel well and free of tensions. This was exactly what happened. She smiled and looked very pleased and happy. Sandy expressed her thanks several times before leaving the office ... just about the time when she was ready to leave, I rang the little gong and she started rotating her hands—one around the other. She looked a little silly so we both laughed breaking the spell and then she left.

### THIRD SESSION

Sandra seemed to be much happier when she appeared for this visit. She was also more relaxed. She had received some hypnotic suggestions that may have helped her. She looked and showed none of the anxiety that she demonstrated initially.

I decided to give Sandy the California Test of Personality, a test described elsewhere in this book. The results were profiled and they were slightly skewed to the left of normal—but not so much as to cause her to be labeled a maladjusted girl. Here are the scores that she obtained.

| PERSONAL ADJUSTMENT | PERCENTILE* |
|---|---|
| Self-reliance | 30 |
| Sense of Personal Worth | 30 |
| Sense of Personal Freedom | 40 |
| Feeling of Belonging | 50 |
| Withdrawing Tendencies | 40 |

| PERSONAL ADJUSTMENT | PERCENTILE* |
|---|---|
| Nervous Symptoms | 20 |
| TOTAL Personal Adjustment Score | 40 |
| **SOCIAL ADJUSTMENT** | |
| Social Standards | 80 |
| Social Skills | 50 |
| Anti-social Tendencies | 30 |
| Family Relations | 20 |
| School Relations | 20 |
| Community Relations | 70 |
| TOTAL Social Adjustment Score | 40 |

*Percentile means that number of all those who received the test initially (when it was developed). That Sandy performed 80 percentile means that she did better than 80% (very good) and 30 percentile would be very poor—50 percentile would be in the middle.

Sandra did better in some categories than was expected for a girl who was raised in her circumstances. Her social standards were high and she was self-reliant. The latter could be expected, but that she scored so well on Social Standards was surprising. Where did she acquire these standards, I wondered?

The test indicated that the girl was nervous and that could be verified by being with the girl. The test also revealed that she had headaches and at times walked and talked in her sleep. That was something that she had not told me about ... perhaps I hadn't asked her.

The test also indicated that she had difficulty with her family relationships. Of this there was no doubt. Sandy did not like her parents. In fact she claimed to hate her stepfather. Hopefully, during the coming age regression session, I would uncover some family dynamics that hadn't yet been talked about.

She tested poorly in the school relationship section. Like many other students she felt that her teachers were overly strict and were sometimes unreasonable and unfair. If it wasn't for this, she claimed that she would like school better. She didn't belong to any teams or to any school organizations. She didn't belong in the sense that she didn't take part in any of the many activities available to students.

## SUICIDE

I felt that Sandra should have a complete physical examination—one that looked for physical causes for the indicated nervous symptoms even though it seemed clear enough that her manifested nervous difficulties were symptoms of tensions that came from her maladjustment in some key psychological areas. Sandra was insecure and felt inferior to her associates.

The girl's parents had rejected her. She didn't even know the name of her real father. The girl was intelligent and old enough to appreciate her position. But there was good reason to feel optimistic about the girl—she was not absorbed in self-pity.

Sandra was a good subject for hypnosis. A few waves of the crystal ball before her eyes were sufficient to send her into a trance where she was unable to move her hands or open her eyes. Her ability to accomplish this was reinforced with amnesia.

"You will remove one of your shoes but upon awakening you will be unable to recall doing it. You will find your shoe on the floor and wonder how it got there."

This was exactly what happened. At the end of the hypnotic session, she looked at her foot and remarked, "My shoe must have fallen off." She could not remember what had happened to it.

Sandra smoked cigarettes and claimed she wanted help in breaking the habit. I gave her this suggestion. "You realize that to smoke is harmful. You know that smoking is considered to be a cause of cancer and that cancer is a dreadful disease. Cancer spreads so that parts of it are often carried to all parts of the body to start new cancers. Women sometimes find them growing in the breasts. When this terrible thing happens it is often necessary to have a surgeon cut out one or both breasts. Don't you think that you had better stop smoking and never run the risk of this happening to you?" Sandra nodded her head. Her lips almost curled in disgust at the thought of another cigarette.

Like other girls of this age, Sandra wanted to be thin. She asked for help and received this suggestion. "Your digestive processes will speed up and you will be able to digest your food more rapidly than you have in the past. Fatty foods and candy will not appeal to you. Your metabolism will increase to the point where you will cease to store fat in the body. Your elimination will be rapid. Tomorrow morning you will have a complete evacuation of all waste materials from your body. It will be this way all week long . . ." I have read how other hypnotherapists have succeeded in helping clients stop smoking and overeating but success had so far eluded me and I had previously come to the conclusion that hypnosis alone was useless unless the client had made a firm decision and only wanted some reinforcement to aid in their accomplishing their own goals and reinforce their own decision—so I was not over-confident—it was worth a chance.

Sandy needed redirection with her school work. I suggested, "You will feel a compulsion to do your homework each night, not to help your teachers but to help yourself. Someday you will need to work, for this you will need training, and a high school diploma. Doing your homework each night is getting ready for the future. Your homework will improve because your mind will be free to study. Your mind will not wander . . . you will remember the things taught to you each day and be able to recall the information when tested." These suggestions were repeated several times for emphasis and reinforcement.

Sandy came out of hypnosis just as easily as she went into it. At the count of ten she opened her eyes and remarked that her foot was cold. She was surprised to find a shoe upon the floor.

## FOURTH SESSION

Sandra was facing a big problem. The family with whom she was living planned to move to another state. She was not sure that she would be able to go with them, but the idea of going back to her "own" home was repugnant. During a recent school vacation, she returned "home" for a visit but was afraid to go inside. She waited outside for a while in fear of her stepfather but did go in eventually. "Once I got in I was all right. He wanted me to come and sit on his lap. I wouldn't do it. He said that he missed me and wanted me to come home to stay."

"Did he try to make love to you?" I asked.

"No," she protested, "he knows that if he did anything like that I would go right to the police station and complain about him . . . we have had some outs before. He knows that is what I would do." She appeared firm on that, but was she?

We went over the California Personality Test together. Everybody wants to know the results of the tests that they take. If Sandra didn't get an opportunity to review this test she would always wonder why and perhaps feel distressed and have negative impressions about their efforts. I informed her that she did well and showed her the profile. "There are a few areas where you need work," I explained them.

"You believe that your family thinks that you are not going to amount to much. Tell me why?" I asked.

"They don't trust me," she answered.

"In what way?" I asked.

"In going out . . . 'she' never wanted me to go out with boys and she hated to leave me home alone," Sandy answered.

"Did she give you a reason for this?" I asked.

"No, she just felt that I was undependable."

"Did you give her any reason to feel that you couldn't be trusted to cope with the advances boys sometimes make?" I asked.

"No," Sandra replied almost indignantly. "She just hated to have me go out with boys . . . she was always like that."

I offered an explanation for this behavior that seemed so unreasonable to her. "Could she have been thinking of how she once became pregnant and wanted to keep that from happening to you?"

"When did you start biting your fingernails?" I changed the subject and picked up her hands.

"It started last year," she answered, "we used to fight a lot (stepfather). I was afraid of him . . . he threw my brother out and I knew that I was the next to go."

"Did your nightmares start at about the same time?" I asked, still leading the conversation.

"Yes, although I used to dream about getting killed before having the nightmares."

"Tell me about these dreams," I requested.

"It was always the same . . . that I was being stepped on by huge caterpillars." I wondered if the many legs of the caterpiller represented a man's probing hands?

"What were the nightmares about?" I asked.

"I had three of them and they were all the same . . . I was being strangled," she replied.

"How were you being strangled?" I asked.

"By a pillow . . . there was a shadowy figure bringing a pillow down over my face . . . I would wake up screaming."

All of the dreams and nightmares that she talked about formed a pattern, a hostile impending tragedy. She saw death coming, threatening her. She lived a life of anxiety, always under a threat. No wonder she dreamed as she did of death. Did she want to die? Was this a death wish?

"Was there anything unusual about your bedroom while your dreams were frightening you?" I asked.

She continued, "The windows were always open and the curtains were blowing." It sounded rather melodramatic, like some old movies. Had she been watching some old thrillers on the television just before her nightmares?

"It is not uncommon for some people to have bad dreams . . . we all do at times," I lied rather lamely. "You are an impressionable young lady and about the time that you were having unhappy home experiences there were a lot of stories in the newspapers about the Boston strangler. Girls all over the state have been concerned and probably had disturbances of their sleep too." With this weak explanation I continued. "You say that you have walked in your sleep, tell me about these episodes," I requested.

"My mother told me about most of them. I would get up and walk about the house. If anybody touched me while I was walking I would wake up . . . one time I got up and unlocked the front door and went down the steps before they stopped me. When they asked me where I was going, they say I told them that I was going for a drink." Sandra smiled at this joke. I explained that sleepwalking is a way of running away from a problem—a subconscious flight from an uncomfortable situation. Now that she was in another more pleasant environment where there was nothing to run away from, her night walking would end.

"Your parents are not getting along together," I commented. "Do they physically strike at each other?"

"No," she answered.

"Do they swear at each other?" I pressed.

She admitted that they not only swear at each other but also swear at "their" children. I asked Sandra to mention some of the profound words that her parents used but she refused, "I don't swear."

Our time together was running out so we went to the hypnotic part of our hour. I told Sandra that she was going to be responsible for much of the therapy and to help her prepare for that responsibility, all of my suggestions would now be made with personal pronouns. I told her to think of my words as being her own. It wouldn't be long before she would be expected to learn self-hypnosis and to place herself under her own hypnosis so that she could make suggestions to herself. She listened carefully as I intoned, "I am now going to place myself under hypnosis. I am now going to relax my body starting from the top of my head. The muscles in the back of my neck are now relaxing . . . the muscles of my jaws are now relaxing . . . the muscles in the back of my head are now relaxing . . . the muscles in my chest are now relaxing . . . all of the muscles in my stomach are relaxing . . . the muscles in my thighs are relaxing as well as the muscles of my calves and feet. My whole body is comfortable and completely relaxed. My eyes are sleepy and the lids are going to close . . . I will count to ten and as I do my eyes will get so heavy that they will close completely and I will not be able to open them until I release myself from hypnosis." I counted to ten and at times her lips could be seen to move slightly. She was counting along with me. It was obvious that she was cooperating. Her eyes closed tightly so I continued, "Now that my eyes are closed I shall test them to see how well I did." It was apparent that we had obtained a good eye closure. "I have tested my eye closure and found that I have been successful . . . I will now clasp my hands together and test my ability to make them stick . . . my hands are sticking together . . . sticking . . . sticking . . . etc. . . . etc. . . . I will be unable to pull them apart." I told Sandy to test her hands. She did and found that she was not able to pull them apart. "Now that I have found that I cannot pull my hands apart I will go on to another test . . . I am going to be forced to swallow by an action of my subconscious mind and when this happens I will then pass into a deeper trance" . . . as I talked, I saw Sandra's throat swallowing . . . "I have done very well this evening in bringing about this trance and so I am now able to make suggestions that will help me." With this prologue, I restated the suggestions that were given to her the previous week. She was awakened in the usual manner at the count of ten.

## FIFTH SESSION

Sandy brought her report card to show me the improvement in her marks. It was not very impressive . . . her conduct mark went down.

| Subject | First Quarter | Second Quarter |
|---|---|---|
| English | 60 | 70 |
| U.S. History | 65 | 65 |
| Geography | 65 | 75 |
| Science | 55 | 65 |
| Cop 1 | 60 | 60 |
| Conduct | S | U |

Sandra was absent nine times during the first quarter and 16 times during the second quarter, but it was in the middle of winter. She may have been out because of the common cold, a winter time affliction. There had been some improvement in her work but the improvement wasn't enough to cause rejoicing, even so it was a trend. Her mark in conduct had sadly dropped but according to Sandy this drop resulted from her being caught smoking. I guess that my hypnotic suggestion, aimed to curtail her smoking, had failed. She believed that her behavior had not changed for the worse. Her response to the school situation in the California Personality Test indicated that she was in conflict with her teachers. There was not much doubt about that. Although I had already discussed the results of the California Test with her, I reviewed portions of it again. This test was intended to constitute a part of her reeducation and would be used repeatedly to try and secure a better social adjustment for her.

I congratulated Sandra for doing so well. "I know girls who haven't had your kind of problems and who have not scored nearly as well as you did. There must be a lot of strength to your personality."

Sandra had done poorly on the test section that related to nervous symptoms. I commented, "You told me that you used to walk in your sleep. Now you know that this was a form of running away from something that you can't escape from while you are awake because there was no place to run to."

She smiled a little and asked, "Is that something like trying to commit suicide?"

"Yes, I suppose that it is. In both instances we have an individual attempting to escape from something."

"Because I've started to kill myself several times," she responded, holding up her wrists to expose some scars.

Without any hesitation I went on, "I suspect that all of us at one time or another have thoughts of doing something like that ... you must have been pushed very far to have actually attempted it. Why don't you tell me about the first try?"

"It was about a year ago when I took four bottles of aspirin ... I got sick and dizzy and couldn't hold my eyes open. I finally must have felt that I really didn't want to die so I tried to throw up."

"How did you manage that?" I asked.

"I got a finger down my throat ... I did throw up but it was some time before I got over the sickness."

"Have you told anyone about this?" I asked.

"No," she replied.

"Didn't your mother notice that something was wrong with you?" I asked.

"Yes, but she thought that I was just sick."

"Did something special happen that made you want to take your life?" I asked.

"There was nothing special," she returned, "I just felt that everyone was against me ... my brother cut his wrist one time too," she continued, showing her strong identification with him. "Once I was in the car with him and he was driving like a wild man. I was sitting beside him in the car, I didn't know that the car was stolen ... he would drive over a hundred miles an hour, then look at me and slow down. He would then speed up, but every time he looked at me he would slow down ... I could see the tears coming down his face ... finally he drove me home and went off by himself. He was arrested by the police for stealing the car sometime later ..." She was anxious to talk about this episode. Later I asked her to tell me about the second time that she started to commit suicide.

"That happened last summer. I cut my wrists with a razor blade."

"Can you tell me why?" I calmly inquired.

"I was sick of everything ... I was sick of life," she explained. "But when the blood came and got all over everything I stopped and bandaged myself up."

She admitted that once again she had successfully concealed an attempt to take her own life. I asked her if these self-destructive efforts had occurred around the time she was having nightmares. She said that they had.

"Now that you are able to look back upon these actions, how do you feel? Do you now wish that you had been successful and able to carry them out?" I asked.

"No ... I feel guilty ... why life is something wonderful," she answered.

It seemed to me that there was still a strong wish to die lying dormant in her mind but so far it had always been overcome by an even stronger wish to survive. Would the balance ever be tipped in favor of death? Was her comment, "Why life is wonderful," a platitude made up for my benefit. Did she mean those words?

"I would like to talk about the last time you started to kill yourself. Tell me as much as you can about it," I asked.

"It was only four months ago," she answered. "I cut my wrist with a razor blade ... This time I cut deeper and exposed the vein (artery), I could see the vein throbbing ... I was dizzy ... and blood was all over the place. It was Larry who found me. (Larry may have been a cousin of the family she now lives with.) He came in the bathroom ... I don't know why. He slapped me across the face several times until I seemed to know what was going on ..."

"Why did you do it?" I asked. Sandra at first wouldn't mention the triggering event. I persisted, "You no longer live in B——— where you were under so much stress. Did you break up with a boyfriend?" I probed.

Sandy looked sheepish and grinned, "Yes, but it wasn't so much the fact that he broke off with me but the way that he said it, 'It's all over now.' I kept thinking about those words ... and I went home and did it."

"Were you able to keep the third abortive suicide a secret?" I asked.

"Yes," she responded. "We bandaged it up and I wore long sleeve dresses and sweaters so that no one could see ... after it got better, Larry's mother asked about the mark on my wrist. I told her that I had been playing with a cat and he scratched me. It does look something like a cat scratch," she insisted. I didn't think so.

Sandy's suicidal activities had caught me by surprise. Except for a tendency to bite her fingernails she didn't display any outward manifestations of such an unusual anxiety, but teenage suicide is not a rarity. In fact, it is getting commonplace. Her inclinations should have been anticipated.

After having discussed the suicide attempt and the various reasons why she could look ahead to a brighter future, we moved on to a lighter subject. "Your responses to some of the school-related items on the California Test are interesting. You feel that many of your teachers are unreasonable and unfair to their students, and that some of these teachers prefer other students to you. At least, that is the impression that they have given you." Sandy didn't comment so I continued, "Of course if I told you that all teachers were fair and had no pets . . . you and I both would know that I lied. Unfortunately, it is true that there are some people in the teaching profession who should not be there. There is no doubt that you are right about some of your teachers, but hopefully you are not right about all of them. Do look again and ask yourself, what would you do if you were the teacher? Could you organize better, could you manage the dicipline better? Think about it and see what you come up with."

Sandra had nothing to say but did appear receptive to the thoughts. I wondered just how receptive she really was?

Sandra became involved with the TED test that has already been discussed in detail. She did well on the first five tasks, although in the aggression story she did indicate a personal resignation, "The (neutral child) fights back and eventually gets her own way . . . cause she is younger." Sandra was the older stepchild in the home of younger sisters and had emerged second best many times in her arguments with them.

Sandra went through the "learning task" with good responses but seemed to have a small problem with the conscience task. The girl, as imagined by Sandra, felt guilty and afraid when presented with temptation. Except for those negative feelings, Sandy's projected image probably would have stolen the money.

Sandy failed the task of "separation" from the mother figure. As a matter of fact she failed to score high enough to warrant scoring the other dimensions of the picture. Sandy failed to perceive a girl leaving her mother. Instead she saw a girl coming in. The mother in the picture was waiting up for her daughter who had "snuck out."

Toward the end of our hour together, I had Sandra affix her eyes to a spot on the wall of my office, and then with just a minimal suggestion, she entered into the trance. I told her, "You don't need to feel guilty of anything . . . you are a young lady growing up with usual problems . . . nothing to be ashamed of but much to be proud of . . . you will learn to relax and be free of all anxiety . . . you have many friends who like you just as you are . . . school will open many doors for you. In order to take full advantage of your school opportunities you will do you homework faithfully ... there are many things in store for you ... travel to foreign lands ... people to meet and things to do ... you will look forward to having many of the good things in life ... you are interested in quitting smoking, therefore you will find that the smell of tobacco will make you sick and its taste will be bitter and unpleasant." Sandy was awakened from her trance with the usual ten count and suggestions for well-being. I was confident that all of my suggestions were well received, except the last one.

### SIXTH SESSION

Sandy was extremely quiet during this visit, almost uncommunicative. Had she told me so much during her previous visit that she was now embarrassed and reluctant to see me? This has happened with others. Perhaps she felt ashamed of some of the things that she had said and was now determined not to reveal any more. Her mouth was set in a grim line ... perfectly straight, although, at times, in reponse to questions it would change into a position that could be described as a typical teenage cynical "shrug of the mouth."

She had failed the sixth test of the TED test so I decided to discuss this in relationship to her mother. "Separating from your mother seems to be one of your problems," I remarked, showing her the scored responses to that picture. Sandra agreed that this was one of her greatest troubles. She explained that her mother had never trusted her to go out and always wanted to know where she had been. Later, under hypnosis, we explored this thought and seemed to make some progress towards her understanding her mother's protective attitude.

I told Sandra that she would spend most of this hour in hypnosis. "We want to go back into the past," I explained. Possibly she wanted to retain her past in private as she was surprisingly slow to enter the hypnotic trance. On previous visits she had entered the trance in just a few moments, but this time she took a full ten minutes before successfully passing the eye closure, hand clasp and arm stiffening tests. Later in the evening to see if she had remained in the trance, I suggested that her arm would extend itself in a poker-like fashion. This happened. She was unable to move it from the suggested position. But even so, she was unable to hallucinate and see the suggested motion picture screen. Hypnosis was piled upon hypnosis at least three times but Sandra still could not hallucinate. I made a posthypnotic suggestion that with practice she would on another day be able to see the screen and view pictures of her past life upon it . . . was it possible that she could hallucinate but for reasons of her own wouldn't admit it? I began to explore her memory without using the instrument of choice.

"Tell me about some of the important things that happened during your sixteenth year," I asked.

"I moved to Q———," she answered laconically.

"Why was this move so important?" I continued.

"My stepfather didn't want me home anymore," was her short answer.

"Did he have a reason for feeling the way he did?" I questioned. Sandy replied that she didn't know why he felt that way.

"Were you having nightmares?" I asked.

"Yes, I was," she admitted.

"Tell me about them," I requested.

"I dreamed that I was on a railroad track and when the train came down the tracks I laid down in the middle so that it would run over me."

"What finally happened in your dream?" I asked, wondering why she hadn't mentioned this before.

"I woke up crying," she answered.

"Did you have any other nightmares?" I asked, remembering those she had spoken about earlier.

"Yes," she continued, "I used to dream about green caterpillars stepping on me. We had a lot of them around the house and I was always stepping on them."

"A few weeks ago you told me about a dream of someone coming into your bedroom to try to suffocate you with a pillow. Now you tell me about a train. Why do you have a different dream to relate tonight?" I asked.

Sandra's expression didn't change as she answered, "I had both dreams."

"Tell me about your fifteenth birthday," I requested.

"It was just an ordinary day," she replied.

"You mean that there was no cake or party," I persisted.

"Yeah, I had a cake," she admitted.

"If this had been just an ordinary day then someone must have baked you a cake every day," I remarked.

"No, I didn't have a cake every day," she protested.

"Then someone thought enough of you to have baked a cake to keep this day from being just an ordinary day," I corrected. Sandra made no further comment.

"Tell me about the most important thing that happened to you during your fifteenth year," I requested.

"I guess that it was the trouble that I got in," she responded. She had to be prompted to continue. "I got drunk at a party and the police picked me up . . . I was with a girl friend, but she was the only one that got arrested. I was only a material witness."

"How did you get caught?" I asked.

"Some women complained that there was an unchaperoned party going on at the Veterans' Building," Sandy continued, in a disjointed fashion. "We got N——— out of the building when we found out that they were coming . . . we got her to the bowling alley, but she passed out when we got there and wouldn't come out of it. Someone took her to the hospital where they pumped her stomach out." I wondered if there was more than just alcohol in her stomach that had to be pumped out but didn't wish to pursue it.

I commented, "Of course your mother found out about this. You were in the police station and later in court. What did she say?"

Sandy continued, "She was upset but finally calmed down . . . she said that she hoped that I had learned a lesson."

"I believe that you told me earlier that your mother didn't trust you to go out, that she tried to keep you in and at times you felt that she was wrong. You also mentioned that your stepfather was wrong when he tried to keep you from going out. If you could change positions with your mother and you were in her place and she was in your place would you let her go out as you apparently would do at times?"

"Sandra hesitated before answering, "I would keep her in."

"Why would you do that?" I asked.

"To watch out for her," she softly replied.

"Do you think that is what she was doing for you?" I asked.

"Yes," Sandra replied, but her face changed to a petulant expression.

I didn't want to end this conversation that was so interesting, but our time together was expiring. I had made some suggestions throughout this session that included some positive thoughts about her relationship with her parents. All suggestions were made to relieve her tensions and anxieties.

"You will feel calm and experience a peace coming over you such as you have never felt before . . . I will remove all anxious thoughts from you and leave you at rest . . . relax . . . relax . . . dream sweet pleasant dreams . . ."

Sandra was awakened but complained, "I don't think that I am fully awake yet."

Once more I repeated the awakening process, which always consists of counting to ten with the counts interspersed with positive suggestions about feeling refreshed and better than ever. She was more communicative as she left the office, but not by much.

## SEVENTH SESSION

This time I again directed Sandra's attention to the *California Test of Personality*. "As explained before, you did very well on this test. Your responses to the social relationship section indicated a high level of adjustment. There were a few troubled spots so let's reexamine them." We discussed her nervous symptoms and offered another explanation for her nightmares.

Sandra's dreams all seem to be related in some way with death. Perhaps a study of her dreams could have predicted her abortive attempts to bring about her own death. The dream of strangulation occurred in her own bedroom. I don't know how to interpret dreams . . . I'm not sure that they can be really interpreted. Her bedroom was the setting of a bad dream. There was the threat of a shadowy figure coming with a pillow planning to suffocate her. This dream was extremely hostile and aggressive. The questions arose, did the girl feel that she was in mortal danger of being killed or did she want to suffocate the life out of someone? There was the extremely hostile dream of a train coming down its tracks with Sandra deliberately lying in the middle of them so that the oncoming train would pass over her. There was also the dream of being stepped on by huge caterpillars. Was she really the target of her dream threats?

Sandra's dreams were terrifying and appeared to reflect both fear and guilt. Possibly they released some of the tension that stemmed from the daily conflict that she faced, living in a home where she was the illegitimate half-sister. Maybe they saved her life. She did abort self-destruction. Did each of her terrible dreams permit some tension to escape from her troubled mind? Was her subconscious mind acting out some of the unresolved conflicts that disturbed her? The girl listened carefully to these suggested explanations of her dreams. "That's fascinating," she commented.

"Your scores on 'family adjustment' suggest a need to reorganize your thoughts. If you will think back, you will notice that some of the problems that at one time seemed hopeless were not as bad after all. Yet with the special difficulties that surrounded your early childhood it is not surprising that you found growing up difficult. Perhaps the difficulties you have mastered strengthened you because you have done well." Sandra listened intently to my words but didn't offer much comment.

"You don't need to stir up old wounds by examining past family relationships, but you should examine your thinking as it affects your present schoolwork. You need to be successful there so that some day you will be able to earn your own way." Sandra seemed to be accepting these conscious suggestions. Later they would be repeated under hypnosis.

We examined the TED test. "You also did well on the picture test, especially on the first four pictures. There seemed to be a problem in the development of a conscience ... this needs to be examined. Would you refrain from doing something that you know is wrong because you might get caught or just because you know it is wrong?"

Sandra smiled and replied, "I probably would be worried about getting caught..."

"Yes," I answered, "Fear might be your motivation, but a better reason for doing right instead of wrong could come from your own conscience. You should choose the right thing because of the simple fact that it is right and not because of fear of getting caught and punished."

We examined the sixth task, separation from the mother figure. "This appears to be your greatest difficulty in growing up—getting along with your mother." The girl nodded in agreement. "You believe that she was too restrictive ... she didn't always let you do the things that you wanted." Again, Sandra indicated complete agreement. Her attitude was reflective, not at all rebellious ... "Do you not think that there is a possibility that she was concerned for you; that she wanted to prevent you from making some of the mistakes that she might have made as a girl?" Sandra agreed. "Perhaps there were times when you misunderstood your mother's demands and wondered if she really loved you."

"There were times when I did feel that way," she added. It seemed to me that she emphasized the word "did." I hoped so.

"Perhaps at times when you doubted your mother's love, deep inside you felt her love just as someday the children you have yet to bear will feel your love for them ... even though they may not yet understand you any more than you understood your mother." The young lady seemed reflective and responsive to the words that, in spite of everything, seemed to have become a lecture.

Sandra reclined in the chair and fastened her attention upon a small neon light glowing from the far wall. I directed her to relax and to enter the hypnotic trance. The induction of hypnosis took longer than I expected. Why, when we have had so many successful experiences with hypnosis? It seems that she would not go speedily into the trance. With her experience with hypnosis it seemed to me that she should have gone into the trance more readily. Others usually did. Ten minutes elapsed before Sandra entered a good medium trance. Again she was given several tests of trance depth.

First, her eyes became tightly closed and she admitted that she was unable to open them. I then stroked her arm and made the suggestion that it would stiffen poker-like. It stiffened instantly and she stated that she was unable to move it until it was released by another suggestion. I asked Sandra to hallucinate the theater screen so that we might start the age regression process using the reverse motion picture idea, but again she could not hallucinate. "I can't see the screen." It would seem that this is the one thing that she can not do under hypnosis.

We tried amnesia and were successful. "You are personally acquainted with three boys, James, Phillip and Joseph. You like all three of these boys until one day Phillip does something that you do not like. What are the names of the three boys?" I asked.

"James, Phillip, and Joseph," she replied.

"Good," I continued. "James, Phillip and Joseph ... those are the names of the three boys, but Phillip does something that you don't like and as a result you have determined to forget all about that boy. You still like James and Joseph, but you have forgotten all about the other one. You no longer like him so that you have forgotten all about him including his name ... all you can remember are the names of the two good boys James and Joseph, James and Joseph, James and Joseph. What was the name of that other boy ... the one you don't like?" Sandra struggled but could not remember the name of the third boy.

I decided to try anesthesia as still another proof of the power of hypnotic suggestion. I stroked her right hand, "There is no feeling in this hand, it will be just as if a doctor had taken a needle and injected something to deaden pain, the way a dentist does before he extracts a tooth ... you will no longer feel anything through this hand. It is asleep. You will not feel anything with it." I pinched her left hand hard and she flinched. Her right had was pinched much harder but there was no reaction.

"I can't feel a thing," she said. Again the back of her hand was pinched so hard that the impression remained. Sandra didn't react. Her hand was without feeling, and it remained that way until it was returned to normal with the simple suggestion, "Your hand is all right now." Again I pinched her right hand, but this time she flinched and pulled her hand away. There was no doubt the girl was solidly in the state of hypnosis, but still unable to hallucinate. It seems that there are some subjects who can do this and others who cannot. Yet they are all into hypnosis. I congratulated Sandra again upon her success and told her that the next time we met she would be able to go deep enough into hypnosis to see the motion picture screen. I really didn't believe it. Still this post-hypnotic suggestion might bring it about the next time.

"I have told you that while you are under hypnosis you can go back to your earliest memory. Practice in doing this is helpful so let's once more explore this unusual experience. Move into your past as you might move into some kind of tunnel ... go back to 16 years old, 15 years old, etc. until at last you are just one year old." Sandra's memory was blank at this age so we advanced to the age of two.

"I could talk before I was two," she volunteered.

"To whom did you talk?" I asked.

"To my grandfather."

"What was his name?" I asked.

She smiled and replied, "Bumpy."

"Do you play with your brother?" I asked.

"I would like to play with him, but he doesn't want to play with me," she answered.

"Why do you suppose he won't play with you?" I asked.

"Because he can go out of the yard, but I can't ... but I sneak out anyway."

"What happens when you do that?" I asked.

"I usually get caught and spanked . . . I still go . . . sometimes I get put to bed."

"Why is your mother concerned about you when you sneak out of the yard?" I asked.

"She is concerned about something happening to me," Sandy replied.

"Your mother wishes to protect you?"

"Yes," she admitted.

"If she is concerned about you and wishes to protect you then she must love you," I stated but in a questioning manner.

"Yes," the girl softly replied.

"When you became five years old do you have a birthday party that you can tell me about?" I asked.

"We had a little party, just my brother and me and Mommy and Daddy."

"Do you like it when your Daddy is with you?" I inquired.

"I don't like him," she answered.

"What has he done to you to make you feel that way?" I asked.

"He just looks mean . . . especially when he is mad," she answered.

"Does he hit you?" I asked.

"Sometimes he hits us and makes us kneel on the stairs," she replied.

"Tell me about one of these incidents," I requested.

"My brother and I were fighting . . . I guess that he had a headache because he hit us with his belt and then made us kneel with our knees on the stairs. We had to stay that way for a long time . . . maybe an hour . . . when he finally let us go to bed we could hardly get up the stairs."

"When you were 15 you had some trouble with the police," I remarked moving to speed up through the years."

"Yes," she answered. "My girl friend got drunk and we had to go to court."

She told this story before when she was in the waking stage and under hypnosis, the story was the same. Each time she spoke of her girl friend getting drunk and her appearance in court as a material witness, but is she telling the truth? Could she have been the one who was drunk and is she concealing it? She isn't clear on her role as a material witness. Would the police have brought a young girl to court because she was drunk? Mabe not, but they certainly would charge someone who was supplying young girls with alcoholic drinks. I wonder how old her girl friend was?

When we came to the sixteenth year, her hour with me had ended and there was just enough time for her to remark voluntarily, "I see my mother's viewpoint better now ... I realize that she did things for my own good."

Just before the girl was taken out of her trance, she received the following reeducative suggesions made throughout her session.

"Your tensions and anxious moments are leaving you ... you will awake feeling relaxed and at peace with the world. Tonight you will go to sleep just as you head touches your pillow, you will find that problems will vanish with the dawn, you will have sweet dreams. Remember that school is for you ... it is the place where you will learn skills that will enable you to earn your own living. The whole world is before you with countless pleasures and places to go. You will study and get ready for the wonderful things in life that are to come. Do your homework, it is for you, not for your teachers, that you do this work. Work hard in school and you will be rewarded by good marks and, most importantly, knowledge that will help you in the future."

I gave Sandra pretty much the same thoughts regarding smoking that she received last week. She still smoked but claimed that the cigarettes tasted bitter and the smoke sickening ... she was awakened in the usual manner.

## EIGHTH SESSION

Sandra had made great progress during the past few weeks. She was free of tensions and appeared well able to face the problems that had bothered her during most of her life. She was so pleased with herself and the success that she found through hypnotherapy that she asked for permission to bring a girl friend to this lesson. The presence of an additional person in the room prevented us from delving into some things that had been exhumed during the earlier sessions but perhaps this was just as well. Her ghosts didn't appear to be effective any more.

I told Sandra, "The time has come for you to begin work on your own self-hypnosis." She looked dubious. "You will want to be able to dispel your own anxious moments by entering a trance with the special feature of being able to make your own good suggestions.

This doesn't mean that you can't come here if you need to . . . but I don't believe that you will need me any more."

The girl leaned back in the chair with just an occasional glance at her friend.

"Tonight I shall use the personal pronoun saying, 'I' instead of saying 'you' when making suggestions. The suggestions will be made slowly so that you can repeat them after me. Hopefully you will be able to put yourself to sleep and I won't do the same for myself." The girls laughed. "I shall put myself into hypnosis . . . my rapport will be with myself . . . I will be able to make helpful suggestions to myself . . . my body is now relaxing all over from head down to my toes . . . the muscles and nerves in the back of my neck are relaxing as well as the muscles and nerves in my lower jaw. The muscles and nerves along my back are relaxing . . . soon I shall feel a pleasant tingling sensation running all through my body . . . my breathing is deeper." With this her breasts moved up and down in a more pronounced manner. "The muscles and nerves in the thighs of my legs are relaxing. My body feels heavy although it is a pleasing heaviness . . . The calves of my legs are completely relaxed as well as my feet . . . I am entering into a completely relaxed peaceful state . . . My mind is at rest . . . Tensions are leaving my body . . . A sweet calm is coming over me such as I have never known before . . . I know that my eyes are getting tired and will soon close only to open again when I tell them to . . . I shall now count to ten when I will be forced to swallow. Immediately following this swallow I shall go into a deep trance and will be able to make suggestions to myself . . . suggestions that will help me resolve problems . . . ."

Sandra swallowed on cue, her eyes closed and she entered into a suggestible trance.

"Will you silently suggest to yourself that your right hand is getting lighter and will soon rise up in the air?" I asked. In a moment or two her hand did rise up to remain until I commented, "You have done very well. Why don't you let your hand come down." To my surprise the hand soon started to lower slowly but then dropped with a bang.

I gave the girl additional suggestions like those she heard on the previous sessions. I told her to count to ten, "Just like me," and to awaken herself. When she accomplished this I remarked, "You know that you worked this session almost alone . . . You are now ready to do it all alone."

At first Sandra protested, "I couldn't remember all the things that you say."

"It doesn't matter whether you do or not. It is just the general ideas that are important. Give it a try," I insisted.

She responded and her eyes blinked but did not close. It seemed best to help. "Count to ten and then if you say so your eyes will close completely." Her eyes did close and she raised her hand to indiate that she had truly hypnotized herself. She awakened herself when it was suggested. "You have done so well that you don't need my help anymore. Try it and make some good suggestions to yourself."

This time the girl put herself into a hypnotic trance without any help. We can presume that she made the suggestions that were previously presented to her. I did not question her about this. I felt that her developing independence should not be questioned. Soon, and without prompting, Sandra opened her eyes and looked at her friend as if to say, "See how easy it is."

## CONCLUSIONS

Sandra's intelligence was limited, at least as far as the Otis-Lennon Mental Ability Test was able to determine for me. Her I.Q. was only 89 according to that test. We can assume that a more orderly home life would have helped her to display a greater amount of intelligence. I think that her potential I.Q. is higher than indicated on that test. She hasn't done well in school, but it has been pointed out that a child laboring under the bewildering question, "Do my parents really want me?" can hardly be expected to compete successfully in school with a child who has no such problems.

She proved to be a good subject for hypnosis and this helped me to establish the rapport that quickly enabled her to expose her suicidal attempts. The fact she went readily into hypnosis may also have indicated that she had more intelligence than was demonstrated by the intelligence test. Children with low levels of intelligence have proved to be difficult subjects for hypnosis.

The California Test of Personality helped point out some of her special emotional problems, nightmares, running away, sleepwalking, etc. I used this test as a teaching tool to explore some of the problems that were disclosed through the testing. This was therapuetic and even without the use of hypnotism would have helped her through some of her difficulties. The discussion of her frightening nightmares dispelled much of the darkness surrounding them.

The projective TED test pointed out the problem that existed between the girl and her mother, enabling me to come to grips with one of her fundamental difficulties. Again this test provided a learning vehicle for the girl.

Sandra was a good hypnotic subject but was unable to go into age regression with any real success. This particular phenomenon of hypnosis did not come to her as it has to others. There may exist special individual resistance to segments of the various hypnotic phenomenon in different individuals. The resistance may result from previous conditioning of some kind unknown to the therapist or the subject. It appears that some consent from the subject is needed before the therapist can pry into parts of the subject's mind. The intimate knowledge that Sandra imparted to me was first made in the waking state and later repeated in the sleep state. The TED test responses were almost the same in the waking state as they were in the sleep state.

Sandra's response to the suggestions given under hypnosis were well received but with some exceptions. I told Sandra that she should give up smoking, that the taste of tobacco would be bitter and that the effects of smoking would be injurious to her health. I would like to say that she stopped smoking but the truth is that she did not. Sandra still smoked but did admit that the cigarettes tasted bitter. She smoked in spite of the bitter taste. Her compulsion to smoke was strong enough to overcome the bitter taste of the tobacco.

Hypnosis did not solve all her school problems. Her work did show some improvement but nothing spectacular appeared quickly. I gave her some suggestions to help her appreciate the efforts of her teachers and be less critical of them. This may have taken effect. There was some evidence that this had happened.

Another suggestion I made to her that failed to be effective was the one designed to cut down her intake of fatty foods; that her basal metabolism would increase and that her elimination of waste would be facilitated all to cause her to lose weight. I made this trio of suggestions several times, but my attempts proved to be ineffective. Her weight did not change and her intake of fatty foods remained about the same. I don't believe that hypnosis is a miracle tool that can magically be used to wave away pounds of fatty body tissue.

Of great significance is the fact that Sandra improved emotionally and was able to return to the home of her mother and enjoy her company. In her eight lessons, she acquired an understanding of her mother's concerns that had at one time seemed overly restrictive. Through her knowledge of self-hypnosis, she acquired the ability to relieve herself of destructive tensions. She informed me that she no longer required help since she was "all right now." I believed her. She could even cope with her stepfather's improper advances. Sandra never returned after her eighth lesson. She said "good-bye" and with a happy expression disappeared from my life.

# CHAPTER TEN
# JOE: STEALING

The causes for stealing are numerous and have to be specified before therapy can begin. The therapy for stealing has to fit the presumed motive. A child may steal food because he is hungry. He may steal clothes because he wants to keep up his social appearance, he may steal as a form of revenge upon someone because he thinks that person has done something to him. The child may also have an uncontrollable urge to steal as a dare.

The general therapy for stealing begins by telling the child that he is suspected or is known to have stolen something and as a result is facing the loss of certain privileges.

Joe was looking for the secret thrill of being mischievous and he gave in to that pressure.

## JOE

All of the young people who come for therapy have some kind of educational problem and sometimes their educational problem is secondary to some other more pressing problem but the educational problem is often the cause of the other one. Sometimes it's the child's secondary difficulty that brings him in to see me.

Joe was not yet twelve years old. He had been labeled pre-delinquent. Joe was in trouble with the law, but he didn't understand why he did the things that got him into trouble with the law. Joe was brought to me just after he had been arrested for breaking into a neighbor's house to commit a burglary. It was hard to understand why Joe had committed this crime. Joe was the pride of a financially secure family. His father was doing well in his own business. Joe loved his father and mother. Joe spent a lot of time with his father and frequently went to work with him. The family owned a fine pleasure boat and they all loved to go sailing together.

Joe's parents were good to him. They gave him presents and spent a lot of time with him. His father ran the family business and his mother ran the home. Both parents enjoyed their responsibilities, but things were going wrong for Joe.

Joe had two siblings to live with. He had a sister who was four years older than he was and a brother who was ten years younger. This handsome age span may be the reason why there were no particular rivalries existing between the siblings.

Joe had repeated the primary grade and this failure provided him with his only hateful experiences. Joe explained, "She (the teacher) had a spite against me."

"Why do you think so?" I asked.

"I don't know why," he replied, "maybe it was because we moved here from ——— " (he named the town).

Joe had entered kindergarten and stayed through the third grade in this other town. When the family business improved they moved to a more affluent neighborhood and Joe entered a new school where he did so poorly that he was asked to repeat the grade. Joe talked a lot about his new school. Just about everything he hated most in this world centered about his new school and its teachers. "I hate it when the teachers bother me . . . I feel like telling them off . . . I get real mad . . . I don't like it when Miss ——— (he named the teacher) took my pen away . . . She came by my desk and slammed the lid down. She almost got my fingers. The desk is too small for my legs to fit under so I like to keep the lid up a little way."

As Joe talked on and on about his school and his teachers I couldn't help but reflect upon the ways that many school teachers use to contribute to the negative feelings that children have about school. Many teachers are eager to blame the child's parents when something goes wrong with a child's education, but teachers and parents equally contribute to a child's education and they both share the joy of a child's success and the blame for a child's failure when that occurs too.

"Do you get along well with your friends?" I asked.

"Not really," he replied, "when I get in trouble they don't want any part of me."

"You are having some trouble getting along with your teachers," I continued.

"My teachers don't understand me. They give me U's in conduct (unsatisfactory). I think that my parents understand me but I'm not sure. They did some things when they were kids too. They don't hit me much. Only when I am real bad."

"You mean when you steal something?" I asked.

"Yes," he breathed.

"Tell me why you steal money from your mother's pocketbook when she gives you everything you need," I stated. (I really didn't know if he had stolen anything from her or not.)

"Sometimes they forget to give me my allowance and I am broke so I take some money from her. She doesn't know about it," he hastened to add, as if to say, "Please don't tell her about it."

"What about the time when you broke into . . . house. Were you looking for money or something to drink?" I asked.

"We wanted money," he quickly replied.

"But you boys already had something to drink, didn't you?" I persisted not knowing if they had or not.

"Yes, we did," he replied. "I was with ––– (Joe named another boy).

"How old were you when you started stealing money from your mother's purse?" I asked.

"I was just a young kid, about seven or eight . . . I am getting a little warm now," he added.

Joe had been given a placebo at the beginning of the session in hopes that it would encourage his quick responses to meditation/therapy.

"I expected that you would have become warm before now," I returned pleasantly, "and by now you would feel kind of drowsy." Joe wiped his hands across his brow that was beginning to sweat and we continued to talk about his early childhood experiences.

Joe examined my previously prepared word association list and there were no significant associations but after he finished he volunteered, "There is something that you don't have down here. The thing I am mostly afraid of is cops when they are chasing me."

"Tell me about this," I requested.

"The first time it happened was when we were lighting fires, and the second time was when we were taking Christmas tree bulbs from the decorations down town."

"Did the cops chase you after you broke into the house?" I asked.

"No, they didn't chase me. They came to my house. Someone told them about me," He replied.

I administered the Otis-Lennon Mental Ability Test Intermediate Level, Form J, to determine his intelligence. Joe did very well, getting 39 correct responses out of 80 possible ones. This raw score, when coupled with his age of eleven years and ten months gave him a derived I.Q. of at least, 106. This ranked him above 65 percent of the thousands of other young people of his age who had taken the test. Joe was mentally equipped to do well in school. Why had he failed?

I decided to use the hypnotic technique of age regression and try to locate hidden motivations for his antagonistic attitude and subsequent delinquent activities. While Joe was meditating I returned him to his earliest days saying, "Let's try something different tonight. Get a picture of yourself sitting in the front seat of a motion picture theater and looking at the screen. When you do that you will be able to review many of the important events that occurred during your childhood. Remain deep in meditation, but open your eyes and look ahead through space to the motion picture screen. Let me know when you can see it."

Joe wrinkled his brow trying hard to see the screen. He was straining to see when he exclaimed, "I can see the screen." Joe was surprised to see it.

"That's fine," I replied. "Focus upon your last birthday. Can you look back to that day?"

Joe was led, step by step, back through his life to the age of two years when his sentence structure became too juvenile and his thoughts too childish to continue. He was two when he told me of a little swing that his mother placed in front of the television set so that he could swing back and forth in front of it and become amused by the television programs. There were no revelations that could be labeled significant.

Near the end of the session and while Joe was still deeply engrossed in meditation I talked to him about the almost secret voice of his conscience. "Do you sometimes seem to hear a voice within you speaking to you and telling you right from wrong?" I inquired.

"Yes," he softly admitted.

"After tonight you can expect to hear it more clearly than you have ever heard it before. It tells you right from wrong doesn't it," I reminded.

"Yes, it does," he admitted.

"You will notice that when you accept the voice of your conscience you will feel good about yourself. We have found that you are a very intelligent boy. There is nothing to stop you from using your intelligence and becoming one of the best students in your school. You have a good memory. You can use it to remember the lessons taught in school. You can catch up with your school work and soon get into the top reading group in your class."

I only saw Joe eight times and in the course of these visits decided that Joe's delinquent activities were partly and perhaps equally the result of adjustment problems in his home and his school. Joseph had a separation problem from his mother and that may be one of the reasons why he stole money from her. Joe was anxious to develop a masculine image and he tried to do this by rebelling against society. He was trying to act tough and at the same time gain independence from his mother.

Joe didn't know how to handle aggression and that was part of his trouble. He didn't know what he should do when he felt threatened. He knew that he would rather fight than appear to be a sissy, and as a result he got into a lot of fights around the school. This got him in to trouble with his teachers. Joe may have been right to believe that his teachers didn't understand him. They only thought of him as a troublemaker and never considered the fierce inner tensions that were causing Joe to act out with angry and destructive actions.

Joe's future was encouragingly bright. He was in the process of working out some of his problems. After school, Joe was going to work with his father and earning five dollars per week. His father was pleased to have the boy around. Joe was lucky. His delinquent acts were momentary impulses.

Joe and I eventually lost contact with each other, but we had a mutual acquaintance who told me that Joe was going along fine in school; that there were no more delinquent activities. It seemed that Joe had changed his life. I was told that his attitude toward school had improved and that his marks had shot up.

# EPILOGUE

There is nothing to stop an individual from learning all there is to know about hypnosis and using that knowledge upon another person who is willing to become hypnotized. There is no shortage of individuals who want to submit to the experience of becoming hypnotized. Hypnosis possesses a tremendous potential for good, but in the hands of an unscrupulous person the potential for evil is also there.

During my undergraduate college days, my interest in hypnosis matured and as a premedical student the subject of hypnosis was considered a powerful conditioning and analytical instrument available to alleviate some of man's difficulties. During those college years I helped some of my friends overcome their fear of examinations. But it wasn't until after many years of service as an educator and after many years of frustrating experiences with child guidance experts that I again turned to hypnotism as a means of helping children overcome some of their problems. I had at last found a place for hypnosis. In this book I have taken my readers through a number of case histories that seem to be typical of the kinds of problems that exist with children. I've tried to show how elementary hypnotism can work. Several instances of my own unsuccessful efforts have been deliberately included. I haven't succeeded with everyone but that doesn't mean that another hypnotherapist would have failed. There have been times when I have succeeded when a colleague has failed with the same subject.

There may be some real dangers if negative suggestions are made to the "sleeping" subject, but there are no dangers to hypnosis itself. Any abnormal situation created by a post-hypnotic suggestion and left with the subject upon awakening might create a problem for the subject. An arm that has been made stiff during hypnosis should always be restored to normal before awakening. The therapist should have a good understanding of psychology and most importantly he must be the kind of person in whom the subject can place his trust.

Throughout this book I have used the word, suggestion ... because this is the basis upon which hypnotherapy is built. It is not the foundation for analysis although it is the tool that enables an analysis to be more quickly made. It is said that hypnosis is the result of conditioning and that the relief of symptoms comes from reconditioning rather than suggestion. I have used the word, suggestion rather than, conditioning in this context because it has the advantage of long usage.

Almost all of the suggestions were given to the subjects verbally although in producing the hypnotic state I have used many objects that suggested the trance. The subjects were conditioned to think of the objects as trance producing otherwise they would have been useless. Occasionally the suggestions were written down and handed to the subject to read at a later time. Perhaps more should have been made of this technique. Suggestions produced the trance which is a state of augmented suggestibility. During this state of augmented suggestibility, more suggestions were made to affect the relief the subject needed. The relief or change occurred when the subject believed that it would occur. This curative force is in every instance inherent within the subject, but it was activated by the hypnotic suggestions.

Most of the young people that I've written about lived with some kind of situation that has been stressful. Most of them learned to relax as a result of hypnosis and in some instances self-hypnosis. When they were able to gain a measure of self-confidence, their skills increased. It was necessary for them to "let go" of their tensions and negative self-image before reeducation could begin. This process has been referred to as dehypnotization by some writers. Most of the students learned how to concentrate and how to release the mind distractions. Complete relaxation is more than just allowing the body to flop, but it helps. Complete relaxation is a state of body and mind.*

Any other technique that would have released the mind from the

---

*Conditioned Reflex Therapy, Andrew Salter. Capricorn Books. N.Y.

# EPILOGUE

corrupting forces may have served these young people just as well. All it had to do was release the healing forces that always were present in their own bodies. The relaxed state of mind that they obtained through hypnosis might have been obtained through some kind of religious conversion. I don't know ... perhaps in the long run that might have been better for them.

All of our experiences condition us and this conditioning can be bad or it can be good. Fortunately, the bad conditioning can be unlearned and new patterns of thinking can be installed in place of the old ones. Everything we have learned can be thought of as some kind of conditioning experience. Dr. Andrew Salter wrote in one of his many books that everything that has been learned can be unlearned and that is the philosophy behind the reeducative therapy in the case histories written about in this book.

Most children worked with in the usual school situation don't receive as much testing as those reported here. One such boy was in the fourth grade and I only saw him once. His case history was reported by his classroom teacher. His father had died the year before I saw him. His mother had several other active boys to bring up. Her hands were full trying to make a living and raise her family at the same time. This boy needed a male with whom he could identify—one that his mother was unable to fulfill. He reacted to the loss of his father's firm hand by acting out at home and in his school. He was failing in school and he disturbed the other children. The teacher complained about the boy to the mother. She made many attempts to discipline the boy. He had lost most of his privileges if not all. He had been spanked. He had been kept after school. He had been sent to his principal's office. This was to no avail. The boy continued on his way downhill academically and socially. He associated with other boys who were also doing wrong things.

I will call him Michael although that was not his name. Michael was brought to me just once and that only for about 15 minutes. He turned out to be a good subject and quickly entered into the trance. I gave him suggestions similar to these, "You know that your school work is important to you. It is the key to your future. It is not only important to you, but to your mother and to your father if he was here with you. Your parents want you to do well in school because they love you and are concerned. You can do well in school and you will if you want to. Tomorrow, when you go to school you will try very hard. You have it within you to be the best student in the class. You will work harder in school than you have ever done before. You will be so busy doing your school work that you will not have time to 'fool around.' You will work hard ... hard ... hard ... and not waste your time. It is too valuable to waste fooling around."

The boy left the office not really sure of what had happened to him. The hypnosis had been induced without any introduction. In fact it wasn't even mentioned. It seems possible that the boy didn't really know what had happened to him nevertheless the boy did exactly as he was instructed. He obeyed the post-hypnotic suggestion for the remaining two or three months of school. He worked harder than he had ever worked before. The teacher reported to his mother that she didn't know what had happened to him. "He was working hard and not disturbing the class at all."

It would be nice to say that the boy's school problems were permanently resolved, but unfortunately this was not the case. Towards the end of the next school year the post-hypnotic suggestion seemed to have worn off because the boy reverted back to his old behavior. Had the boy been brought to me again to receive the same suggestions he might have been all right, but this wasn't the case. I never saw him again.

## REINFORCEMENT

The reappearance of symptoms is something that may occur with this therapy, but the reappearance can be handled again and in the same way as before. To make a permanent change, the old ways have to be erased and erased over and over again until they are no longer important to the individual. Erasing a symptom does not mean that something else will erupt to take the place of the old symptom. In most cases the cause of the old symptom has vanished to leave only the physical or emotional manifestation of the long since lost problem.

The "bedwetter" had completely overcome his apparent "dyslexic" symptom of reversing his 5's only to have them reappear again one year later. He returned for additional therapy and again received the necessary suggestions to correct this symptom. This time the correction was permanent.

## EVERYONE BENEFITED

All of the students seemed to have gained something from their experiences in hypnotherapy. There was never an unhappy experi-

# EPILOGUE

ence. The most striking benefits were gained in modifying the old personality of the students. The young people gained a better outlook upon life. They became more independent. They became success-oriented instead of failure-expectant.

## CORRUPTING POWER

There is one thing that the hypnotherapist must guard himself against. It is an odd kind of power problem. When a subject has submitted himself to the therapist and has successfully reached a trance there can be no doubt that the therapist has achieved considerable power over the individual. He hasn't as much power as feared by those uninformed individuals who are influenced by the Svengala fiction, yet his influence is considerable. There is very little doubt in my mind that a competent hypnotist could, in time, condition his subject to a new frame of reference. Just how far he could go with this conditioning is questionable. If anyone has found out, he hasn't published the results.

We know that power is corruptible. The hypnotherapist must guard against that possibility. He must keep his work fenced in with high standards. Anyone planning to use the services of a hypnotist would be wise to inquire about his prospective hypnotist, not so much his credentials, but his references.

# INDEX

Age Regression, 56-59, 62-64, 151-155
Ambrose, Gordon, xvii, xxix, 145
Amnesia, 19, 185
Anesthesia, 156, 185

Baroff, G., 120
Bender, Gestalt (test), 118-121
Bender, J. F., 41
Bensberg, C. G., 120
Bond-Clymer-Holt (test), xxxvii

California Personality Test, xxxvi, xxxvii, 2, 80, 107-108, 116, 169-170, 175, 183, 190
Capricorn Books, 85, 200
Chemotherapy, 125
Children's Hospital (Boston), xxxi
Clawson, Aileen, 118
Cohen, H. (TED), xxxi
Coleman, James C., 22
Concentration, xiii
Consulting Psychologist's Press, 4
Coue, Emile, 95

Durell Sullivan Reading Test, 12
Dyslexia, 1, 5, 6

Emotional Blocks, xvii, xxiv
Enuresis, 1, 3, 6

Feldman, I., 120
Flannagan Aptitude Classification Test, xxxvii, 93, 94
Freud, Sigmund, xxiv, xxxii
Frostig, Marianne, 4

Gates, A. J., xx
Gindes, Bernard, xxix, 134
Grune and Stratton Publishers, 120

Hallucinate, 19, 61-64, 95, 96, 99, 181
Hanvick, L., 120
Harcourt Brace and World Publishers, xxxvii
Houghton Mifflin, xxxvi, xxxvii
Howard, Melvin, 1
Hypnotherapy, xxvii
Hypnosis, xxviii

International Congress of Psychosomatic Medicine, xviii
Iowa Every Pupil Test of Work Study Skills, 8, 20, 129, 139, 143

Jackson, Lydia, xxvii

Koppitz, Elizabeth, 120
Krippner, Stanley, v

Lindner, Robert M., xxxi, xxxiii, xxxiv
Lyons and Carnaham Publishers, xxxvii

Maltz, Maxwell, 99-100
Mann, Herbert, xvi
Memorial Memory, 153
Michigan Department of Mental Health, 121
Michigan Picture Test, 113, 118, 121, 122, 125
Moire Patterns, xxix, 166
Motivation, xiii, xxiii, 66

Oral Sadistic, 123

INDEX

Otis-Lennon Mental Ability Test, 5, 7, 8, 25, 39, 50, 118, 129, 144, 167
Otis Quick Scoring Test, 102

Pittman Publishing Co., 41
Post-Hypnotic Suggestion, 13, 31, 66, 69, 70, 77, 79, 151, 159
Powers Publishing Co., xxviii, xxix, 156
Powers Melvin, xxvii, xxviii
Pupil Adjustment Inventory, xxxvii

Regressive Memory, xxiv
Revivified Memory, xxiv
Richard, G. (TED), xxxi
Role Playing, xxiv
Rorschach Test, xxxvii

Salter, Andrew, xxvii
Saybrook Institute, xvi
School Phobia, 18, 21, 22, 23, 38
Science Research Associates, xxxviii
Scott Foresman Reading Inventory, xxxviii, 22, 51, 131, 144, 146, 162
Schizophrenia, 111, 116, 126
Self Concept, 141
Self-Hypnosis, 65, 69, 74, 159, 161, 188
Sibling Rivalry, 89
Stanford Binet, xxxviii
Stealing, 193
Stuttering, 41
Suicide, 163

Tasks of Emotional Development Test, xxxi, 15, 17, 47, 48, 134-136, 147-149, 180, 184

Van Pelt, S. J., xxv

Western Psychological Service, 118
Wilshire Book Co., xxx, xxix
Woodward, L. T., xxviii

Word Association, 133, 145, 158
Wright, Erik, M., xv